Modern English

MODERN ENGLISH

A User's Guide to Grammar and Style

Michael Beresford

Duckworth

First published in 1997 by
Gerald Duckworth & Co. Ltd.
The Old Piano Factory
48 Hoxton Square, London N1 6PB
Tel: 0171 729 5986
Fax: 0171 729 0015

© 1997 by Michael Beresford

All rights reserved. No part of this publication
may be reproduced, stored in a retrieval system, or
transmitted, in any form or by any means, electronic,
mechanical, photocopying, recording or otherwise,
without the prior permission of the publisher.

A catalogue record for this book is available
from the British Library

ISBN 0 7156 2766 X

Typeset by Ray Davies
Printed in Great Britain by
Page Bros (Norwich) Ltd, Norwich

Contents

Introduction 1
Acknowledgements 4

Part I

1. THE PRESCRIPTIVE TRADITION . . . 7

The betterment of English 7
The imposition of rules 8
The dominance of Latin 9

2. MAIN TRADITIONAL RULES . . . 11

Split infinitives 11
Final prepositions 12
'Shall' and 'will' 13
Subject and object pronouns 14
Fused participles 16

3. LESSER RULES . . . 19

'Due to' and 'owing to' 19
Intensifiers with participles 20
Agreement with 'none' and 'neither' . . 21
'Between', 'among' and reciprocal pronouns . . 22
'Fewer', 'less', and 'not so ... as' 23
Relative pronouns 24

4. GRAMMARIANS' VICTORIES . . . 26

Multiple negation 26
Single negation 27
Double comparatives and superlatives . 28
Regulation of verb forms 29
Adverbs in -ly and numeral combinations . 30

5. CRITERIA OF CORRECTNESS . . . 31

Correct usage 31
Incorrect forms 32

Contents

Logic and grammar	32
Illogical usage	34
Analogy and grammar	35
The Latin model	37
6. USAGE AND NORMS	**39**
Doctrine of usage	39
The usage doctrine opposed	41
Doctrine of the norm	42
Need for better prescriptivism	43
7. DIVIDED USAGE	**46**
Attitudes to usage	46
New coinages	48
Flawed expressions	49
8. RULES OF STYLE	**53**
Campbell's rules	53
The Fowlers' rules	54
Quiller-Couch's rules	56
Orwell's rules	57
Gowers's rules	58
9. GOOD ENGLISH	**60**
Features of good English	60
Rules of good English	61
Qualification of the rules	62
Teaching English grammar	63

Part II

10. HYPERCORRECTION	**67**
Phonetic hypercorrection	67
The nob's pronouns	67
Nob's pronouns after prepositions	68
The nob's adverbs	69
Adverbs for adjectives	70
Hypercorrect 'whom'	71
'Who' and 'who(so)ever' after prepositions	72
Gentrified 'as' and 'as with'	72
Pseudo-subjunctive 'were'	74
11. FALSE AGREEMENT	**76**
Collective nouns	76
Plural and compound subjects	77

Contents

Plural anomalies	78
Attraction	79
'Each', 'either', 'neither' and 'none'	80
'One' in subjects	81
Epicene pronouns	82
Faulty pronoun use	83
Pronoun anomalies	84

12. FALSE ATTACHMENT — 87

The rule of attachment	87
False apposition	87
Common misattachments	88
Misrelated participles	89
Participial absurdities	90
Common participial misconstructions	91
Absolute and loose participle phrases	92
Generalizing participle phrases	93
Participles converted	95

13. FALSE ELLIPSIS — 97

Acceptable ellipsis	97
Omission of 'as' and 'than'	97
Omission of prepositions	98
Omission of verbs	99
Abbreviated clauses	100
Absent connectives	101
Instructionese and advertese	102

14. FALSE COMPARISON — 105

Elliptical comparisons	105
Like-phrases and unlike-phrases	106
Inclusive exclusion	107
False 'than'	108

15. FALSE NEGATION — 111

Multiple negation	111
Acceptable multiple negation	112
Negative transference	112
'Neither', 'nor' and 'not'	113
Underreaching and overreaching negatives	114
Redundant negatives	115

16. CROSSED CONSTRUCTIONS — 118

Blends	118
Tautological blends	119

Contents

Verb harmonization	120
Object swapping	120
Miscellaneous blends	122

17. BROKEN CONSTRUCTIONS — 125

Grammatical dislocation	125
Syntactical non sequiturs	125
Broken questions	126
Mixed voices	127
One-legged constructions	128
False sequence of tenses	129
False inversion	130
Logical gaps	131
Sentence fragments	132

18. WORD CONFUSION — 134

Malapropisms	134
Confusable adjectives and adverbs	135
Confusable verbs	136
Confusable nouns	137
Sesquipedalian substitutes	138
Pseudo-synonyms	139
Semantic reversal	140
Mixed metaphors	141

19. MISCOUPLING — 144

Gradability and secondary grading	144
Elatives	145
Absolutes	146
Downgrading and upgrading	147
Odd couples	148
Weakening intensifiers	149
Miscellaneous miscouplings	150

20. MISPLACEMENT — 152

The rule of proximity	152
Parallel constructions	153
Adverb placement	153
Back-to-frontery	154
Detached relative clauses	155
Exiled phrases and participles	156
Misleading arrangement	156

21. AMBIGUITY — 158

Ambiguous speech and writing	158

Contents

Disambiguation	159
Categorial confusion	159
Pronoun ambiguities	160
Verb ambiguities	162
Structural ambiguities	162
Negative ambiguities	164
Miscellaneous ambiguities	165
22. REDUNDANCY	168
Redundancy in speech and writing	168
Pleonasm and tautology	168
Types of tautology	169
Abstract appendages	170
Redundant adjectives	171
Redundant adverbs	172
Redundant particles	172
Redundant prepositions	173
Other redundant function words	173
Redundant affixes	174
Verbosity and circumlocution	175
23. GRAMMATICAL PRAXIS	177
24. STYLISTIC PRAXIS	183
Punctuation	190
Basic Grammatical Terms	199
Name Index	207
Subject and Word Index	209

This book is dedicated to
my wife Maureen and my son David.

Introduction

English in all its glory holds a unique, commanding position among the languages of the world today. It is more widespread and influential than any other tongue; it has a greater vocabulary than any other; and it can express most ideas in fewer syllables than any other. It is unsurpassed, indeed unmatched, in its richness, resilience and resourcefulness.

Inevitably, it also displays the defects of these qualities. Its richness spawns confusion as well as profusion; its resilience admits much vagueness of expression; and its resourcefulness allows some forms to be overburdened with uses. Most faults of English, however, lie not in the language itself but with people who use it carelessly or ignorantly. The English language affords all the means needed for clear and effective exposition on any subject whatever. It is not in decline, as some believe; on the contrary, it is vigorous, adaptable and inventive, as in the past.

It is a sad fact that many people speak and write miserable English. Much of what is written is cobbled together, rambling, repetitive and overloaded with words. Misuses and misconstructions abound in speech and writing. Yet a mastery of good English is within the grasp of every literate native speaker. All that is required to achieve it is patient practice in observing a modest number of basic principles, ascertained without difficulty and of proven value.

The first part of this book deals with traditional grammar and rhetoric, dispelling some common misconceptions about language in general and English in particular. The rules of grammar and style laid down in the past are examined in detail and most are found wanting; some of them are not just unhelpful but downright harmful to the promotion of good English. Prescriptivism as it was practised earlier is shown to be inadequate, not because it was prescriptive but because it was based neither on sound criteria nor on an accurate description of usage. The remedy for unsatisfactory prescribing is not to abandon the prescriptive approach, but to establish reliable rules of good English, based on sound criteria and precise description. This book offers a set of such criteria and rules, followed in the second part by chapters on each of the main faults of grammar and style.

It is quite wrong to suppose, as many linguists do, that the precepts of grammarians have no effect on usage. One of the chapters of this book is devoted to showing how standard English was changed in several significant ways under scholarly influence, especially in the 17th and 18th centuries. There is nothing unrealistic, therefore, in striving to improve the language by prudent selection. Where the usage of educated people is not uniform but divided, we have an opportunity to help linguistic evolution in a Darwinian sense, by ensuring the survival of the fittest forms.

Many manuals of English usage have been published hitherto, but unfortunately they contain much questionable guidance. The usage they recommend is in many cases that of idealized speakers who say 'It is I', 'He is bigger than she', 'Whom are you calling?' and never split an infinitive, even in anger. Some authors attempt to come to terms with present-day usage, but most of them adopt an authoritarian approach, perpetuating linguistic myths and clinging to outmoded 'correct' forms. Their rules appear to be more often imposed on the contemporary language than derived from it. And, as they rarely lay down any principles of good usage, their works are usually a ragbag of assorted faults, ordered alphabetically instead of being classified by type. This 'dictionary' method is bound to lead to gaps, overlaps, and tedious cross-references.

Pre-eminent among these arbiters of good English is Henry Fowler, whose *Dictionary of Modern English Usage* (1926) still makes instructive and stimulating reading, enlivened as it is by his pungent and witty comments. But it does not reflect the usage of educated people in Britain or America today. The book contains material drawn exclusively from novels, journals and newspapers of the late 19th and early 20th centuries, but in the last seventy years or so written English has changed a good deal, drawing closer in many ways to the spoken language. On some points of usage Fowler is deeply conservative, on others remarkably liberal, and some very common features of bad English he ignores altogether. A revised version by Sir Ernest Gowers, published in 1965, adds instances from a later period, cuts out some dead wood and challenges or modifies some of Fowler's views. By contrast, the third edition, compiled by Robert Burchfield and published in 1996, is a root-and-branch revision which, while scholarly and up to date, retains little of the original Fowler.

The present book sets out the commonest defects of today's English, classified according to type. It deals with points of both grammar and diction. Most chapters illustrate not only bad or inappropriate usage but also good, acceptable usage; thus false agreement, false comparison and false ellipsis are placed in a context of valid agreement, valid comparison and valid ellipsis. Reasons are given for judging forms to be good or bad and, wherever possible, an attempt has been made to explain how the bad usage comes about. Most cases of such usage can be traced in fact to one of three causes: (1) the extension of a rule beyond its appropriate domain, (2) the operation of false analogy, and (3) confusion between forms that are similar in sound or sense. In addition, many cases of bad English arise from a faulty placement, omission or inclusion of words. Some bad English is simply the result of muddled thinking, for clarity of expression can only proceed from clarity of mind. And much writing is marred by the presence of irrelevant detail.

The examples of English given in this book come from a great variety of sources, both spoken and written; from radio, television and casual conversation as well as from books, newspapers, journals and other printed matter. Most of the examples, drawn from authentic late 20th-century English, are unattributed, but sources and dates are cited for specimens of earlier English, which are given to shed light from the past on present usage. We in the English-speaking world are especially fortunate in possessing an unrivalled body of material on our mother tongue, for it has been recorded, described and analyzed in greater detail than any other language, ancient or modern. In particular, we have two scholarly works of great distinction, the *Oxford English Dictionary* in its second, twenty-volume edition (1989) and *A Comprehensive Grammar of the English Language* (1985) by Randolph Quirk, Sidney Greenbaum, Geoffrey Leech and Jan Svartvik. These two works form a sound descriptive basis for offering prescriptive guidance on modern English usage and both have been consulted extensively in the writing of this book.

Language is, after life itself, the greatest gift we possess. It is the most characteristically human of all our attributes, setting us apart from all other living creatures. It is central to all our experience and enters into every aspect of our lives; our civilization and culture would not exist without it. For these reasons we need to cherish and safeguard this priceless possession that is our native language by cultivating its best forms and rejecting the inferior. If this book furthers those ends it will have served its purpose.

Acknowledgements

For his generous help and advice in the preparation of this book I wish to thank my colleague Dr John Dalingwater. To my wife I owe a special debt of gratitude for her constant encouragement and assistance.

Part I

1. The Prescriptive Tradition

The betterment of English

The earliest English grammars, written in Latin or under its direct influence, go back to the end of the 16th century. Latin, for many ages the sole medium of intellectual discourse, still dominated the learned world of that time, but was gradually yielding to the force of the vernacular. Until late in the 16th century English had generally been described as a crude, poverty-stricken language, lacking the expressive powers possessed by the classical tongues of ancient Greece and Rome.

This deficiency was gradually made good by the coining of new words and by borrowing from other languages, chiefly Latin and Greek. For well over a hundred years, in the late Renaissance, English went through a period of augmentation and refinement. During the Elizabethan and early Jacobean reigns in particular the language was enriched by men of learning, who greatly increased its vocabulary, and enhanced by men of letters, who added to its other virtues that of elegance. By poets such as Shakespeare it was, wrote Francis Meres, 'gorgeously invested in rare ornaments and resplendent habiliments' (*Palladis Tamia*, 1598).

As a result, by the end of the 17th century learned men were mostly agreed that in its recent past English had attained a state of near-perfection, its attributes rivalling those of the classical languages. 'For elegance, for fluency, and happiness of expression,' wrote Edward Phillips, 'I am persuaded it gives not place to any modern language spoken in Europe, scarcely to the Latin and Greek themselves' (*The New World of English Words*, 1658).

To the cultured minority in the early 18th century it seemed that England was enjoying an Augustan Age of literary eloquence and polish, like that of the Roman Empire under Augustus Caesar. Among the educated class many now feared lest the highly wrought English language fall into barbarism under an onslaught of illiterate changes. It must be saved from corruption, which had already set in, by being purged of impurities and fixed in an agreed form. To this end several eminent writers, among them John Dryden, Daniel Defoe, Joseph Addison and Jonathan Swift, at various times advocated the foundation of an academy, like those already established in Italy and France, to regulate and stabilize the language.

Their proposals, like later attempts to create such an academy in the United States, came to naught. No authoritative body was set up to legislate on the use of English, but the gap was largely filled by the imposing figure of Dr Samuel Johnson, acting as a one-man academy. The publication of his *Dictionary of the English Language* in 1755 was a landmark in the history of English. Long regarded as the standard authority on the forms, meanings and uses of words, it was followed by other works whose authors set out to reduce the language to order and furnish a standard of correctness. Grammar came to be seen essentially as the choice of 'proper' forms or, as Dr Johnson has it, 'the art of using words properly'.

The imposition of rules

Thus it came about that in the latter half of the 18th century, when English grammar began to be taught in schools as an independent subject and not as a preparation for the study of Latin and Greek, there was no dearth of books on correct usage. Well over two hundred grammars and rhetorics, devoted to stigmatizing solecisms and systematizing syntax, complemented an ever-increasing number of dictionaries. The combined influence of all these works soon made itself felt among the rising middle classes, who were keen to have firm linguistic norms laid down for them. The hitherto unregulated English language was subjected to scholastic discipline. Where anarchy and instinct had reigned before, order and logic were now imposed.

Most of the prescriptive rules of English were framed by writers of this time, such as Robert Lowth, George Campbell, Hugh Blair and Lindley Murray, whose chief concerns in language were precision and 'propriety' [correctness]. Like the literary oligarchs of the same period, they sought to confer decorum on the language. In pursuit of this goal they formulated rules of grammar and style, which they modified as they went along, agreeing with each other on some points and clashing over others. They eagerly ferreted out misuses of words and errors of grammar, rejecting what they deemed to be improper terms and low expressions. Believing grammar to be but applied logic, they repudiated usage, even that of the most celebrated authors, as the sole standard of correctness. They based their rules on logic, analogy and above all on Latin, which they took to embody the principles of universal grammar and revered as the paragon of linguistic virtues.

By the 19th century a tradition had been established as to what constituted good English, namely the practice of the best speakers and writers, subjected to tests devised by self-appointed guardians of the language. Unlike most of their predecessors, however, the Victorian arbiters of usage were inclined to regard good grammar more as a moral imperative than as a matter of linguistic etiquette. To be sure, they did not always see eye to eye, and feuds were fought in which one grammarian's prescription was another grammarian's proscription.

1. The Prescriptive Tradition

Besides a good deal of plagiarism, there was much fault-finding with the English both of great writers and of fellow grammarians. For example, Lindley Murray was attacked on many points by Noah Webster in his famous *American Dictionary of the English Language* (1828) and by Goold Brown, another American, in his vast work *The Grammar of English Grammars* (1851). After these attacks came an acrimonious transatlantic polemic between Dean Henry Alford, author of *The Queen's English* (1864) and George Washington Moon, who criticized him severely in *The Dean's English* (1864). Goold Brown, Alford and Moon refined the art of detecting errors in English to the point where few utterances would escape censure. But despite all their differences most grammarians continued to take Latin as their chief model. Thus it was considered bad style, if not bad grammar, to begin a sentence with the word *however* (meaning 'nevertheless'), merely because the masters of Latin prose never used the equivalent words, *autem* and *tamen*, in first position.

The dominance of Latin

It was this Latinate tradition that dominated and distorted the teaching of English for nearly two hundred years. Only when the science of linguistics came to the fore in the late 19th century was it generally realized that English could not be satisfactorily described or explained in terms of the rules governing Latin. The 'Latin fallacy', the belief that what applies in Latin must also apply in English, was abandoned as the prescriptive approach to grammar came under challenge from linguistic scholars, especially those of the structuralist school. In the 20th century it has come to be recognized that all aspects of language are relative to time and situation, that grammatical rules are not sacrosanct for evermore, and that each variety of English is correct in its own sphere of use. This has led some linguists to regard the inculcation of standard English in schools as a form of linguistic snobbery. To this view must be added the belief, common among educationalists, that grammar teaching has a harmful effect on creative writing and cramps the pupil's style. All the grammar that pupils are likely to need, it is argued, will be picked up from the spoken language and from reading. To quote from the Newbolt Report, *The Teaching of English in England* (1921), 'English should be taught through the study of good literature rather than through definite grammar lessons'.

All this created uncertainty and a loss of confidence among many teachers of English. As a consequence the teaching of formal English grammar began to lose ground in British and American schools from the close of the 19th century. After the First World War there was a significant retreat from the teaching of English grammar. As a result, the one thing that could be said with certainty about the pupils of progressive English grammar schools is that they knew little or no English grammar. This retreat continued after the Second World War until finally, in the late 1960s, most British schools abandoned the teaching of English grammar altogether. Now, a generation later, the pedagogical pendulum has swung back in favour of treating grammar in English lessons, albeit in a more informal manner, without resort to the cognitive grind of parsing and clause analysis.

In many ways the reaction against prescriptive rules was understandable and justified. These rules were handed down from on high as if written on tablets of stone, despite the fact that many of them had long been flouted in practice, even by the best speakers and writers. It is instructive to look at some of these traditional rules, to note the historical ignorance on which they were based, and to recognize the extent to which they went unheeded.

2. Main Traditional Rules

Split infinitives

For many years the most frequently and fiercely denounced 'error' of English usage was the so-called split infinitive. Grammarians, teachers and newspaper editors all thundered against it. Let no one dare write or say *to fully understand*, *to flatly refuse* or *to at least consider*. Yet the rule condemning it is of relatively recent origin. The first known objector to its use was the printer Richard Taylor, who complained in 1840: 'Some writers of the present day have a disagreeable affectation of putting an adverb between to and the infinitive' (*Tooke's 'Diversions of Purley'*, 2nd edition). Another writer, at the end of the 19th century, named Byron as the father of the split infinitive, quoting in evidence his line, 'To slowly trace the forest's shady scene', from Book II of *Childe Harold* (1812). In fact the split infinitive was not a Byronic invention, nor was it anything new in the language, for it is found as far back as the 13th century. It was used by early translators of the Bible, by Donne, Dickens and others, though it was not common before the 19th century.

It is nonsense to suppose that the word *to* is an inseparable part of the infinitive, that the two are joined together in a kind of holy matrimony, not to be put asunder by any man. *To* is no more an integral part of the infinitive than the article *a* or *the* is a necessary part of the noun. This is shown by the use of the 'bare infinitive', i.e. unaccompanied by *to*, with modal verbs, as in *he may come, he should see, he must know* and so on. The reason for this mistaken belief in the indivisibility of *to* and the infinitive is not hard to find. In English grammars of Latin the translation of the infinitive always included the word *to*, simply as a mechanical device to make clear the part of speech. Learners of grammar inferred from this that there was an indissoluble bond between *to* and the infinitive proper. Accordingly they treated any separation of the two as a gross solecism, and the avoidance of split infinitives became a fetish, often pursued at the price of clarity and naturalness.

Consider the sentences 'I cannot bring myself to really trust him', 'She grew to rather like him', 'He is likely to far outstrip his rivals' and 'We expected him to at least defend our interests'. The words *really, rather, far* and *at least* cannot be placed elsewhere without altering the sense or emphasis of these statements. And in the sentence 'We expect to more than double our output' the words *more than* would make no sense anywhere else. In short, there is no good reason for objecting to such adverbial enclaves; on the contrary, they enrich the language by increasing its pliancy and range of expression.

Final prepositions

Almost as heinous a crime as splitting an infinitive, in the eyes of Latinate grammarians, was ending a sentence or clause with a preposition. So familiar was this precept that it became a standing joke among schoolboys to define a preposition as a word you must never end a sentence with. Apparently the rule was invented by the poet John Dryden towards the end of the 17th century. Dryden had been a man of letters for many years when, in his *Defence of the Epilogue* (1672), he declared the use of a final preposition to be a fault, one which he had but recently noticed in his own works. He would often test his English by turning it into Latin and in so doing was obliged to move any preposition standing at the end of a sentence. As a result, when revising his *Essay of Dramatic Poesy* (1668) for the second edition of 1684, he 'corrected' his own syntax. For example, he altered 'the age I live in' to 'the age in which I live', because in Latin one must say *aetas in qua vivo*, the order *aetas qua vivo in* being quite unknown. English was once again pressed in the mould of Latin, the language of scholarship.

The use of a final preposition was deemed to be inelegant by Robert Lowth in *A Short Introduction to English Grammar* (1762), the most widely used English grammar book of its time. The same view was popularized by Lindley Murray in his *English Grammar* (1795), a derivative compilation that served for decades as the standard pedagogical authority in its field. The very etymology of the word *preposition* (Lat. *praepositio*, from *prae* and *posit-*, 'fore-place') supported Dryden's rule. A postposed preposition was a contradiction in terms. Thus the Latin sense and use of a preposition was foisted on English. As a consequence many generations were taught to believe that prepositions must be kept true to their name and placed before the words they referred to, never after.

However, practice was very often at variance with precept here, as with the split infinitive. Like it, the final preposition goes back to the 13th century. Examples of its use can be found in all our greatest writers, from Chaucer onwards. In the writings of Joseph Addison, one of the finest stylists of his age, it occurs so often that it was sometimes called the Addisonian termination, a name bestowed on it by Bishop Richard Hurd, who edited his works. The use of a final preposition is, and has long been, normal in idiomatic English. It is natural in *wh-*questions like 'Where is it from?', exclamations like 'What a mess you are in!' and is unavoidable in passive constructions such as 'He was laughed at' and in infinitive clauses such as 'He is easy to work for'. Nor can it be avoided with phrasal verbs in such sentences as 'Here's a competition I must go in for' and 'That's enough to be going on with'; the 'prepositions' here are in fact adverbial particles which cannot be divorced from their partners.

It is said that Winston Churchill, on reading a sentence in which some official had clumsily avoided a prepositional ending, wrote the marginal comment: 'This is the sort of bloody nonsense up with which I will not put'. Henry Fowler, the greatest popular authority on English in this century, likewise rejected the Dryden rule. 'To shrink with horror from ending with a preposition,' he wrote, 'is no more than foolish superstition.' In his opinion, 'the remarkable freedom enjoyed by English in putting its prepositions late ... is an important element in the flexibility of the language' (*Modern English Usage*, 1926). Like Churchill and Fowler, we can confidently discard this tired old shibboleth.

'Shall' and 'will'

Failure to distinguish between *shall* and *will* was another cardinal sin in the book of the old prescriptive grammarians. In the 18th century the 'proper' use of these forms was taken as an infallible sign of good English, so much so that Alexander Pope and other editors 'corrected' the errors in Shakespeare, who had unwittingly sinned in this respect. The twofold distinction between *shall* and *will* was first noted by George Mason, a Frenchman writing for foreigners, in his *Grammaire Angloise* (1622). The rules were then formulated by John Wallis in his *Grammatica Linguae Anglicanae* (1653), the most influential English grammar of its time. The basic rules are that with first-person subjects *shall* expresses the plain future, making a prediction ('I/we shall go'), and *will* expresses a coloured future, signifying the speaker's intention, promise or threat ('I/we will go'); with subjects in the second and third persons the converse applies.

The use of *shall* and *will* in questions was first expounded by Michael Maittaire in *The English Grammar* (1712). Finally, the fully elaborated rules, including the use of *should* and *would* in conditional clauses and reported speech, appeared in James White's *The English Verb* (1761). These works reflected a usage developing among cultivated speakers in the south of England in the early 17th century. During the previous hundred years usage varied considerably, but *shall* was much more often used than *will* to express the plain future. Thus the rendering of the 23rd Psalm in the Authorized Version of the Bible (1611), like that of Coverdale in the Great Bible (1539), ends with the words: '... and mercy shall follow me all the days of my life; and I will dwell in the house of the Lord for ever'. The rules framed later would require *shall* and *will* to change places here.

At no time did the grammarians' rules for *shall* and *will* reflect universal usage. Most speakers of English outside England itself did not and still do not distinguish between the two auxiliaries in the way prescribed: for example, in the English of most Americans *will* is generalized to cover both predictions and promises, but whereas Americans regularly use *shall* in first-person questions like 'Shall I call you?', Scottish and Irish speakers say 'Will I call you?' The dividing line between *shall* and *will* has always been blurred in places, and the rules are breached even even by the best writers. The existence of two paradigms with the same forms in complementary distribution (*shall, will, will* and *will, shall, shall*) was bound to lead to confusion, which was further compounded by doubt about whether the *'ll* in colloquial contracted forms such as *I'll* and *you'll* stood for *shall* or *will* (historically it derives from *will*). In this situation insistence on the rules smacked of insular pedantry.

Schoolmasters used to tell the cautionary tale of a man (variously given as Scottish, Irish and French) who fell into the water and met his end, solely through crying: 'I will drown and no one shall save me'. He would have been rescued, so the lesson ran, if he had exchanged the positions of the auxiliaries. For us today the story has lost its point, since neither the *shall* nor the *will* suggests volition here and the *shall* sounds quaintly old-fashioned. The tale may well also prompt the reflection that a man in distress who could not simply shout 'Help!' deserved to drown.

Nowadays *shall* is rarely combined with second- or third-person subjects, whereas formerly it was regularly used, to express a command ('Thou shalt not kill'), promise ('You shall go'), or threat ('You shall pay for this'), or where anticipating *shall* in the answer ('Shall you go?' i.e. 'Do you expect to go?'). The fact is that *will* has gradually gained ground at the expense of *shall* and has now all but displaced it. Where it has not done so, other means of avoiding *shall* are to hand. The first-person question form 'Shall I ...?' can be as well expressed by such turns of phrase as 'Should I ...?', 'Am I to ...?', 'Would you like me to ...?', 'Do you want me to ...?', 'Do you think I should ...?' and so on. In short, *shall* is now a dispensable word whose disappearance, far from depriving us of valuable nuances of meaning, as some believe, would be a gain for simplicity, ridding the language of a sore that has plagued it for several hundred years.

Subject and object pronouns

A long, confused battle has been waged between *I* and *me*. Until very recent times the use of 'It is I' was considered a touchstone of linguistic propriety. But while purists insisted that we should say 'It is I' and 'He is bigger than I', for several centuries most people, including the educated, have persisted in saying 'It is me' and 'He is bigger than me'. Some scholars have surmised that this use of the object pronoun *me, him*, etc. came about in imitation of the French disjunctive pronouns *moi, lui*, etc., as used in 'C'est moi' and 'Tu es plus grand que lui'. The fact is, however, that the use of *moi* and *lui* in these constructions was established in French a good 200 years before *me* and *him* began to oust *I* and *he* from the same positions in English. The Old French 'Ce suis je' gave way to the form 'C'est moi' in the second half of the 14th century; by contrast, the Old English 'Ic hit eom' (I it am), after giving way to 'It am I' and then 'It is I', began to be challenged by 'It is me' only at the end of the 16th century.

In Tudor times the object pronoun forms began to be used alongside the still predominant subject forms to express the complement of the verb *to be*. Both occur in Shakespeare's plays, for instance, indeed in remarks by Sir Andrew they are almost cheek by jowl: 'That's me, I warrant you' and 'I knew 'twas I …'. (*Twelfth Night*, c. 1600). The comparative *me* also appears in Shakespeare, as when the heroine of *Antony and Cleopatra* (c. 1606) asks about Octavia: 'Is she as tall as me?' With third persons this usage in comparisons occurs somewhat earlier. Thus Coverdale's rendering of Proverbs 27:3 in the Great Bible of 1539 reads: 'The stone is heavy and the sand weighty; but a fool's wrath is heavier than them both', but *they both* in his Bible of 1535.

Considering the wide time-gap between these changes in the two languages, we may here rule out any French influence on English, for this had effectively ceased long before the 16th century. The shift from *I* to *me* in such cases was evidently a native development, parallel to that of French, but independent of it. Two factors must have contributed to a gradual change in usage. First, after the English noun had shed most of its case endings in the late Middle Ages only the personal pronouns retained a formal distinction between subject and object. In this situation case confusion became rife, especially in the second-person pronouns, where it was aided by the cross-association of forms with identical vowels, i.e. subject *ye* and object *thee*; object *you* and subject *thou* (then pronounced 'thoo'). It is not surprising that *you* and *ye* came to be confused, so much so that Shakespeare and other Elizabethan writers used them indiscriminately for both subject and object. Confusion between *thou* and *thee* was likewise common. Among Quakers it led to the curious practice of using *thee* for both subject and object and, since they rejected the formal *ye* and *you*, for the plural too, then making the verb agree in the third person singular, to give such forms as *thee knows*. Role reversal in pronouns is found in dialect to this day, as is illustrated by the words of the West country lad who signified his willingness to marry by saying: 'Us'll 'ave she if 'er'll 'ave we'.

The other factor, besides lexical confusion, is syntactical convention. The normal word order of statements, in medieval as in modern English, is subject – verb – object (SVO). Thus verbs are usually followed by *me*, whether it be direct object, as in 'He saw me', or indirect object, as in 'He told me', and likewise with impersonal forms such as 'Woe is me' and 'It likes me' (= I like it), which superseded 'Me liketh' (= to me it is pleasing). It would be natural in these circumstances to substitute *me* for *I* in the post-verbal position, which was seen as object territory. The combination of these two tendencies is sufficient to explain the use of *me* and other object pronouns, both in the predicate and in the second term of comparisons.

Until late in the 18th century there was much vacillation in the use of pronouns after *than* and *as ... as*. James Boswell, in his famous *Life of Samuel Johnson* (1791), used the pronouns *I* and *me* indifferently at the end of comparisons. The grammarians of his day, who strove valiantly to regularize English, disagreed on this point. Some ruled that the case before *than* and *as ... as* should also be used after them; others treated these words as prepositions and thus to be followed by the object pronoun; yet others thought the case of the pronoun should be decided by expanding the construction, as in 'I like her better than he (likes her)' and 'I like her better than (I like) him'. This last rule found favour with later prescriptivists, but was commonly disregarded in practice, like many of their rules. The general tendency is to use the object pronouns everywhere except where the pronoun is directly bound to a finite verb as its subject. In other words syntax, not case, largely determines the choice of pronoun forms.

Despite the prescriptive dogma that the verb *to be* can never take an object, people persist in saying 'It's me'. Over 100 years ago Dean Alford wrote: ' "It is me" ... is an expression which everyone uses. Grammarians (of the smaller order) protest: schoolmasters (of the lower kind) prohibit and chastise; but English men, women and children go on saying it' (*The Queen's English*, 1864). Today 'It is I' sounds archaic, pedantic and pseudo-genteel. To insist on its use is to turn back the clock of history; it is like telling people to say 'Whither goest thou?' instead of 'Where are you going?' By contrast, the *I*-form is still common in comparisons, but is always followed by a verb in natural speech. Thus we say either 'He's taller than me' or 'He's taller than I am'. Similarly in adverbial comparisons we say either 'He knows more than me' or 'He knows more than I do'.

Fused participles

A point of grammar once vigorously contested is the use of a noun or pronoun with a participle as one unit, as in 'I don't like him whistling' and 'Women copying men annoys me'. Learned opinion was long divided over the acceptability of this construction, but most grammarians of the 18th and 19th centuries preferred it to the alternative form using the possessives *his* and *women's*. In the 20th century Henry Fowler launched a vehement attack on the non-possessive construction, which he called the 'fused participle' and described as an ignorant vulgarism in its simplest form, where the first part is a proper name or pronoun. In his view the only correct locution was the possessive gerund, i.e. 'I don't like his whistling' and 'Women's copying men annoys me'. The fused particle, he argued, defied analysis and was 'rapidly corrupting modern English style'.

Otto Jespersen, an eminent Danish scholar, sprang to its defence and in the mid-1920s a battle of the giants was joined on the issue. The victor was the Dane, who showed that the fused participle construction was grammatically analyzable and that it was not a novelty, as Fowler had supposed. In fact, though not as old as the gerund construction, it has been in use with nouns since the beginning of the 13th century and with pronouns since the late 15th century, when William Caxton, the father of English printing, wrote the object phrase *me so presuming* in at least three different works.

The fused participle has a much wider range than the gerund construction, especially in expressing the object of a sentence. For example, we say 'I don't like anything (not *anything's*) disturbing me', 'I don't like all of you (not *your*) watching me', 'He enjoyed this (not *this's*) being done to him', 'He died without his work (not *work's*) being recognized', and 'There is no chance of her and John (not *John's*) getting married'. The sentence 'I like him singing' is synonymous with the accusative and infinitive construction 'I like him to sing', and since we allow the infinitive as the complement of an object it seems perverse to disapprove of the participle in the same role. In both cases the pronoun is linked with the verb to form a single syntactical unit. 'I do not like him singing in the bath' does not mean, as some insist, 'I do not like him (when he is) singing in the bath', but 'I do not like (the situation of) him singing in the bath'; in other words we are referring not to the person engaged in the activity but to the activity itself.

The use of a fused participle as a sentence subject is much less common. We say 'His (not *he*) coming late annoyed me'. If the personal pronoun is used, as it is colloquially, we say *him coming late*, using the object form by 'phrase transference' from its object position ('I don't like him coming late'). With a noun or name before *-ing* we use both constructions, saying 'John's/John winning a prize amazed me'. In the first case we have a gerund (*winning*), which takes a direct object (*a prize*), unlike the verbal noun, which requires a dependent genitive (*the winning of a prize*). In the second case we have as subject a noun phrase (*John winning a prize*) making up a single unit, the fully articulated form of which would be introduced by some abstract term (*The fact/thought of John winning a prize*).

In the second edition of Fowler's *Modern English Usage* (1965) Sir Ernest Gowers showed himself to be more indulgent towards the fused participle than Fowler, who had confessed to an 'instinctive repugnance' for it. While allowing that it was necessary in some cases, Gowers fought a rearguard action against it in others. 'Fowler is right,' he wrote, 'in deprecating the use of the fused participle with a proper name or personal pronoun in a simple sentence: *upon your giving* is undoubtedly more idiomatic than *upon you giving*.'

Gowers gave no reason for this judgement and had no warrant for saying that one is more idiomatic than the other: they are both long-established idioms. But as Robert Burchfield rightly observes in the third edition of Fowler (1996), the possessive with gerund is on the retreat. Since the end of the 19th century there has been an increasing preponderance of fused participles. Nowadays the gerund type is mainly found in the writings of a small number of people who are sticklers for what they regard as the 'correct' form. In fact both constructions are valid and sometimes they have their separate uses. If we say 'I don't like his singing' we refer to the way he sings; but on the other hand, if we say 'I don't like him singing' we refer to the fact of his singing, regardless of whether it is well or badly done. Distinctions of this kind enrich the language and justify the survival of both forms.

3. Lesser Rules

'Due to' and 'owing to'

Other, albeit minor, points of grammatical dogma were held sacred by the old prescriptive authorities. The use of *due to* as a preposition was until recently a notorious bugbear of the purists, who conducted a long campaign to stop it being used in the same way as *owing to*. *Due to*, they dogmatized, is an adjective and should only be used as such. In their view, it was acceptable to say (1) 'Leaks that occurred in many places were due to faulty valves' and (2) 'Leaks, due to faulty valves, occurred in many places', but not (3) 'Leaks occurred in many places, due to faulty valves'. In the first two sentences *due* is an adjective qualifying *leaks*, predicatively in (1) and attributively in (2). But in (3), they argued, *owing to* is the proper form: *due to* is wrong here because *due* refers to *many places*, which makes nonsense since many places cannot be due to faulty valves. The same objection, of course, could be made against *owing to*, since *owing* may likewise be taken adjectivally to refer to *many places*.

It is easy to see how type (3) developed, by 'phrase transference', from type (2), and the shift in usage would be reinforced by analogy with *owing to*, which had established itself as a compound preposition early in the 19th century. Where *owing to* led, *due to* was almost bound to follow. By the end of the century *due to* had come to be used, especially in American English, in the same way as its near-synonym *owing to*. No cogent reason has ever been given for accepting *owing to*, but rejecting *due to*, as a preposition. It has been said that the use of *due to* can lead to ambiguity, but in the few instances where this is so, it would also be the case if *owing to* were substituted.

The old distinction between the two constructions is thus both arbitrary and artificial. Moreover, *due to* has the advantage of greater brevity. Fowler condemned the prepositional use of *due to* as illiterate, while acknowledging that it was 'as common as can be'. Gowers, in his revised version of Fowler's work, showed that the usage had attained the status of respectability. It was established usage in America by 1930, according to an article by Professor J.S. Kenyon in Volume 6 of *American Speech* for that year. And in England it received the royal seal of approval, so to speak, when it was used by Queen Elizabeth II in her speech at the opening of the Canadian Parliament in 1957. 'Due to inability to market their grain,' said Her Majesty, 'prairie farmers have for some time been faced with a serious shortage of funds to meet their immediate needs.'

Intensifiers with participles

Another 'error' eagerly seized upon by the old champions of linguistic purity was the use of *very* with a past participle. The purists objected to such combinations as *very pleased* and *very interested*, which had been in use since the middle of the 17th century, and insisted on *much* or *greatly* in place of *very* here. Now it is true that we do not say 'He was *very* criticized' or 'The chances were *very* increased': here we must use *much* or *greatly*. But when the participle has lost its verbal force and turned into an adjective there is no reason why it should not be qualified by *very*. It is just as acceptable to say *very pleased, very determined* or *very complicated* as to say *very glad, very resolute* and *very complex*, which mean much the same.

The reasoning behind this rule is that the adverb of degree *very* cannot modify a verb. We do not say 'They *very* admire him', hence we should not say 'He is very admired' but 'He is much/greatly admired'. But the rule proves unsound if one applies such a transformation test to all cases. We do not say 'They *very* amuse her', but we do say 'She is very amused by them'. This last is an example of a past participle used to make the passive voice, i.e. used verbally, not as an adjective. Idiom allows this, but only when some emotional reaction is being expressed. Thus it is acceptable to say 'We were very shocked by this news' and 'I was very annoyed by her remarks'.

In other cases it is quite unidiomatic to use *very* with a passive construction. No one would say, for example, 'The house was *very improved* by the extension', but *much improved* or *greatly improved*; nor would one say 'The crops were *very affected* by the drought', but *badly affected* or *severely affected*. Of course, some past participles, by their meaning, preclude the use of any adverbial modifier. Thus nothing can be *very annihilated* or *greatly devastated*, just as nothing can be *very unique* or *highly impossible*. But the old linguistic taboo on using *very* with participle-derived adjectives, being too restrictive and at variance with normal educated usage, has been abandoned and the language has been enriched by this greater freedom of collocation. Sometimes a difference of meaning is marked by the use of *much* with a past participle and *very* with the same word used as an adjective. Thus *a much disappointed man* has been many times disappointed, but *a very disappointed man* is disappointed to a high degree. Similarly, there is a world of difference between *a much married woman* and *a very married woman*.

3. Lesser Rules

Agreement with 'none' and 'neither'

Strongly defended for a long time was the rule that the word *none* must be construed with a verb in the singular, and this despite the fact that Lindley Murray, the high priest of prescriptivists, had allowed a singular or a plural verb here. Our ancestors, heedless of grammatical consistency, freely used both forms of the verb with *none*. The use of a plural verb is first recorded in the 9th century in the writings of King Alfred the Great, and later examples of it abound. In Shakespeare's *Love's Labour's Lost* (c. 1590) Dumaine remarks: 'For none offend where all alike do dote'. A century later Dryden wrote: 'None have been so greedy of employments ... as they who have least deserved their stations' (*Dedication of the Georgics*, 1697). Even the great Dr Johnson used both singular and plural verb forms in his novel *Rasselas* (1759), in one place writing 'none ever varies his opinion', and in another 'none are wretched but by their own fault'.

The use of *none* with a plural verb was objected to on the pseudo-logical grounds that *none* contains *one*, which is singular. *None*, it is true, derives from Old English *nan* (= *ne an*, 'not one'), but so too does *no*, a shortened form of *none*. Therefore one could equally well object to the combination *no men*, which contains an etymological *one* just as much as *none* does. But etymology is as unreliable a guide in resolving grammatical difficulties as it is in establishing the present meanings of words. The fact is that with *none* the verb may be in either number, depending on whether the singular or plural idea is uppermost in the speaker's mind.

In formal agreement *none* is treated as the equivalent of *not one*, hence the singular is used; in notional agreement it is seen as the equivalent of *not any*, hence the plural is used. The tendency to use a plural verb is increased by the force of attraction when *none* goes with a dependent plural noun or pronoun (*none of the men, none of them*). By contrast, when *none* goes with a dependent singular noun or pronoun the verb is always singular. Thus we say 'None of the eggs were used', but 'None of the butter was used', *eggs* being a countable noun (one with a plural form) and *butter* being uncountable (one with no plural). Similarly we say 'None of them matter', but 'None of that matters'.

With grammarians of the past it was an article of faith that the word *neither*, like *none*, should take a singular verb, whether it is used alone, with a dependent genitive, or in combination with *nor*. *Neither* is singular pronoun, therefore it requires a singular verb, so the argument ran. In present-day practice, however, a singular verb is regularly used only when *neither* qualifies a singular noun. Thus we say 'Neither book is missing', but 'Neither of the books (them) is/are missing' and 'Neither is/are missing', with the plural form of the verb far commoner than the singular.

The use of the plural verb goes back to the middle of the 16th century. Shakespeare, for example, has 'when neither are alive' (*Cymbeline, c.*

1610) and Dryden has 'Neither were great inventors' in the preface to his *Fables* (1700). *Neither* may be seen as an alternative singular (not this or that) or as a cumulative plural (not this and not that). It is perfectly reasonable to take it either way, and the modern preference is for the plural. This is even extended to using *neither* with a plural subject or complement as well as a plural verb, as in 'They neither trust the other' and 'Neither of us are swimmers'.

The correlative pair *neither ... nor* poses special problems of agreement. A singular or plural verb may be used with two singular noun subjects, as in 'Neither father nor son is/are to blame'. Most grammarians have preferred the singular here, but as the idea of addition is just as strong as that of separation there is good excuse for those who use the plural. Dr Johnson did not shrink from using the plural when he wrote: 'Neither search nor labour are necessary' (*The Idler*, 1759). When both subjects are plural, a plural verb is naturally used, as in 'Neither parents nor pupils like him'. But with mixed subjects there are complications. We would say 'Neither the men nor the dog were hurt' since *men* and *dog* may be subsumed under *they*, but it is not clear whether it is better to say 'Neither she nor they know' or 'knows', 'Neither John nor I am afraid' or 'is afraid'. The old rule in such cases was that the verb agreed with the nearer of the two subjects, but common sense suggests the use of the plural in all cases, and this practical solution has prevailed against the strictures of the precisians. The consistent use of plural agreement is wholly acceptable and defensible, for *neither ... nor* can quite reasonably be regarded as the negative of *both ... and*.

'Between', 'among' and reciprocal pronouns

It was a fixed principle with traditional grammarians that the preposition *between* should be used for two things or persons, and *among* for more than two. Thus we divide property between two persons and among three or more. But in actual usage, whereas *among* always refers to more than two, *between* is by no means restricted to two. Indeed we are advised by no less an authority than the *Oxford English Dictionary* (*OED*) to ignore this restriction and continue to observe the following distinction. *Between* expresses the relation of something to many surrounding things individually; *among* expresses a relation to them collectively. We would not say 'the space lying *among* the three points', 'the choice lay *among* the three candidates', or 'to insert a needle *among* the closed petals'. We speak of 'a treaty between four powers' because it links each one to each of the others. Furthermore, *between* is used to express the result of some collective action, regardless of the number of people involved. For example, we would say 'Between them the passengers managed to get the car to a garage'. Purists will point out that *between* comes from *by-twain* (='two'), but despite that fact the word has, from its earliest appearance, been extended to more than two. We should not allow ourselves to become victims of the etymological fallacy.

3. Lesser Rules

We may likewise reject the artificial rule according to which *each other* refers to two things or persons, and *one another* to more than two. To quote Fowler: 'This differentiation is neither of present utility nor based on historical usage'. If there is a distinction in practice between the two forms, it is that *one another* (like *one*) is more likely to be used in general statements, such as 'People should help one another', and *each other* is more usual when referring to particular people, as in 'The children help each other'. In all contexts, however, the two reciprocal pronouns may be used interchangeably.

'Fewer', 'less', and 'not so ... as'

Another prescriptive rule sometimes invoked by writers on usage draws a distinction between the comparatives *fewer* (not so many) and *less* (not so much). Thus *fewer* is assigned to countable nouns, while *less* is reserved for uncountables: *fewer eggs* but *less bread*, and *fewer delays* but *less waste*. In fact the use of *less* with a plural has a venerable history going back to Old English, where the word *fewer* is not found. And when measured against modern usage, the rule is still only a half-truth, for whereas *fewer* is used only with plural nouns, *less* is by no means confined to singulars. It is at least as common to hear *less eggs* and *less delays* as *fewer* of them. And this is understandable because the word *more* is used for number and quantity alike. There is no separate antonym of *fewer*, no word *many-er*, used solely for countables. Thus, since *more* can be used with both singular and plural nouns, there is no reason why *less* should not do double duty in the same way, *fewer* being retained as an alternative for use with countables. The fact is, however, that *fewer* and its superlative counterpart *fewest* are linguistic luxuries we could well dispense with, as their work can always be done by *less* and *least*.

A curious rule, first enunciated in Lowth's grammar of 1762, decrees that the first of the comparative correlatives *as ... as* should be replaced by *so* after a negative: *as good as*, but *not so good as*. This distinction did not accord with earlier usage, which had *as* or *so* as the first correlative, whether the comparison was affirmative or negative. Thus *so ... as* had been commonly used, as in Shakespeare's 'Look I so pale ... as the rest?' (*Richard III*, c. 1593), though it was going out of use.

No doubt Lowth's intention was to take the two coexisting forms and put each to a separate use. Unfortunately, his mechanical rule conflicted not only with the free usage of previous ages, but also with contemporary usage, in which a distinction was made, as it still is, between *as* and *so* in negative comparisons. 'It is not so far as York' implies that York is far away. 'It is not as far as York' gives no indication whether York is far or near; it may in fact be only a short distance away. Similarly 'He is not so tall as his son' implies that both are tall, whereas 'He is not as tall as his son' gives no indication of how tall they are; both may be short, tall, or of medium height. In other words *so* is an intensive, marked adverb, and *as* is a neutral, unmarked adverb in the negative construction. We no longer use *so* in the affirmative construction except in a few conjunctions which have preserved this old form, for example *so far as* (= as far as) and *so long as* (= as long as). Thus we may regard Lowth's rule as a grammatical fiction, without validity now or in the past. Happily, since most people are ignorant of it, the rule is generally ignored.

Relative pronouns

Last in this inventory of minor grammatical precepts comes a recommendation rather than a rule. Since the 19th century many normative grammarians have urged us to use the relative pronoun *that* in defining (or restrictive) clauses, but *which* and *who* in commenting (or non-restrictive) clauses. We are advised to say, in a defining way, 'The books/boys that arrived late were sent back' and, in a commenting way, 'The books/boys, which/who arrived late, were sent back' (commenting clauses need commas or pauses). This is a neat division of linguistic labour – in theory.

The trouble with the scheme is that it accords only in part with actual usage. In practice the use of *that* is, and long has been, confined almost exclusively to defining clauses. We do not say (with pauses) or write (with commas) 'The books/boys, *that* arrived late,...' i.e. to supply further information about the antecedent. Unfortunately, however, the converse does not hold true. Although *which* and *who* are used in commenting clauses, where *that* rarely occurs, they are also quite common in defining clauses, especially in written English. It is normal and acceptable to say 'The books which (= that) arrived late', meaning those books and no others, and similarly 'The boys who (= that) arrived late'.

Another difficulty is this: there are conditions in which *that* cannot be used in defining clauses. In conversation it is usual to say 'This is the house that I was born in', with the preposition at the end. But if we wish to adopt a more formal style, with the preposition at the head of the clause, we cannot say 'This is the house in *that* I was born'; we must say 'in which I was born'. Similarly 'He is the man that I spoke to', but 'He is the man to whom (not *that*) I spoke'. As with preceding prepositions, so in the possessive, the use of *that* is ruled out, as it has no other forms. For persons we have *whose* and for things we have *of which* (often replaced for convenience by *whose*), but there is no possessive form *thats*. Thus we say 'He's the man whose son was killed' and 'This is the house whose owner (= the owner of which) has died'.

These constraints on the use of *that* make it impossible to distinguish between defining and commenting clauses by pronoun selection alone. Since the pronouns *that*, *who* and *which* cannot always be used with distinctive functions, only stylistic guidance can be given about their use. The best advice in this matter is quite simple and it is grounded in idiomatic custom. Avoid using *which* or *who* where *that* will do just as well, and do not use any relative pronoun if the sentence makes sense and runs smoothly without one: 'This is the key that (rather than *which*) fits the lock', 'It was Tom that (rather than *who*) came to see me' and 'It is John I want (rather than *that* I want)'.

4. Grammarians' Victories

Multiple negation

It may be thought, from the catalogue of discredited rules in the previous two chapters, that the grammarians and teachers suffered defeat on all fronts. Not so: they achieved some triumphs over vernacular usage, and from among competing forms they determined in many cases which were acceptable in standard English.

The change from multiple to single negation is a shift in educated usage largely attributable to the efforts of teachers and grammarians. In Old English multiple negation, though not always used, was normal in most constructions; certainly whenever other negative words occurred *ne* always preceded the verb. In Middle English two or more negatives together were still widely used. Thus, in his Prologue to *The Canterbury Tales* (c. 1386) Chaucer wrote of a 'verray parfit gentil knight' (true perfect well-born knight) that 'He nevere yet no vileynie ne sayde' (never spoke rudely), using three negatives.

For a long time, in order to make the negation clearer, the generally unstressed particle *ne* was often strengthened by the addition of *not* (from *noht*, earlier *nowiht*, 'not a thing'). In late Middle English *not* frequently lost its emphatic force and subsequently it displaced *ne* as the negative marker. Multiple negation, now with *not*, continued to be used during the 15th and 16th centuries, but less frequently than before in the written language. By Shakespeare's time it still occurred quite often with *not*, as when Mercutio says: 'I will not budge for no man's pleasure' (*Romeo and Juliet*, c. 1595). But its chief remaining use was in coordinate constructions with *nor*, as when Mistress Quickly says: 'I will bar no honest man my house, nor no cheater' (*Henry IV, Part 2*, c. 1597).

By the 17th century double negatives of the 'sentence element' type ('I don't want no meat') had been reduced to the status of unacceptable literary English. And by the end of the century multiple negation rarely occurred in the standard language, though it lingered on there well into the 18th. Thus the *Gentleman's Magazine* in 1764 (vol. 34) told of a 'person of no mean appearance' losing his hat at a ball and crying: 'Pray, Gentlemen, has not nobody seen never a hat nowhere?' And in a letter written as late as 1797 Charles Lamb told Coleridge: 'I can't see no wit in her', but by then the construction was both an archaism and a solecism.

Single negation

The change that had taken place in educated usage between 1500 and 1700 was brought about by grammar teachers, assisted by translators of the Latin classics and editors of English literary works. Cultivated young men were trained at school and college in the forms of classical grammar, and the English they wrote and spoke was strongly influenced by the structure of Latin. The single negation of Latin was thus transferred to English, a change made possible once the strong negative *not* finally supplanted the weak *ne* in the 16th century.

Single negation was adopted as a textbook rule by prescriptive grammarians, chiefly because it conformed to the Latin model, but for other reasons too. Clearly, it was unsatisfactory to have two opposed methods of negation existing side by side within the same system, for this could lead to ambiguity. Clearly, too, all the advantages lay with choosing the single type. Single negation was free of redundancy, a thing frowned upon by prescriptivists as unnecessary and inelegant. Nor did the choice involve the loss of a valuable emphatic device, as some have supposed. Multiple negation, where it is the norm, cannot be emphatic. It is in fact a kind of verbal blunderbuss, used to ensure that there can be no possibility of misunderstanding. Whichever type of negation is used, emphasis can only be achieved with certainty in the spoken language, where stress may be placed on the appropriate word or words.

Single negation was far superior, being clear, logical and non-redundant. Contrary to what is often said, it is not based on the mathematical principle that two negatives make a positive. In arithmetic two negatives make a positive when multiplied, not when added, as they are in language. It is in logic that two negatives cancel each other, and the 18th-century grammarians believed that grammar should follow logic. The conflict between logic and usage was noted as early as the 16th century by Sir Philip Sidney: 'For grammar says (to grammar who says nay)/That in one speech, two negatives affirm' (Sonnet 63 of *Astrophel and Stella*, 1591).

The principle of cancellation was first set forth in a grammar book by James Greenwood, who stated that 'two negatives, or two adverbs of denying do in English affirm' (*An Essay Towards a Practical English Grammar*, 1711). It was illustrated by Hugh Jones, who wrote: 'Two negatives affirm, as "you have not no money" is really "you have some money" ' (*Accidence to the English Tongue*, 1724). Robert Lowth made the same point in the second edition of his grammar (1763), where he stated: 'Two negatives in English destroy one another, or are equivalent to an affirmative' and quoted in evidence Milton's lines, 'Nor did they not perceive the evil plight/In which they were ...' (*Paradise Lost*, bk I, 1667). And putting the case against multiple negatives, John Clarke ruled that they 'absolutely prove what you mean to deny' (*The Rational Spelling Book*, 1773).

Thus redundant negation was effectively schoolmastered out of standard English and replaced by logical negation, as happened in German. But the piling-up of negatives persists to this day in all non-standard varieties of English. It has survived in rustic dialect, as in the recorded remarks of two countrymen, 'He nivver said nowt neeaways ti neean on em' and 'Neeabody's neea bisniss ti thraw nowt inti neeabody's gardin'. It lives on in popular songs, as in the lines 'And I'll play the wild rover no more; no, nay never, not never no more'. But the palm for negative repetition must surely be handed to the American from one of the southern states who said: 'I ain't gonna sit in no chair and let no crazy lawyer tell me no lies about no law that no judge has in no law-books that no smart politician wrote, or nothin' like that, nohow'.

Double comparatives and superlatives

Like double negatives, double comparatives and superlatives were driven out of standard English. They arose in Middle English and became especially common in the 15th and 16th centuries. Sometimes they were emphatic, but most often they were merely a blending of the two types, *more* with *-er*, and *most* with *-est*, which resulted in double marking. Shakespeare freely used the double comparative, making various characters say *more better*, *more elder*, *more safer*, *more worse*, *more nearer*, *more corrupter* and, anomalously, *less happier*, also adverbially *more proudlier*. The most famous Shakespearean double superlative is Mark Antony's bitter reproach: 'This was the most unkindest cut of all' (*Julius Caesar*, c. 1599), where the *most* clearly intensifies the expression. Double superlatives were commonly used when addressing those of exalted rank, e.g. 'most noblest knight' and 'the Most Highest', meaning God, the Supreme Being.

The playwright Ben Jonson defended the use of these double forms in his treatise *The English Grammar* (1640), where he compared them to similar ones used for emphasis in ancient Greek. Here, however, he was out of step with most contemporary and later grammarians, who viewed such forms as untidy tautologies. The works of Shakespeare and other writers soon came under corrective treatment. Thus in the Second Folio (1632) edition of Shakespeare's plays *more richer* was altered to *more rich* in *Hamlet*, and *more* was removed from *more braver* in *The Tempest*.

The use of both forms of the comparative or superlative together was censured by grammarians, teachers and editors alike from the beginning of the 17th century, and since the 18th century has been regarded as unacceptable in standard English, though it still occurs sporadically in literary works, as well as in speech. Tennyson, perhaps consciously archaizing, wrote as late as 1833: 'But Paris was to me/More lovelier than the world beside' (*Oenone*).

Regulation of verb forms

The grammarians of the 18th century had much success in establishing the standard forms of 'strong' verbs, i.e. those with internal vowel changes like *sing*, *break* and *drink*. Since the 16th century there had been a marked tendency to level the simple past tense and past participle forms of such verbs. Thus we find *are broke*, *have chose*, and *have spoke* in Shakespeare, and similarly in later writers, e.g. 'a spider *has wove*' in Gibbon, and 'will *have stole* it' in Swift. Contrariwise, we find *I seen*, *I done* and *I begun* for *I saw*, *I did* and *I began*.

Under the spell of Latin, with its numerous inflections, the prescriptive regulators resisted levelling and laboured to preserve inflectional differences in English wherever they could. Since Latin distinguished the past tense and the past participle, they believed that English should do likewise, where possible. In this way they managed to arrest the reduction of irregular verb forms, preserving the distinction between *sang* and *sung*, *wrote* and *written*, and many other pairs. Where a 'weak' verb, i.e. one with a past in -*ed*, had developed a strong alternative by analogy, the second was chosen as standard. Thus the forms *catched* and *digged*, though original, were abandoned in favour of *caught* and *dug*, in order to keep as many irregular forms as possible in use. For the same reason strong verbs such as *blow* and *throw* were not allowed to retain the regular forms *blowed* and *throwed* that were widely used. In nonstandard English, however, the levelling tendency persists; sentences such as 'I *seen* her yesterday', 'He's *broke* his leg', 'They've *took* it all' and 'She *done* nothing wrong' are still commonly heard.

The verb forms *you was*, *ain't* and *he don't*, freely used by people from all walks of life in the 18th century, were routed by the purists. Robert Lowth condemned *you was* as an 'enormous solecism', though his contemporary George Campbell testified that it was 'ten times oftener heard' than *you were* in addressing one person (*Philosophy of Rhetoric*, 1776). In fact it made sense to distinguish singular *you was* from plural *you were*, but there was no corresponding distinction in the present, no *you is* to contrast with *you are*, and no matching distinction in number between *you has* and *you have*.

Again, it made sense to level *am not* and *isn't* to *ain't* (from *aren't*), a contracted form of long standing in south-eastern English dialect. But there was no levelling to parallel this in the affirmative forms, which remained separate as *am*, *is* and *are*. Moreover, *ain't*, by the dropping of *h*- from *hain't*, was also used for *haven't* and *hasn't*, while *have* and *has* obstinately remained separate forms.

By contrast, the third-person auxiliary form *he don't*, which appeared late in the 17th century, had its affirmative counterpart *he do*, first recorded 200 years earlier. This brought the verb *do* into line with other auxiliaries such as *can't* and *shan't*, which have but one form in the present; its closest analogue is the auxiliary *won't*, which arose at much the same time and with which it came to rhyme by imitation. The difficulty with *do* is that it is used not only as an auxiliary, like *can* and *shall*, but as a main or 'notional' verb, and in this primary use its third singular form is always *does*, even in the negative.

For these and possibly other reasons *you was*, *ain't* and *he don't* were considered unsatisfactory and came under the prescriptive ban in the 19th century, though they still flourish in the vernacular and in dialect. The word *ain't* has long been a bugbear of teachers, especially in America, where it is still widely used in informal speech, even by well-educated speakers, especially in the phrase 'Ain't I?' and in common sayings like 'Ain't that something?' and 'You ain't seen nothing yet'.

Adverbs in *-ly* and numeral combinations

The legislators of correct usage, favouring distinct forms for different grammatical functions, were responsible for the spread of adverbs in *-ly* at the expense of 'flat' adverbs, i.e. those identical with adjectives. In particular they disliked the combination, often found in earlier English, of flat adverb with adjective, as in *exceeding small, uncommon grateful, wondrous strange* and *monstrous cruel*. As a result, the use of adverbs in *-ly* has steadily increased in standard English over the last 250 years, but in colloquial speech the old form lives on in such phrases as *mighty fine, proper poorly, real good* and *sure glad*.

In Old and Middle English, when cardinal and ordinal numbers were combined the cardinal always came before the ordinal, as in 'the two (three) first'. Then in the 16th century the reverse form, 'the first two (three)', began to be used too. Both variants remained current, but from the middle of the 18th century the older form came under increasingly frequent criticism and was gradually driven out of general use by grammarians and their classroom allies. It was argued that both combinations normally mean not the two first (two equally first), but the first two (the first and second), hence the latter is the appropriate form. Thus modern logic prevailed over ancient idiom. Of course, in the much rarer instances where we refer to two things or people, each of which is first, we still say 'the two first'. We speak in such cases of 'the two first secretaries' and 'the two first prizes', thereby differentiating them from 'the first two secretaries' and 'the first two prizes'.

*

The examples given above show that language change, though for the most part spontaneous, is sometimes consciously directed. Precepts inculcated in the classroom can help to check or counteract natural tendencies and thus have an influence on linguistic development.

5. Criteria of Correctness

Correct usage

Clearly, many, indeed most of the rules laid down in the past by grammarians and teachers were artificial ones, based not upon current usage but upon the usage of an earlier time or usage as the prescriptivists thought it should be. Ignorance of linguistic history and personal prejudice, sometimes dressed in pseudo-rational guise, played no mean part in the framing of these school rules. However, the fact that most old rules are outmoded or misconceived does not mean that all of them are. Nor is the concept of grammatical norms discredited because the old prescriptivists were quite often mistaken in their attempts to establish them. The truth is that the prescriptive tradition, though it has made only a modest impact on spoken usage, has succeeded in creating a broad consensus on the norms of written English.

Nowadays the relativity of these norms to the period and to the variety of English being considered is acknowledged by all grammarians. What is stigmatized in the language at one time may be approved at another, so that the barbarisms and slang forms of one generation may become accepted usage in the next. Moreover, the stigma attached to such forms is often purely social, and has nothing to do with such criteria as communicative efficiency or euphony.

Some linguists, holding that there is nothing in language that can be called correct or incorrect from a scholarly or scientific point of view, have rejected the idea of standards altogether. This notion of language as a free-for-all in which 'anything goes' was first expressed by R.G. Latham, a professor of English. Latham believed, quite rightly, that usage is learnt from habit, not from rules, and that as usage changes, so do the rules. But he went on from this to draw the extraordinary conclusion that 'in language whatever is, is right' (*The English Language*, 2nd edition, 1848).

In our own century Robert A. Hall, a professor of linguistics, has propounded the same view. Wishing to assure his readers that their English was as good as anyone else's, Professor Hall wrote: 'There is no such thing as good and bad (or correct and incorrect, grammatical and ungrammatical, right and wrong) in language' (*Leave Your Language Alone!* 1950). This anarchic dogma, designed to comfort the linguistically insecure, will deceive none but the naive, for it is demonstrably false. No eclipse of the solecism has taken place, as we can see by looking at a few deviant utterances.

Incorrect forms

The foreigner who says 'I am here since two month' is clearly using incorrect, wrong, ungrammatical English. Likewise a native English child who says 'I buyed some mouses' shows incomplete mastery of the language by using incorrect grammatical forms. The foreigner and the child are both saying things that are recognizably wrong in any variety of English. Native adult speakers can go wrong too. The sentence 'He stated unequivocably that he would use force irregardless of the consequences' is doubly incorrect; *unequivocally* has been confused with adverbs in *-ably*, and *regardless* has been contaminated by *irrespective*. In the sentence 'He decieved the ennemy' both the verb and the noun are incorrect according to the accepted spelling conventions. The sentence 'It were them kids what done it' is incorrect in standard English, though normal and correct in many non-standard varieties. The question 'Does you does or does you don't take Access?', modelled no doubt on the song 'Is you is or is you ain't my baby?', uses deliberately ungrammatical English as an eye-catching device in an advertisement, but it has no validity outside this sphere.

The concept of correctness, of 'obeying the rules', is intimately bound up with language, which is essentially a rule-governed system of communication. Being a human invention sanctioned by convention, language depends on norms. Thus the observance of norms is a fundamental characteristic of natural language use. However, the terms 'correct' and 'incorrect' have connotations inappropriate to linguistic judgements, for they suggest a mathematical rigour and certainty not found in language. Likewise the words 'right' and 'wrong' have moral overtones which, when applied to language, seem to commend or condemn other people's linguistic behaviour. For this reason, to avoid misleading associations with mathematics or morality, linguists nowadays prefer to use the terms 'acceptable' and 'unacceptable', or 'appropriate' and 'inappropriate', which mean the same thing but are free of any such suggestions. What remains to be decided is by what criterion or criteria we may judge linguistic forms to be acceptable and determine which among them are better or worse.

Logic and grammar

The oldest yardstick used in making judgements about grammatical propriety is logic, which has been linked with grammar since antiquity. The foundations of grammar in Western Europe were laid by the ancient Greeks, for whom it was originally but one aspect of philosophy. The Greek philosophers, especially Plato, Aristotle and the Stoics, associated grammar closely with logic. A logical proposition must be expressed grammatically, hence for them grammar was an indispensable tool in the search for truth.

During the later Middle Ages grammar again came under the sway of philosophy. Medieval scholars believed that the grammar of all languages was essentially the same, being based on two universals: the nature of the external world and the properties of the human mind. In their 'speculative' (i.e. theoretical) grammars they sought to reinterpret Latin grammar in conformity with scholastic logic and metaphysics. The application of Aristotle's logic to grammar began about the middle of the 11th century and spread in the 12th century, when Europe experienced a great rebirth of learning. The grammarians of the following two centuries, who are known as modistae, continued this work of classification and analysis, but added little to grammatical theory. The penetration of grammar by Aristotelian logic brought both good and ill. It proved helpful in the refinement of syntax, but harmful in fostering the beliefs that language is solely the creature of reason and that all languages resemble Latin in their grammar.

The ideal of marrying grammar with logic was revived in the 17th century by French scholars at the Convent of Port-Royal, near Paris. For the Port-Royalists logic was the principle underlying all languages, regardless of the many surface differences among them. The true logical form of a sentence could thus be quite different from its grammatical expression in a given language. As there is one logic for all, they argued, so there is one general grammar for all languages. The Port-Royal grammar of 1660, in many ways a successor to the medieval speculative grammars, was the most influential grammar book of post-Renaissance times.

In the 18th century, the so-called Age of Reason, it was commonly held that man is a rational being whose language reflects his rationality. Accordingly, the study of grammar was equated with the study of the universal 'laws' of the human mind. This view of grammar as a form of logic was still common in the 19th century. Samuel Taylor Coleridge, challenging Wordsworth's espousal of rustic diction, remarked in parenthesis that the rules of grammar 'are in essence no other than the laws of universal logic, applied to psychological materials' (*Biographia Literaria*, XVII, 1817). In his book *On the Study of Words* (1851) Richard Chenevix Trench, an eminent linguistic scholar, wrote of man from earliest times being, without knowing how, the possessor of 'the great logical, or grammatical framework of language (for grammar is the logic of speech, even as logic is the grammar of reason)'.

This opinion was articulated in greater detail by the philosopher John Stuart Mill in his inaugural lecture, delivered at the University of St Andrews in 1867. After praising Latin and Greek as superior to modern European tongues, Mill went on to say: 'Consider for a moment what grammar is. It is the most elementary part of logic. It is the beginning of the analysis of the thinking process. The principles and rules of grammar are the means by which the forms of language are made to correspond with the universal forms of thought ... The structure of every sentence is a lesson in logic.'

The truth is, however, that natural language is not governed by pure reason, for it is not constructed entirely in accordance with strictly logical principles. Contrary to what Mill asserts, the forms of language do not correspond to the forms of thought, nor do grammatical categories always tally with logical ones. Languages have different grammars, and the grammar of a living language changes, but logic does not change. In short, logic is the servant of grammar, not its master. As such, it is not a safe guide in deciding grammatical questions.

Illogical usage

Illogicalities are not hard to find in English, as in any other natural language. Logic would require us to place the word *only* next to the word it qualifies. Thus we should say 'I want only two' or 'I want two only', but most people say 'I only want two', introducing the qualifier early in order to mark the modesty of the request. Similarly, the early use of *only* gives warning of a later restriction in statements such as the following: 'Any such request will only be considered by the managers if it is accompanied by a doctor's note'. In each case the displaced adverb is psychologically more effective in conveying the speaker's meaning.

In the sentence 'He is not an artist like his brother' the word *like* is used illogically, for the intended meaning is 'He, *un*like his brother, is not an artist'. The statement 'I wouldn't be surprised if he wasn't right' logically means 'I would be surprised if he was right', but we all understand it to meant the opposite ('if he was wrong'). We say 'Don't be longer than you can help', influenced no doubt by such sentences as 'Don't be long if you can help it'. Logically, however, we should say 'Don't be longer than you *can't* help', with the unavoidable expenditure of time expressed in the negative, but to speak so would be false to idiom, which often cocks a snook at logic.

Constructions embodying a double negative of the type *not un-* and *not without ...*, if strict logic applied, should have a full affirmative meaning, but in fact they express a diluted affirmative. Thus *not uncommon* does not mean 'common', but 'occurring, though not very often', and *not without influence* means not 'possessing influence', but 'with some small influence'. George Orwell, in his essay 'Politics and the English Language' (1946), poured scorn on the *not un-* construction and advised us to cure ourselves of it by memorizing the sentence: 'A not unblack dog was chasing a not unsmall rabbit across a not ungreen field'. This is amusing, but misses the point. 'He is not unknown to me' means 'I have some slight acquaintance with him' and suggests a certain hesitation on the part of the speaker which is absent from the direct 'He is known to me'. The reason for this is that the periphrasis involves a detour via two mutually destructive negatives, which weakens the force of the expression.

As a further refinement, this type of expression is often used in understatements. The *OED* illustrates this use with a quotation as early as 1671, from a translation of Erasmus's *Colloquia*, published under the initials H.M. (Gentleman): 'We say well and elegantly *not ungrateful* for *very grateful*'. Thus, if we say a woman is not unattractive we may mean, depending on the woman, that she has a few attractive features or that she is extremely attractive. Understatement, sometimes strikingly effective, can be found too in the use of the *not without* ... construction. Early in the Second World War Winston Churchill stated that the British navy was hunting German U-boats 'with zeal, and not without relish', expressing himself much more pungently than if he had merely said *with relish*.

The progressive passive construction 'The house is being built', which began to compete with 'The house is building' at the end of the 18th century, was long frowned upon by most grammarians. They objected that it was illogical to combine a continuous active participle with a completed passive one. Despite this, by 1900 the newer form had won the day, almost extinguishing the earlier, 16th-century construction, which was prone to ambiguity ('He was hunting', for example, could be construed in an active or passive sense).

The relationship between language and logic was well described by Jespersen. 'Language,' he wrote, 'is neither perfectly logical nor totally alogical. Language is never illogical where strict logic is required for the sake of comprehension, but neither is it pedantically logical where no ambiguity is to be feared in ordinary conversation: it steers adroitly between these two dangers' ('Logic and Grammar', 1924).

Analogy and grammar

The second criterion of linguistic propriety is analogy, a principle much argued over by the ancient Greeks when they discussed the nature of language. Some, such as Socrates and the Stoics, held that there is a natural affinity between words and the things they stand for; others, following Aristotle, saw words as arbitrary signs, connected only by convention with what they signify. This led to a dispute about the role of analogy within language itself. In the second century BC there emerged two schools of thought, the analogists and the anomalists. The analogists, seeing language as essentially regular and obedient to a strict law of analogy, insisted on absolute, fixed rules of grammar. The anomalists, by contrast, maintained that language is fraught with exceptions and contradictions, that grammatical rules are sanctioned only by custom and therefore subject to change.

This dispute lived on among Roman scholars, who borrowed most of their grammatical concepts and categories from the Greeks, and historically it was decided in favour of the analogists. In Alexandria at the end of the second century BC Dionysius Thrax, a pupil of the analogist Aristarchus, wrote a grammar of Greek, the earliest to survive. This brief work served as a model for the Latin grammars of Donatus (*c.* 350) and Priscian (*c.* 550), which were standard textbooks for most of the Middle Ages. Thus, besides the speculative grammars there existed in medieval Europe teaching manuals of Latin and Greek. These practical grammars inherited from the Alexandrian school of post-classical Greece a prescriptive character, which persisted through the Renaissance down to modern times, in the teaching of the dead languages and later the living vernaculars. And this traditional prescriptive approach was grounded in the belief that each language has correct, classical forms and meanings which should be preserved unaltered.

Now there is no doubt that analogy plays a major part in the shaping of language, for analogical changes are the means whereby it attains greater regularity and simplicity. The application of analogy gradually brought about the spread of the plural ending *-s* to nouns which in Old English had plurals in *-a, -an, -e, -u* or without change. The verb *bake*, by analogy with verbs such as *rake*, changed its 'strong' past forms *book* and *baken* to the 'weak' form *baked*. Conversely, the weak verb *wear* altered its past *weared* to the strong forms *wore* and *worn* on the analogy of verbs such as *bear* and *tear*. The non-standard possessive pronouns *hisn, hern, ourn, yourn* and *theirn*, still heard in some dialects, were obviously formed analogically, by borrowing the *n*-sound from the end of *mine* and *thine*. The emphatic and reflexive personal pronouns *himself* and *themselves* are often replaced in dialect and popular speech by *hisself* and *theirselves*, formed on the analogy of the other pronouns of this type, namely *myself, herself, ourselves* and *yourselves*, in which the first part is possessive. Children and foreigners often say *buyed* for *bought*, but the analogy with *try – tried* breaks down. So too does the analogy with *switch on* and *switch off* when they make the opposite of *plug in* to be *plug out*, instead of the actual *unplug*. Clearly then analogy is a force, but not a rule. We can never be sure when and how it will operate. Moreover, several analogies, all of them valid, may suggest themselves in a particular case. Thus disputed points of usage cannot always be settled by recourse to analogy, since each of the competing forms may be justified in this way.

Schoolchildren were long taught to say *different from* (after *differ from*), but in fact *different to* (after *dissimilar to*) is 'found in writers of all ages' (*OED*), and many good writers since the 17th century have used *different than* (after *other than*). This last, though condemned by purists, is valuable as a means of avoiding the clumsy expression sometimes necessitated by the use of *from* or *to*. 'It has a different look at night than in the daytime' is undoubtedly neater than 'It has a different look at night from/to that which it has in the daytime'. Similarly with the adverbial form: 'She behaves differently with me than with you' is preferable to 'She behaves differently with me from/to the way (in which) she behaves with you'. Another example: should the verb *doubt* be followed by *if*, *that* or *whether*? Here again there are three analogues 'do not know *if*', 'believe *that*' and 'wonder *whether*' none of which is intrinsically superior to the others.

Analogy can thus suggest two or more different forms, but cannot tell us which variant is best. Indeed, there may be no 'best' form, for each may have a valid function. It is fallacious to suppose, as the old prescriptivists did, that the rightness of one form entails the wrongness of its alternatives. 'Of two modes of expression,' wrote Dean Alford, 'if one be shown to be right, the other must necessarily be wrong' (*The Queen's English*, 1864). That this is not so is proved by the co-existence of many synonymous expressions which are not in dispute. We may equally well say 'He likes to chat' or 'He likes chatting', using the infinitive or the *-ing* form without distinction of meaning. The past tense form of the verb *light* may be *lighted* or *lit*, and the past participle of *sow* may be *sowed* or *sown*. We may speak of a *tight-knit group* or a *tightly knit group*. These and numerous other examples of acceptable free variation demonstrate that analogy is not a reliable principle in deciding matters of disputed usage.

The Latin model

As criteria of correct grammar both logic and analogy were overshadowed by Latin example. For centuries scholars were steeped in Latin, and its influence pervaded every aspect of English grammar in both book and classroom. The first grammar of modern English, William Bullokar's *Pamphlet for Grammar* (1586), is a brief outline based on Lily's famous Latin grammar, which appeared earlier in the 16th century and which was itself based on the works of Donatus and Priscian.

Several English grammars of this early period were modelled, wholly or in part, on Ramus's Latin grammar (1559), in which word classes were distinguished by form, not meaning. This model was followed most closely by Paul Greaves's *Grammatica Anglicana* of 1594 and Ben Jonson's *English Grammar*, published in 1640 but written before 1633. A compromise between Ramist principles and traditional semantic criteria is found in Alexander Gill's *Logonomia Anglica* (1619) and Charles Butler's *English Grammar* (1633). But none of these followers of Ramus could overcome the problems involved in applying his Latin-derived categories to a description of English.

Most English grammars written before the end of the 19th century were in thrall to Latin, notable exceptions being those of John Wallis (1653), Christopher Cooper (1685), Joseph Priestley (1761), Robert Lowth (1762) and William Cobbett (1818). J.C. Nesfield's *Manual of English Grammar and Composition* (1898), widely used in schools both at home and abroad for many years, was firmly based on Latin. Even in the 20th century the redoubtable Henry Fowler was still deferring to Latin in settling points of English usage.

The normative grammarians of the 18th century sought to apply the principles of a universal grammar, derived from the structure of Latin, to their analysis of English. And since any divergence between Latin and English was seen as a defect in the mother tongue, various expedients were employed to preserve an appearance of similarity. Inevitably, the categories and distinctions adopted in most grammars were often ill-suited to English. Latin grammatical terms were generally retained, but the eight parts of speech distinguished in Latin were often varied in number for English. The 18th-century view of English grammar is typified by Dr Johnson's remark: 'I always said Shakespeare had Latin enough to grammaticize his English'.

In one respect Dr Johnson was right. Shakespeare must have had more than a nodding acquaintance with Latin, for it was used exclusively as the medium of instruction in the schools of Elizabethan England. The aim of their teachers was to enable pupils not only to understand Latin literature, but also to speak and write in the language. Later, when English grammar was introduced into the curriculum, it was taught in the same way as Latin. The parts of speech formed the most important element of study, hence parsing was the chief exercise used in class. Second in importance was the correction of false English, mostly mistakes of spelling and concord.

The inappropriateness of all this can be seen by comparing Latin and English. Though they both belong to the Indo-European family of languages, they differ in many fundamental respects. Latin nouns have no articles and three different genders; English nouns have two articles and no grammatical gender. There are five noun declensions in Latin, with six cases in both singular and plural. Allowing for 'shared' endings, a Latin noun may have up to eight different forms, whereas English nouns have only three forms: singular, plural and possessive. Adjectives in Latin agree in gender, number and case with the noun they qualify; English adjectives do not alter form to agree with the noun.

With verbs the contrast between the two languages is even more striking. English has several auxiliary verbs; Latin has none. A Latin verb has four sets of subjunctive forms for both active and passive voices; in English the subjunctive is little used and nearly always avoidable. A complete Latin verb has nearly a hundred different forms; by contrast English verbs have a mere four or at most five different forms. Latin, which uses inflection to express grammatical relations, is a synthetic language with relatively free word order. English, with few inflections, is predominantly an analytic language in which grammatical relations are shown by fixed word order and the use of function words, especially prepositions and pronouns.

Attempts to force English into the Procrustean bed of Latin do violence to its nature and sometimes produce ludicrous results, such as the discovery that English nouns, like Latin ones, have six cases, including a vocative (*O table!*) and an ablative (*from a table*). Each language constitutes a unique system and must therefore be described in terms of its own characteristics.

6. Usage and Norms

Doctrine of usage

Since antiquity grammarians have regarded established usage as the criterion of correctness. The Stoics of ancient Greece proclaimed usage to be the supreme authority in matters of language. In like manner the Latin poet Horace affirmed that 'usage is the arbiter and the law and standard of speech' (*Ars Poetica*, c. 20 BC). In modern times the same position has been taken by many grammarians, in particular those, such as Joseph Priestley and William Cobbett, who rejected Latin as a model for English. Priestley maintained that 'general prevailing custom [i.e. usage], whatever it happens to be, can be the only standard for the time that it prevails' (*Theory of Language*, 1762). Cobbett gave it as his opinion that 'what a whole people adopts and universally practises must ... be deemed correct' (*A Grammar of the English Language*, 1818). Henry Sweet, who brought English grammar to a high level of scholarship, expressed the same view when he wrote: 'Whatever is in general use in a language is for that very reason grammatically correct' (*A New English Grammar*, 1892).

Now it is undeniably true that usage is the basis of all correctness, but it is equally true that not all usage is approved as correct. The Horatian maxim thus begs the question by equating usage with the standard, for it fails to tell us whose usage sets the standard. To say that custom is the only correctness is rather like saying that morals are the only morality. Not all usage is viewed with favour, any more than all morals are. There is usage and usage. Language is judged acceptable or not, depending on whose usage it is and how effective it is, that is to say not by linguistic criteria, but by social criteria in speech and stylistic criteria in writing.

Ben Jonson, paraphrasing Quintilian's *Institutio Oratoria* (AD 92-4), wrote that 'custom is the most certain mistress of language, as the public stamp marks the current money' (*Discoveries*, 1641). After these golden words he went on to make clear that by custom he meant, as did Quintilian, the agreed practice of educated men, what he called 'the consent [= consensus] of the learned'. This doctrine of usage, as it has come to be known, was further developed by George Campbell in his *Philosophy of Rhetoric* (1776). There Campbell laid down the principle that good usage must be 'national, reputable and present'. This classic dictum, which confers authority on the prevailing usage of contemporary good speakers and writers, was accepted by nearly all 19th-century grammarians, though they often ignored it in practice, like Campbell himself.

It will be readily agreed that usage, to be acceptable, should embrace the whole speech community, and not be confined to some regional variety. Dialect forms must be excluded not because they are bad or inferior, which they are not, but because they are non-standard and not always intelligible to outsiders. It will also be agreed that whereas usage should not be restricted in place, it should be limited in time, to the present and the recent past. A living language changes, as we know, and with it so do its norms. We no longer say 'It likes me not', nor – except in jest – 'I like it not', but 'I do not like it'. In linguistic, as in other matters, the past cannot dictate to the present. Thus, to base our judgement of what is acceptable or good on older usage is as unsound as basing it on Latin usage. Writers of the past may have furnished models for their own times, but cannot serve as guides for us today. Their standards should no more be imposed on us, than ours on them. It was a form of scholarly sport with some grammarians in the past to hunt for 'errors' in the works of older writers, especially the famous, in the mistaken belief that their rules were valid for all time, even retrospectively. And it was not difficult, by such means, to make even Shakespeare and Milton seem illiterates.

The remaining requirement of good usage laid down by Campbell is that it should be reputable, that is to say the usage of good speakers and writers. At this point we must be careful not to fall into the trap of circularity by then defining good speakers and writers as those who use good English. This danger is easily avoided, however, if we define good English as that used by people whom the English-speaking community in general recognizes as good speakers and writers of the language. The people who enjoy this linguistic prestige can be readily identified as the most highly educated and cultivated members of society, broadly speaking the professional classes.

There are two points to be noted about good English speech and writing. First, in Britain by no means all educated speakers use the standard received pronunciation (RP), associated with radio and television newsreaders; most in fact have a regional, modified-RP accent. In the United States the closest analogue to RP is Network Standard, the classless and largely regionless accent of newscasters. As for the norms of educated spoken usage, they are all but the same in both countries. Second, some kinds of writing must be ruled out of consideration owing to their use of deviant, unconventional English. Works in which the writers go beyond the confines of ordinary language cannot serve as models of grammar or style. In particular poets, who are creative artists with words, often rebel against the tyranny of custom in language and indulge in poetic licence, using archaic or unusual diction and aberrant syntax.

In determining what is standard written English it is necessary to exclude some of the best imaginative literature, which is a law unto itself, linguistically speaking, because of its wayward use of language. Some modern prose works display markedly untypical kinds of English. For example, the eminent 19th-century historian Thomas Carlyle defied the customary usage of his time in forging a highly eccentric style, a Carlylese larded with archaisms and Germanisms. And in our own century James Joyce invented a whole new language to represent the dream world of his hero in *Finnegans Wake* (1939). This highly idiosyncratic Finneganese, with its mangled morphology and strangled syntax, is totally unsuitable as a model for normal, let alone good usage. It is in fact un-English; some have even called it anti-English. In fixing the norms of the written language we should therefore draw chiefly on non-fiction written by academics, journalists, scientists and other professional people.

The usage doctrine opposed

The doctrine of usage did not go unchallenged. One of its earliest opponents was Richard Grant White, who rejected Latham's dictum that 'in language whatever is, is right'. White, an American arch-purist, took the contrary view that 'in language, as in all other human affairs, that which is may be wrong ... The truth is,' he continued, 'that the authority of general usage, or even the usage of great writers, is not absolute in language. There is a misuse of words which can be justified by no authority, however great, by no usage, however general' (*Words and Their Uses, Past and Present*, 1870). In White's opinion, usage, even of the best authors, is no guarantee of correctness. It is unfair, he argued, to cite isolated passages from eminent writers as examples of poor grammar. Writers should be judged by their general practice, not by their occasional lapses (even the great Homer sometimes nodded, we are told). For White reason, not usage, was the highest linguistic law, and bad usage could be checked by rational criticism.

Another opponent of the usage doctrine was Otto Jespersen, who proposed in its place a doctrine of the norm, after examining the merits of seven different standards of linguistic correctness. Four of these, the geographical (or regional), the aristocratic (or upper-class), the literary, and the democratic, are based on usage. The other three, the logical, the aesthetic, and the authoritative, are extra-linguistic. Rejecting all these standards as unsatisfactory for various reasons, Jespersen concluded: 'That which is linguistically correct is that which is demanded by the particular linguistic community to which one belongs' (*Mankind, Nation and Individual from a Linguistic Point of View*, 1925). But this norm cannot be fixed once and for all, nor does majority usage, though 'correct', always deserve to be copied.

In 1874 E.H.V. Tegnér, a Swedish professor, had written: 'The greatest absurdities in the world become correct as soon as they have got usage fully on their side, just as the worst usurper becomes legitimate as soon as he is completely established on his throne'. To this Jespersen retorted: 'I am not one of those who recognize the worst usurper as legitimate as soon as he is firmly established on his throne ... There is a higher linguistic morality than that of recognizing the greatest absurdities when they once have usage on their side.' Though himself a descriptive linguist, he stoutly defended the rights of prescriptivists. He challenged those who said that usage is king and maintained that we have a right, even a duty, to make our language better if we can. But he failed to address the crucial question: how do we decide what is good and what is bad when educated usage is itself divided?

The most vigorous attack on the doctrine of usage was mounted by the distinguished scholar and teacher I.A. Richards, who described it as 'the most pernicious influence in current English teaching' (*Interpretation in Teaching*, 1938). He believed deference to authority had been one source of our trouble over usage, and drew some telling parallels with various fields of human activity. Good engineering or medical practices are good not because engineers and doctors follow them, but because such practices do the job efficiently. Similarly, a scientific belief is right not because it is held by Einstein or some other eminent scientist, but because the empirical evidence shows it to be so. The same holds true of language. Good speaking and writing are good not because they are practised by good speakers and writers, but because they communicate successfully by achieving a high degree of expressiveness.

According to Richards, the doctrine of usage was put forward to replace the popular clamour for a 'heaven-sent' standard, i.e. one imposed from above. But in his view the tyranny of custom or usage was as great as that of authority. 'Custom is no criterion at all,' he wrote, 'unless it is the best custom – and we can tell which is the best custom, when we meet it or hit on it, only by using a standard with which custom has nothing directly to do, a standard that is not heaven-sent ... but resides in us, as the active principle of communication, and is manifested in our developed skill with words.' The usage doctrine was 'a product of reaction against illegitimate applications of logic and philosophy to language', but it 'took over and perpetuated just those inadequacies that are the real ground for objecting to Rule by Divine Right'.

Doctrine of the norm

Some years later Richards returned to the attack. Viewing the activities of descriptive linguists in the fields of education and criticism as dangerously intrusive, he wrote: 'The appeal to mere *usage*: "If it's widely in use, it's O.K.", is a case in point ... Behind usage is the question of efficiency. Inefficient language features are not O.K., however widespread their use. Of course, to the linguistic botanist it is important to preserve all varieties until they have been collected and described. But that is not the point of view of the over-all study of language, its services and its powers. That over-all view is, I am insisting, inescapably NORMATIVE' (*Speculative Instruments*, 1955).

Richards admitted that there had been 'silly normative prejudices in the past' and did not advocate a return to so-called rational grammar or the old rules, which he looked upon as discredited. Like Jespersen, he espoused the doctrine of the linguistic norm, based on the establishment of standards and improvements in the use of language. In his view, we need not accept everything that is thrown up by usage, however common; we must look at all forms critically, with a discerning eye. He realized that linguistic standards could only be provided from outside language. But, again like Jespersen, he did not propose any principles or criteria by which we might judge usage to be good, bad or indifferent.

Like White and Jespersen, Richards saw usage as an undifferentiated mass that must be sifted by the critical intelligence, so that the best linguistic forms might be found and promoted. This, of course, takes us back to traditional pedagogical grammar. Regulating usage by discriminatory criteria is exactly what prescriptive grammarians have been doing for over 2,000 years, though in modern times with a rigidity that has had seriously distorting effects. Their aims were sound enough, but their methods often crude and unnecessarily restrictive. The prescriptive norms formulated by the grammarians of classical Greece and Rome were descriptively accurate. After them for many centuries European grammarians simply transferred to their own languages whatever framework of description had been found appropriate for Greek and Latin. As a result the modern vernaculars were to a considerable extent misdescribed. The prescriptive rules of English, as we have seen, were often either outlandish or outdated and were usually presented without explanation or justification, on the unsupported *ipse dixit* of some grammarian or rhetorician.

Need for better prescriptivism

The prescriptivists, not surprisingly, came under fire from the modern descriptive linguists, followers of Ferdinand de Saussure and Leonard Bloomfield, who approached the study of language in a strictly objective, non-judgemental way. The besetting sins of the old grammarians were dogmatism and pedantry, but they had other faults too. They were sometimes guilty of laying down rules which betrayed a woeful ignorance of historical or contemporary usage. They were generally content to follow the Latin path trodden by their predecessors. They based many of their rules on inconsistent or irrelevant criteria and paraded their prejudices as matters of 'good taste'. They had no system, but treated all departures from their rules as an unclassified array of errors. Their grammars were often little more than manuals of linguistic etiquette, concentrating on a small number of unrelated points. School grammarians cultivated a narrow briar patch of disputed usage, neglecting the broader terrain of language altogether. But none of these numerous faults are actually inherent in the prescriptive approach to grammar.

In the second half of the present century the attitude of linguists towards prescriptivism has undergone a change. The earlier hostility has given way to tolerance and even acceptance. The value of prescriptive grammar has been recognized by some of the most eminent linguists.

Randolph Quirk, the most distinguished of modern English grammarians, has more than once written in defence of the prescriptivist position. In an article entitled 'From Descriptive to Prescriptive: an Example' he writes, 'It is not for their prescriptivism as such that the older teaching grammars stand condemned ...: it is for the fact that their prescriptions have not been based upon a sound foundation of description' (*English Language Teaching*, XII, 1957). In another article, 'Towards a Description of English Usage', Quirk notes the widespread and deep-seated concern among the educated with concepts of right and wrong, good and bad, in language. 'There must be some investigation of what beliefs and precepts obtain;' he writes, 'they cannot be sneered or shrugged away as the inheritance of prescriptivism, as though this were to demonstrate that they lack significance or influence. They are features of our linguistic morality, as deeply and as complicatedly entrenched as our licensing laws' (*Transactions of the Philological Society*, 1960).

Noam Chomsky, who sparked off a revolution in modern linguistics, has also given his blessing to prescriptive grammar, provided it is well grounded. In a short reply to a critic he remarks that 'a concern for the literary standard – "prescriptivism", in its more sensible manifestations – is as legitimate as an interest in colloquial speech' (*College English*, March 1967). In a similar vein Michael Stubbs, in his preface to Walter Nash's *English Usage* (1986), welcomes good prescriptive works. 'It is a misunderstanding of a linguistic approach,' he writes, 'to think that it necessarily rejects prescriptivism. The real objection is to thoughtless prescriptivism.' Sidney Greenbaum, another eminent grammarian, sees prescriptive activity as a duty neglected by present-day linguists. 'Grammarians have a responsibility, not yet acknowledged,' he writes, 'to address students and the general public on ... matters of linguistic etiquette' (*Good English and the Grammarian*, 1988).

The moral to be drawn from this learned testimony is that we should beware not of prescriptive norms as such, but only of those derived from inadequate descriptions. There is no reason why prescriptive grammar, like prescriptive medicine, should not be scientifically based, with sound, professionally compounded ingredients. Nor need there be any conflict between the scientific work of descriptive linguists and the use made of their results for prescriptive purposes. Nothing in their profession obliges them to shun evaluative judgements or normative attempts to promote the health of their language. Instead of standing aloof and leaving the field to amateur pedants, they should boldly enter the fray and proclaim the standards they value. For it is not true that scientific students of language have no standards; on the contrary they have high standards, based on the best contemporary usage. Significantly, linguists who adopt a strictly anti-normative stance in theory, always in practice follow the norms of good usage, showing that they are on the side of the angels.

What is needed today, therefore, is a new prescriptivism, free of the vices of the old prescriptivists, not shackled to Latin but firmly based on accurate descriptions of current usage. The tasks of the descriptive and the prescriptive linguist are different but complementary. The descriptive linguist is a scholar whose job it is to collect, classify and record the facts of language, like a naturalist observing the facts of nature. In addition he must analyze the facts in order to unlock the laws of the language, discover its underlying patterns and, by delving into the past, explain its peculiarities.

The job of the prescriptive linguist is to sift and evaluate the findings of descriptive scholars in a search for acceptable norms. Where usage is divided he must adjudicate, choosing those variants he considers to be most effective or useful, and giving reasons for his preferences. It is not his business to pontificate, but to make informed value judgements. And since there are no absolute, abiding canons of usage, he must be prepared to revise his judgements in the light of fresh evidence or later changes. Because of the fluctuating nature of language he would be wise to put forward his precepts as recommendations, rather than as strict rules. Prescriptivism, properly practised, steers a middle course between dogmatic purism and anarchic licence.

7. Divided Usage

Attitudes to usage

Of the need for prescriptive grammar there can be no doubt. The prescriptive approach of necessity informs all teaching of English as a foreign language, an activity conducted today on a world-wide scale. Foreign students often use English words and expressions inaccurately, and their mistakes need to be corrected. Most of our own schoolchildren too require some prescriptive guidance in order to extend their limited linguistic horizons by becoming acquainted with the lingua franca that is standard English. As for adult native speakers, their concern is solely with prescriptive grammar; they have no interest in the descriptivists' complicated formulaic chains and intricate tree diagrams.

The detached attitude of professional linguists towards prescription has no effect on the general public, who habitually make value judgements about their language, relying upon dictionaries and usage books to settle their doubts and differences. The substantial number of such books produced over the last hundred years or so testifies to the incessant demand for linguistic guidance. In this, as in other fields of knowledge, laymen naturally look to real or supposed authorities for enlightenment, and it is perfectly reasonable for them to do so.

There are few things people become more passionate about at times than their language, which they feel to be part of themselves. Unfortunately, most people's passion is spent on trivial points of pronunciation and vocabulary. Linguistically speaking, they strain at gnats, but swallow camels with ease. They worry about whether to pronounce *either* as 'eyether' or 'eether', and whether to pronounce the first syllable of *finance* like 'fin' or 'fine'. They harass one another over whether one should say *hárass* or *haráss*, and there is much controversy about whether it is better to say *cóntroversy* or *contróversy*, which *cóntributes* – or even *contríbutes* – nothing to their peace of mind. Many British people insist on *órdinarily* and *prímarily*, condemning *ordinárily* and *primárily* as American forms, quite unaware that the variants with medial stress were normal in England until the middle of the 18th century. People generally still believe, as did the old prescriptivists, that when there are alternants only one can be right, whereas there are numerous cases where both forms are acceptable.

In a similar way many people cling to what I.A. Richards called 'the proper meaning superstition', the belief that each word has a real or intrinsic meaning, namely the etymological one, and that any later change is a corruption or erosion of that meaning. The word *aggravate*, true to its Latin derivation, first meant 'to make heavier' and hence 'to increase the gravity of', 'to worsen'. Purists have long rejected the now commoner meaning 'to annoy', recorded since the early 17th century, but it is only a small semantic leap from aggravating a person's temper to aggravating the person. A greater leap was involved when 'execute a judicial sentence on a person' by transference became 'execute a person', yet the verb *execute* in this secondary sense did not arouse the hostility suffered by *aggravate* in its new sense.

A refusal to recognize that words can acquire new or additional meanings leads to absurd conclusions. Etymologically speaking, *buxom* means 'obedient', *idle* means 'empty', *lewd* means 'ignorant', *nice* means 'foolish' and *silly* means 'blessed'. Judged by the yardstick of etymology, the word *journal* should not be used of a weekly or monthly publication, *December* should be the tenth month, as it was for the Romans, and *anecdotes* should be only heard, not seen in print. We must not be seduced by what Thomas Lounsbury called 'the demon of derivation' (*The Standard of Usage in English,* 1908).

The very common use of *disinterested* to mean 'uninterested' is often castigated, yet this is merely a revival of the older, original sense of the word and should thus be welcomed by purists. It has obvious parallels in *disinclined, disliked, disadvantaged* and many other words in which *dis-* means 'not'. The two senses can in fact co-exist peacefully, for language is generally well protected against misunderstandings by context and the existence of synonyms. If the distinction should disappear, i.e. if *disinterested* and *uninterested* fall together in sense, the lost meaning can be readily supplied by words like *impartial, unbiased, objective* or *neutral*.

It is within everyone's experience that word meanings change, for vocabulary alters more rapidly than any other aspect of language. But like change of all kinds semantic change meets resistance, and defensive battles are often fought to preserve old meanings from extinction. The unfamiliar is viewed by many people with alarm, if not downright hostility. In the 1960s and 1970s, first in America, then in Britain, there was a great outcry against the use of the word *hopefully* to mean 'it is to be hoped' or 'I hope'. Its proper meaning, insisted the protesters, is 'in a hopeful manner'. Yet the role of disjunct or comment adverb is found quite acceptable in other words, such as *mercifully*, so used since 1836, together with *thankfully* and *sadly*, extended in use more recently. It is absurd to fuss about this useful extension of meaning in *hopefully* when comparable cases can be found. The sentence 'Hopefully, the plan will succeed' is criticized on the grounds that the plan is not full of hope; but by the same token when we say 'Mercifully, the plan failed' the plan is not full of mercy either.

By a curious coincidence, a hundred years before this onslaught on the word *hopefully*, the word *reliable* was subjected to similar attacks by purists, who branded it as an illiterate coinage. Their objection was that you do not rely something, but rely on it, therefore the thing should be *rely-on-able* (like the colloquial *get-at-able*). Against this there were many analogous forms such as *accountable*, from *account (for)*, *dependable*, from *depend (on)*, *dispensable*, from *dispense (with)* and *disposable*, from *dispose (of)*, to which no one took exception. But for some obscure reason, quite arbitrarily the word *reliable* was singled out for disapproval. After examining the question at great length Fitzedward Hall concluded, 'That the English-speaking world has benefited by the introduction of *reliable* is beyond question' (*On English Adjectives in* -able, *with Special Reference to 'reliable'*, 1877). It is only recent changes that make some people wince, for the older ones have long been assimilated.

New coinages

Neologisms are met with cries of protest even more often than shifts of meaning. Until recent years purists often protested about new words made up of elements from different languages, which they considered to be linguistic monstrosities. Yet our forefathers, besides borrowing freely from other languages – chiefly French, Latin and Greek, had no scruples about forming hybrids. Indeed it is this hospitality to foreign words and practicality in building new ones that have together given our language its enormously rich and varied vocabulary. In the centuries since the Norman Conquest of 1066 English has acquired hundreds of hybrid words, such as *bakery, bearable, besiege, goddess, starvation, uncertain* (English and French), and *artless, beautiful, dukedom, gentleman, grandfather, justly, nobler, proven, richness* (French and English).

It is not these age-old Anglo-French hybrids that offended the purists, however, but the modern neo-classical compounds comprising elements of both Greek and Latin. Most of these are learned words and technical terms, such as *amoral, automobile, television* (Greek and Latin), and *civilize, feminism, scientist* (Latin and Greek). Equally objectionable to purists are words created by joining classical elements to modern native ones, such as *addressograph, bureaucracy* (French and Greek), *speedometer, stockist* (English and Greek), and *defrost, disbelieve, supergrass* (Latin and English). Because of the decline in classical studies few people today are conversant with the roots of Latin and Greek, so hardly anyone now pleads for purity of forms.

Among neologisms it is verbs that evoke the most violent reactions from linguistic conservatives. In present-day English verbs are generally formed in one of three ways, all of which have made useful additions to our word-stock. The first method is the simple conversion of a noun such as *audition, bottle, garage, hammer, process* and *value* into a verb. The verb *to contact*, described as 'loathsome' and 'an abomination' when it first came into use during the 1930s, is now firmly established, for it usefully combines the multiple senses of 'speak to' or 'write to' (in person), and 'communicate with' (through another person). Other noun-derived verbs that have been condemned are *to guest* and *to host*, which are convenient shortenings of 'to be a guest at' and 'act as host to'. Less obviously useful are *to author, to gift* and *to loan*. Though long attested, they have not gained such a firm foothold, no doubt because they compete with the simpler forms *write, give* and *lend*. Some of these verbs have made a comeback in the language after a long absence, spent by *loan* in America, and by *author* and *host* in linguistic limbo.

The second way of making verbs, by no means a new device, is to add the suffix *-ize* to the stem of an adjective or noun. The chosen victim in this category is, or was, *to finalize*, frequently condemned as ugly and unnecessary, though it has a valid use, meaning 'to put into final form'. During this century there has been a spate of new verbs in *-ize*, such as *accessorize, comprehensivize, hospitalize, miniaturize, pedestrianize, prioritize, robotize* and *slenderize*, which enable us to say in one word what would otherwise require a whole phrase. They are scarcely an elegant collection of flowers but those that are found useful will survive, while the rest wither away after a short life.

The third means of creating verbs is to remove the last part of what appears to be a derivative noun or adjective, thereby producing a back-formation. In this way *edit* was formed from *editor* and *laze* from *lazy*, not the other way round. Similarly formed are *automate* from *automation*, *baby-sit* from *baby-sitter*, *donate* from *donation*, *escalate* from *escalator*, *opt* from *option*, *stage-manage* from *stage-manager*, and *televise* from *television*. The majority of such verbs are now accepted in normal use, but a few such as *emote*, *enthuse* and *reminisce*, used jocularly for the most part, have been stigmatized as vulgarisms. And while we can accept *commentate* as meaning something different from *comment*, we really have no need of *cohese* or *administrate* when *cohere* and *administer* are to hand.

Flawed expressions

We may now turn our attention from the trifling points that agitate many people to more serious ones they would do better to worry about, from the gnats they strain at to the camels they so readily swallow. Let us examine three such camels. First of these is the notorious 'dangling (i.e. misrelated) participle', e.g.

Eating my lunch, the car disappeared

Clearly there is something wrong with this sentence, for it unintentionally raises a smile by literally stating that a car ate my lunch. By conjuring up a ludicrously incongruous picture it evokes the wrong response. The place that belongs to the subject of the participle, i.e. the person eating the lunch, has been usurped by the car. Of course, the tug-of-war between form and meaning is quickly decided by the common-sense realization that cars do not eat lunches. But the sentence as it stands is jerry-built; to be soundly constructed it needs to include the real subject by starting with the words 'As I was eating'.

Once participle phrases are attached to words other than those they refer to, the door is thrown open to confusion. If we replace the car in our example by an animate being this becomes obvious at once:

Eating my lunch, the dog disappeared

Who is now eating the lunch, the dog or the unexpressed subject *I*? If it is the speaker, then again we need the opening words 'As I was eating'; if it is the dog, then the sentence is accurate as it stands. In context the intended meaning would usually be clear, but we should not allow even a potential ambiguity to arise from a mismatch between form and sense. Sound grammatical construction requires that an introductory participle phrase should refer to the subject of the same sentence, not to some other noun or pronoun.

Strangely enough, this syntactical lapse was not pointed out in print until the second half of the 19th century. But the misrelated participle has a long history, going back to Old English, though it was rare in the Middle period, and it can be found in all our best writers down the ages. Examples:

> 'Tis given out that, sleeping within mine orchard,
> A serpent stung me (Shakespeare, *Hamlet*, c. 1601)

> Thus repulsed, our final hope
> Is flat despair (Milton, *Paradise Lost*, bk II, 1667)

> Feeling powerfully as they did, their language was daring and figurative (Wordsworth, Preface to *Lyrical Ballads*, 1798)

> Wanting to be alone with his family, the presence of a stranger ... must have been irksome (Jane Austen, *Mansfield Park*, 1814)

> Going up, the floors were found to have a very irregular surface (Thomas Hardy, *Far from the Madding Crowd*, 1874)

Despite these reputable precedents, however, the fact remains that the misrelated participle is irredeemably flawed and can always be rephrased in a more satisfactory way.

The second faulty construction is the phrase *one of those ... who* (or *that*), followed by a singular verb, e.g.

> She is one of those women who never stops talking

The relative *who* refers to *women*, not to *she*; therefore the verb should be *stop*, not *stops*. The use of a singular verb here is caused by the influence of sentence patterns with much the same meaning, namely 'She never stops talking', 'She is one who never stops talking' and 'She is a person who never stops talking', where *stops* agrees with the antecedents *she, one,* and *a person* respectively. But once *those women* are introduced, it is they who are now the antecedent. This can be simply demonstrated by applying the reversal test, i.e. 'Of those women who never stop talking she is one'. This faulty construction too goes back a long way. Two early examples will suffice.

> Ye be one of them that oweth me homage (Caxton, *The History of Reynard the Fox*, 1481)

> Yet his brother is reputed one of the best that is (Shakespeare, *All's Well that Ends Well*, c. 1603)

The third defective construction takes the form *the reason ... is because*, e.g.

> The reason he shouts is because he is angry

Here we have a confusion between two ways of saying the same thing: (1) 'The reason he shouts is that he is angry' and (2) 'He shouts because he is angry'. The mixed expression, though it has had its defenders, is plainly tautological, as can be seen when the conjunction *because* is paraphrased. 'The reason ... is for the reason that ...' contains a redundant reason, which asks to be removed; strike out *for the reason* and you are left with just *that*, which is all you need. This tautology, now common in both speech and print, is by no means new. Examples:

> His reason is because Poesy dealeth with ... the universal consideration (Sir Philip Sidney, *An Apology for Poetry*, 1595)

> The reason whereof is because the complex idea signified by that name is the real as well as the nominal essence (John Locke, *An Essay Concerning Human Understanding*, 1690)

> You must know (says Will) the reason is because they consider every animal as a brother or a sister in disguise (Joseph Addison, *The Spectator*, April 1712)

These three constructions, illustrating faulty attachment, faulty concord, and faulty diction, could well be described as 'sturdy indefensibles', to borrow a term coined by Fowler. They are all common and have considerable weight of usage behind them. Yet no matter how often or by whom they are used, bad constructions can never become good ones. Even the fact that they are used by good writers does not make them good, for not everything written by good writers is good, any more than everything written by bad writers is bad. With each of these constructions there is a better way of expressing the same idea, and it is better whether most people use it or not. We are not obliged to come down always in favour of majority usage.

The constructions examined above are examples of divided usage. We cannot say categorically that they are wrong and the alternative constructions are right, but we are entitled to say that they are worse and the alternatives better. Sometimes, when usage fluctuates, we may regard the variants as equally good grammatically and our choice of one or other form must then be guided by stylistic considerations. We decide whether *different* should be followed by *from*, *to* or *than*, depending on which of these fits the structure of the utterance best, just as we choose, according to context, whether to use *that, which*, or no relative at all. But most often, when grammatical forms are in competition, one is better and the other worse. In this grey area of divided usage the criterion of custom fails us, for custom here speaks with two voices, sometimes more. The disputed points of usage can only be settled on grounds of grammar, style, or a combination of the two. We therefore need to establish acceptable grammatical and stylistic canons by which to judge the comparative merits of rival forms found in standard use.

8. Rules of Style

Campbell's rules

The criteria of good usage put forward hitherto by writers on English are far from reliable in most cases. For example George Campbell, in his *Philosophy of Rhetoric* (1776), proposed five rules for cases of divided usage:

(1) When two forms compete choose that which is unambiguous.
(2) In doubtful non-ambiguous cases appeal to analogies.
(3) When two forms are equal in other respects prefer that most pleasing to the ear.
(4) If no other norm applies choose the simplest expression.
(5) If none of the above rules apply choose the form that most conforms to previous use.

Here we have a jolly jumble of rules, flawed every one. To answer them in order: few expressions, in context, yield real ambiguities; more than one analogy, as we have seen, can serve the same case; what pleases one ear may displease another; the competing forms may be equally simple or complex; tradition may support each of the rival forms.

Henry Sweet's advice is no more helpful. After asserting the grammaticality of general usage, he continues: 'But whenever usage is not fixed – whenever we hesitate between different ways of expression, or have to find a new way of expression – then grammar comes in, and helps us to decide which expression is most in accordance with the genius of the language, least ambiguous, most concise, or in any other way fitted to express what is required' (*A New English Grammar*, 1892). Here we have three criteria of choice, all of them unsatisfactory. To take them point by point: (1) How does one decide what most accords with the 'genius' (i.e. spirit) of the language, especially one with such a mongrel heritage as English? (2) Ambiguity is rarely a problem in cases of divided usage. (3) Conciseness is certainly a virtue, but if taken too far it can lead to loss of coherence.

The Fowlers' rules

Probably the best-known rules for writing good plain English are those given by the Fowler brothers in *The King's English* (1906). These 'practical rules in the domain of vocabulary', they say, 'are given roughly in order of merit'.

(1) Prefer the familiar word to the far-fetched.
(2) Prefer the concrete word to the abstract.
(3) Prefer the single word to the circumlocution.
(4) Prefer the short word to the long.
(5) Prefer the Saxon word to the Romance.

'All five rules,' say the Fowlers, 'would be often found to give the same answer about the same word or set of words.' The phrase *in the contemplated eventuality*, which they cite as an example, 'is at once the far-fetched, the abstract, the periphrastic, the long, and the Romance for *if so*'. The fifth rule is the one about which they have most reservations, for the Saxon word is not always preferable to the Romance (i.e. Latin or Latin-derived). 'The Saxon oracle is not infallible,' they admit, adding that 'even if the Saxon criterion were a safe one, more knowledge than most of us have is needed to apply it.' They allow that there are difficulties too in applying their second rule. 'Sentences overloaded with abstract words are,' they say, 'effectively not curable simply by substituting equivalent concrete words; there can be no such equivalents; the structure has to be more or less changed.' They cut the ground from under their own feet by acknowledging that different kinds of composition require different treatment and 'in this fact may be found good reasons for sometimes disregarding any or all of the preceding rules'.

The Fowlerian rules are clearly wanting, for if rigidly applied they would produce strange results. Rule (1) needs qualifying. A large part of the vast and varied treasury of English words would languish in neglect if we stuck timidly to those with which we are familiar. The rule also overlooks the simple fact that what is far-fetched (i.e unfamiliar) to one person may be well known to another. And sometimes the unusual or less common word is the only one that fully meets our need. The perfect answer to this precept was given a few years earlier by two Harvard professors, J.B. Greenough and G.L. Kittredge, who wrote: 'Nor is there any principle on which, of two expressions, that which is popular should be preferred to that which is learned or less familiar. The sole criterion of choice consists in the appropriateness of one's language to the subject or the occasion' (*Words and Their Ways in English Speech*, 1901).

Rule (2) alerts us to the dangers of abstract terms, but would be cripplingly restrictive if practised. It is true that advertisers, politicians and sloganeers often use abstract words as a smokescreen in their professional evasions. It is also true that abstractitis can engender pretentious writing like this: 'The utilization of existing resources and facilities is imperative' (i.e. We must manage with what we have), and gobbledygook such as this: 'Problems of implementation logistics have obscured some of the positive potential of competencies' (untranslatable). Yet none of us could do without abstract terms for the most basic function of language, to express our attitudes and feelings. Man does not speak of bread alone, but of joy and sorrow, love and anger, truth and lies, as well as countless other intangible things in his experience. Only occasionally in fact does an abstract word have a concrete equivalent, such as *brains* for 'intelligence', *crown* for 'monarchy', *turf* for 'horse-racing', *guts* for 'courage', *stick or carrot* for 'punishment or inducement', and since most of these concrete substitutes are colloquial they are restricted in use.

Rule (3) is the only one which has the merit of being sound more often than not. A single word, provided that it does the job equally well, is usually preferable to the roundabout phrase. *Poor* is more direct than the euphemism *in straitened circumstances*, just as *No* is quicker to the point than *The answer is in the negative*. Such circumlocutions are generally best avoided, but there are situations in which the periphrasis serves a special purpose, such as sparing someone's feelings (*poor* is too blunt) or making something clearer or humorously elaborate (*No* is too short). Thus even this rule is not absolute, but needs qualification, like the others.

Rule (4) seems sensible at first sight, but in practice it imposes intolerable restrictions, like rule (2). To banish polysyllabic words is to ignore well over half our vocabulary and to overlook the fact that *desire* is sometimes better than *wish*, and that *melancholy* expresses something that *sad* does not. Besides, nearly all the commonest words in English are monosyllables and this of itself ensures a high proportion of short words in any idiomatic text or discourse. Herbert Spencer, writing before the Fowlers, defended the use of long words as follows. 'A word which in itself embodies the most important part of the idea to be conveyed, especially when that idea is an emotional one, may often with advantage be a polysyllabic word. Thus it seems more forcible to say "It is *magnificent*" than "It is *grand*". The word *vast* is not so powerful a one as *stupendous*. Calling a thing *nasty* is not so effective as calling it *disgusting*' ('The Philosophy of Style', 1852).

Rule (5) is the least reliable, on the Fowlers' own admission. Henry Bradley had earlier written against it. 'The cry for "Saxon English" sometimes means nothing more than a demand for plain and unaffected diction ...' he wrote, 'but the pedantry that would bid us reject the word fittest for our purpose because it is not of native origin ought to be strenuously resisted' (*The Making of English*, 1904). This lame-duck rule was attacked later by P.B. Ballard. 'The distinction,' he wrote, 'between the Anglo-Saxon element and the Latin element ... has long ceased to be of any importance to the user of the language. In the commonwealth of letters the pedigree of words is of little consequence;

it is their usefulness in the traffic of ideas that gives them their worth'
(*Thought and Language*, 1934).

Quiller-Couch's rules

In his Cambridge lectures *On the Art of Writing* (1916) Sir Arthur
Quiller-Couch put forward three rules of diction.
> (1) Almost always prefer the concrete word to the abstract.
> (2) Almost always prefer the direct word to the circumlocution.
> (3) Generally use transitive verbs, that strike their object; and use
> them in the active voice, eschewing the stationary passive,
> with its auxiliary *is's* and *was's*, and its participles getting in
> the light of your adjectives, which should be few. For, as a rough
> law, by his use of the straight verb and by his economy of
> adjectives you can tell a man's style, if it be masculine or
> neuter, writing or 'composition'.

After these he cited the last two Fowlerian rules, but added that they
would have to be modified by so long a string of exceptions that he did
not recommend them; in his opinion they were 'false in theory and likely
to be fatal in practice'. Quiller-Couch's rules (1) and (2) are the same as
the Fowlers' rules (2) and (3), except that he qualifies them with the
words 'almost always'. The only rule that is original with him is the
third, advocating the general use of transitive, active verbs because
they strike their object and are hence 'masculine'.

This view of the role of transitive verbs is narrow and blinkered, for
while some like *hit, kill* and *touch* do indeed strike their object, this is
an inappropriate image for the mass of transitives, especially such
verbs as *love, protect* or *save*. It further ignores the fact that an intransitive often cannot be replaced; *to blush, fall, glance, tremble* and many
others have no transitive equivalents. 'She shed tears' is no better than
'She wept' and it takes longer to say or write.

As for the advice to use the active voice, this is an absurd rule which,
if obeyed, would cut out an enormous amount of natural expression.
Hugh Sykes Davies rejected this association of the active verb with
virility and the passive with emasculation. For him the active-passive
opposition is an invaluable resource, one of the chief means of achieving
variety and significance of emphasis. 'The distinction between "active"
and "passive", he writes, 'is not in English primarily or even frequently
a matter of activity as opposed to stillness or inaction. It is much more
often a matter of emphasis, word order, and the smooth connection of
one sentence with another' (*Grammar Without Tears*, 1951). 'John was
attacked by the dog' is the factual equivalent of 'The dog attacked John',
but the sentence perspective is quite different; in the passive form the
focus is on John as victim, while in the active form it is on the dog as
attacker.

The agentless passive, i.e. where the doer or cause of the action is not expressed, has been criticized, notably by Gowers, but it is a convenient construction which has no equivalent in the active form. It has its uses, both good and bad. It serves a useful purpose when the doer of the action is unimportant, unidentified or obvious, as in the following sentences. 'Drugs should be kept in a safe place' (by anyone). 'My flat was burgled last night' (by someone unknown). 'Bloggs was elected MP' (by the electors). On the other hand, the formula 'Your complaint is being considered' in a business letter is merely a weasel expression used to evade responsibility. Ronald Reagan produced a gem of presidential evasion when he remarked 'Mistakes were made'.

Orwell's rules

George Orwell drew on these stylistic precepts, without acknowledging his debt either to the Fowlers or to Quiller-Couch. In his essay 'The English People', written in 1944 but not published till 1947, he took the view that 'there are no reliable rules: there is only the general principle that concrete words are better than abstract ones, and that the shortest way of saying anything is always the best'. Only two years later he had changed his mind and decided that there were rules. At the end of his 'Politics and the English Language' (1946) he proposed six rules which would, he believed, 'cover most cases', curiously omitting his previously mentioned principle of choosing concrete words.

(1) Never use a metaphor, simile or other figure of speech which you are used to seeing in print.
(2) Never use a long word where a short one will do.
(3) If it is possible to cut a word out, always cut it out.
(4) Never use the passive when you can use the active.
(5) Never use a foreign phrase, a scientific word, or a jargon word if you can think of an everyday equivalent.
(6) Break any of these rules sooner than say anything outright barbarous.

This last rule recalls the Fowlerian dispensation to ignore any of their rules if there is good reason to do so. Of the other rules three are Orwell's own.

Rule (1) is clearly a warning against the use of clichés, which he strongly disliked. He failed to see that the cliché has valid uses and overlooked the fact that people disagree about which current expressions qualify for the description. Clichés are original and often striking phrases, seized upon by imitators and so overworked that they lose their potency and become almost meaningless. They are offensive not in themselves but because they tend to be used indiscriminately and sometimes inappropriately. But while they can be used unthinkingly as handy reach-me-downs, they can also be used aptly, as the glove that fits to perfection. They can be enemies of precise expression or they can be deliberately chosen as the most exact way of saying what one wants to say.

Like slang, clichés date rapidly and most of them pass out of use. Many hackneyed phrases that were branded only a generation ago, such as *explore every avenue, leave no stone unturned* and *suffer a sea change*, are now rarely if ever used. In their place we have *at the end of the day, grind to a halt* and *a window of opportunity*. The only safe rule with clichés is to use them sparingly and with discretion. Writers would be needlessly handicapped if they were forbidden to use such expressions as *keep a low profile* or *the thin end of the wedge*. The best writers, though, avoid clichés altogether and coin their own phrases.

Rule (3) has much to commend it, but even here a word of caution is necessary. It is a useful discipline, when one is writing, to cut out superfluous words, for they clutter the text and cloud the meaning if there are too many of them. But compression, to which English lends itself readily, can be taken too far. One can be so laconic as to become Delphic in one's utterances. 'I labour to be brief and become obscure,' wrote Horace. An excess of word-cutting can thus make a text harder to understand, and confuse rather than enlighten. The rule works only up to a point and needs to be applied judiciously, not mechanically.

With rule (5) one cannot but agree, for the needless use of foreign phrases and technical terms is simply an affectation. The use of foreign expressions such as *fait accompli, lingua franca* and *prima facie*, which have no English equivalents, is justified. But we do not need *inter alia* when we can say 'among other things'; similarly *carte blanche* can be as well expressed by 'blank cheque' or 'a free hand', and *la dolce vita* by 'the good life' or 'a life of luxury'. The use of jargon and technical terms is necessary when experts are communicating with fellow-experts, but should be avoided when they are addressing a wider audience. The layman is more likely to understand *bruise* than *contusion, sex drive* than *libido*, and *thigh-bone* than *femur*.

Gowers's rules

In *Plain Words* (1948) Sir Ernest Gowers criticized Quiller-Couch's only original precept, namely the third one, for lacking the crispness that he preached, yet Gowers himself went on to propound three rules that are far from crisply expressed.

(1) Use no more words than are necessary to express your meaning, for if you use more you are likely to obscure it and to tire your reader. In particular do not use superfluous adjectives and adverbs and do not use roundabout phrases where single words would serve.

(2) Use familiar words rather than the far-fetched, if they express your meaning equally well; for the familiar are more likely to be readily understood.

8. Rules of Style

(3) Use words with a precise meaning rather than those that are vague, for they will obviously serve better to make your meaning clear; and in particular prefer concrete words to abstract, for they are more likely to have a precise meaning.

Gowers offers no wholly new rules of his own, but amplifies and qualifies those proposed by his predecessors. In his third rule he tells us to prefer words with a precise meaning, adding that this is more likely to be found in concrete words than abstract ones. This last assertion is quite untrue. Most words with one precise meaning are technical terms like *atom, cholesterol, oxygen, virus*, and many of them are abstract words like *prophylaxis, syndrome, valency* and *velocity*. The vocabulary of everyday English consists largely of 'omnibus words', i.e. those with multiple meanings. Ordinary words denote concepts that tend to be blurred at the edges, and they acquire a specific sense only in association with other words. Precise meanings cannot be attached to concrete words like *creature, material, piece, stuff, thing* or to abstract words like *duty, intelligence, love, value*, least of all to Humpty-Dumpty words like *democracy* and *romanticism*. In short, precision is not more likely to be a feature of concrete than abstract words; it is more likely to be a feature of technical than non-technical words. Precise definition is the chief characteristic of technical terms, be they concrete or abstract. Hence the paradox that the most precise language is the most obscure, for technical discourse is largely unintelligible to all but a relatively small number of specialists familiar with the subject and its terminology.

*

The Fowlers, Quiller-Couch, Orwell and Gowers between them produced ten different rules for writing good English. Of these only three are worth keeping, and the first requires the addition of two provisos, here given in italics.

(1) Omit needless words, *provided there is no loss of clarity or change of meaning*.
(2) Avoid circuitous phrases where a direct or single-word equivalent exists.
(3) Avoid foreign phrases and technical jargon where a native or everyday equivalent exists.

As we have now seen, most recommendations to use one kind of word in preference to another, regardless of context, are wholly misleading and have the effect of putting vocabulary in a strait-jacket. There is only one reliable rule of diction, namely that given by Greenough and Kittredge regarding familiar and unfamiliar words: choose the word or expression most suited to the context, both of language and of situation.

9. Good English

Features of good English

Poor English is common in both speech and writing. There is some excuse for it in speech, for this is a continual improvisation which allows no time to frame one's thoughts with exactitude. But there is no excuse for poorly written English, since the writer can go on altering and reshaping his sentences until they are well articulated.

In much written English scant thought is given to expression. Words are sometimes battered almost senseless. Phrases and clauses are thrown together, regardless of whether the pieces fit each other. Many sentences lack connecting tissue; some are merely limbs severed from the main body and expected to function on their own. Bad writers have simply not learned to use the resources of language competently. They do not artfully strive to avoid clarity; they artlessly fail to achieve it. Writing is an art, but only for those with rare verbal gifts; for everyone else it is a skill that can be learned, like any other skill, given the right guidance and enough practice. Our quest is not for a literary style. What we are pursuing is a plain, serviceable English suitable for most purposes, something without artistic pretensions but better than the poor or the merely passable.

Fortunately, there are ascertainable principles of style, formal and functional criteria by which it may be judged. Good plain English is easy to read, being free from encumbrances such as ambiguity, circumlocution, repetition, unnecessary elaboration and obscurity of reference. The distinguishing marks of good English are clarity, brevity and simplicity. Chief of these is clarity, for without it understanding is clouded and the words then fail in their primary function, which is to convey meaning effectively. Brevity helps to achieve clarity, as long as the compression is not so extreme as to obscure the message. Simplicity is the outward sign of clear thought; the best way of saying something is nearly always the simplest way. The highest forms of English, to be sure, display other qualities besides these, such as elegance, originality of expression, and variety of sentence length and pattern, but these are for the artists with words. We shall be satisfied with English that is clear, brief and simple.

Rules of good English

The following rules have been framed as a guide to fulfilling the requirements of good English. The rules touch both the choice of words and the arrangement of words, both diction and syntax.

Rule of Appropriateness. Use forms of language appropriate to your purpose, to the topic, the situation and those you are addressing. In particular, keep formal discourse free of colloquialisms, slang and abbreviated forms. This rule takes precedence over all the others.

Rule of Attachment. Attach qualifying phrases, especially introductory *-ing* phrases, to the noun or pronoun they refer to.

Rule of Cohesion. When writing, make explicit the relations between clauses, sentences and paragraphs by using connectives. Be orderly: present material in a logical or chronological sequence.

Rule of Compatibility. Avoid semantic incongruity between nouns and their qualifiers, and syntactic incongruity between the first part of a sentence and what follows.

Rule of Concord. Generally make verbs agree in number with their subjects. With collective nouns like *family* and pronouns like *none* use a singular or plural verb according to whether the subject is seen as a single unit or a group of individuals. Ensure that pronouns have a noun of the same gender and number to refer to.

Rule of Consistency. Stick to one style: the formal, semi-formal, neutral, casual, or intimate. When referring to the same noun, avoid mixing singular and plural pronouns or verbs.

Rule of Discrimination. Observe distinctions between pairs of opposites like *imply* and *infer*. Avoid malapropisms, mixed metaphors and crossed constructions. Guard against using a noun in more than one sense in the same context; when you mean different things, use different words.

Rule of Economy. Use the smallest number of words necessary to convey your meaning clearly. Avoid repetition and any kind of redundancy, be it pleonasm, tautology, verbosity or circumlocution. Use epithets and other verbal ornaments sparingly. Eschew irrelevances.

Rule of Omission. Leave out words only if their absence causes no ambiguity, change of meaning or faulty attachment. Omit a noun or pronoun subject only where it is expressed elsewhere in the sentence.

Rule of Proximity. Place words that belong together in sense as close to each other as you can. In particular, place relative pronouns as near as possible to their antecedents.

These rules enjoin us to avoid expressions that are redundant, incongruous or confused, and constructions that are incoherent, disjointed or misrelated. But they are not iron-clad rules, to be obeyed automatically at all times. Like all rules about language, they allow of exceptions and are subject to alteration in the light of later developments. Because of the ever-changing nature of language, there can be no absolute fixed standard of good usage, no linguistic lawgiver whose word is final. However, the amount of change occurring in one person's lifetime will be small and confined in the main to vocabulary. These rules, some of them well established, are chiefly structural and therefore likely to remain generally valid for a long time to come.

Qualification of the rules

The rules set forth above are designed to promote perspicuity, assuming a desire for communication and understanding. But language, which serves a great variety of purposes, is such a complex phenomenon that this assumption is not always sound. What is generally a liability may sometimes be an asset. People can use language to conceal their thoughts or even, as Schopenhauer cynically remarked, to conceal an absence of thoughts. Deliberate obfuscation and mystification are not uncommon, and the double talk of many politicians is notorious.

Even where there is no desire to conceal or mislead, a certain degree of indeterminacy, at least in the spoken language, is needed to ensure the flexibility that oral communication requires. Vagueness is an inevitable, indeed useful feature of ordinary conversation, for it enables us to speak when we do not wish to commit ourselves to anything with precisely defined contours. Hence the common use of woolly phrases such as *kind of, in a sort of way, as it were, seems as if, in a manner of speaking, in due course, much of a muchness,* assisted by a liberal sprinkling of fillers like *you know* and *if you see what I mean*.

Vagueness of expression is a serious defect wherever precision is needed, as in scientific and scholarly writing, but poets and novelists often gain their best effects by hints and suggestions, by elusive and allusive phrases, as well as by manifold ambiguities and multiple associations. The language of theology and mysticism, with their abstract terms which have no verifiable objective referents, is necessarily often vague; about the ineffable one can only waffle.

Like clarity, brevity and simplicity are not always attainable. Sometimes the most economical arrangement of words is not the most intelligible or the most effective. Repetition of words may be desirable, even necessary, if some clarification or emphasis is required. Even the simplicity of a direct statement is not always appropriate; sometimes suggestion is more tactful than the approach direct. And perfect simplicity cannot be achieved if what is being spoken of is inherently abstruse, though a good writer will always strive to expound a complex idea in the simplest terms.

These exceptions apart, however, it remains true for most purposes that speech and writing are best served when they are clear, brief and simple. The rules given above are thus in general a sound guide to good English, which consists of well-chosen words in well-framed sentences. Where educated usage is divided, as it is on a substantial number of points, there is no question of one form being right and the other wrong. Sometimes the variants are equally acceptable, but in most cases one form can be shown to be better than the alternative for some reason or other. And the reason why it is better is that it conforms to the grammatical and stylistic principles embodied in the rules. The preferred form may be clearer, more economical or better articulated than the other variants, and in matters of diction the choice will often be determined by contextual appropriateness.

Teaching English grammar

It should be made clear that the prescriptions given here relate solely to standard English, the form which all enlightened teachers of English will wish to pass on to their pupils. This is not to say that non-standard varieties of English are to be despised; on the contrary they are part of our cultural heritage, to be respected and preserved. In our educational institutions, however, the chief concern should be to enable all students, of whatever background, to acquire a command of the standard language. The plain fact is that in the English-speaking world success in education, and in most other spheres of life, depends crucially upon the ability to understand and use standard English. Young people should not be locked into a linguistic provincialism, but given the opportunity to learn that form of the language which will best enable them to expand their knowledge and equip them to communicate with speakers of English everywhere. And the key which opens the door to that wider world is standard English.

Few things are as fascinating as the mechanics of language. But if we wish to comment on or discuss some aspect of our mother tongue, as most of us do at times, we need the tools with which to do it, and these are supplied by grammar. An acquaintance with basic grammatical terms is thus a prerequisite for any fruitful study or discussion of language, just as a knowledge of biological terms is necessary for the study of biology. Some grammar instruction, however rudimentary, is needed by all children if they are to become truly literate adults.

The abandonment of grammar in English lessons a generation ago was a healthy reaction to the old methods which had failed so dismally—methods involving arid drills and sterile exercises, modelled on the teaching of Latin. If grammar is badly taught it becomes a dry-as-dust subject, but it need not be taught badly; it could and should provide some of the most stimulating activities a school has to offer. All our children come to their lessons with an impressive knowledge and experience of their own language; they should be encouraged to explore how it works, the better to appreciate its complexities and subtleties. Imaginative methods can be devised which will appeal to the young, and material can be selected which is relevant to their needs.

Lessons in which pupils learn to derive rules and discern patterns for themselves will develop their deductive powers and their verbal reasoning abilities. Besides comparing different forms where usage is divided, they could usefully compare standard English forms with those which many of them habitually use themselves. Non-standard forms should not be ridiculed as corrupt or incorrect, but treated as objects of interest and value. 'It ain't no good' is intrinsically no less grammatical than 'It isn't any good' or 'It's no good', but double negation and *ain't*, which once belonged to educated usage, are not accepted in the standard English of today. On no account should such forms be called sub-standard, for this falsely implies inferiority to the standard. The term 'sub-standard' has no place in linguistic description; forms are either standard or non-standard.

Part II

10. Hypercorrection

Phonetic hypercorrection

The linguistically insecure, in their anxiety to avoid one fault, sometimes fall into another that is equally bad; steering clear of Scylla, they sink into Charybdis. Such use of unacceptable speech forms, in an effort to avoid others which are much stigmatized, is called hypercorrection. Most lapses of this kind are grammatical, but phonetic examples occur too, when speakers with a regional accent try to imitate the prestige pronunciation. Thus, some speech-conscious people in the North of England, where *but* rhymes with *put*, correct their *but*, then proceed to mis-correct their *put* to rhyme with *cut*, and similarly make *good* rhyme with *bud*, *butcher* with *toucher*, *cushion* with *Russian* and *sugar* with *bugger* – which rather 'boogers it oop'.

In the United States the pronunciation of *r* at the end of the word or before a consonant once had low status, since it deviated from the English standard where the *r* is not sounded in such words as *car* and *card*. Since the Second World War, however, the position has been gradually reversed, so that the rhotic (*r*-pronouncing) accent is now a prestige marker among Americans. The result is that some speakers from the non-rhotic areas, such as New York City and Southern states, go too far in introducing *r*, saying *carm* for *calm* and *larn* for *lawn*. Similarly, Brooklynites who have discarded the local pronunciation of *bird* as *boid* and *girl* as *goil* can sometimes be heard pronouncing *oyster* as *erster* and *toilet* as *terlet*.

The nob's pronouns

In most non-standard varieties of English *me* is used instead of *I* in a subject partnership, e.g. 'Me and my friend helped him'. This is the result of phrase transference from the object case form, 'He helped me and my friend'. The use of *me* as subject is strongly condemned and this leads to the belief that *me* should never be coupled with a noun or another pronoun, and that the subject form *I* is more grammatical or more genteel. This hypercorrect *I* is the prime example of a 'nob's pronoun', frequently used as the direct object of a verb.

He doesn't like my wife and *I*

If we apply the subtraction test and take away the first object (*my wife*), we are left with 'He doesn't like *I*', which is manifestly unacceptable, since what everyone says is 'He doesn't like me'. Fear of misusing *me* in double subjects makes people misuse *I* for *me* in double objects. Phrase transference of *me and my wife* from object case to subject case leads to its opposite, phrase transference of *my wife and I* from subject case to object case.

    Let you and *I* do it

Those who use this form of words would not say 'Let *we* do it' but 'Let us do it'. *You and I,* like *my wife and I* above, has been transferred as a unit phrase from subject to object function in the erroneous belief that only the *I*-form is correct in combination with a noun or another pronoun.

A similar transference of the unit *he who* or *he that* is found sometimes after the verb *let*. A prominent British politician recently misquoted the Bible, saying:

    Let *he* that is without sin cast the first stone

Let *he* go back to the original, which runs thus: 'He that is without sin among you, let him first cast a stone at her' (John 8:7).

Nob's pronouns after prepositions

Subject noun phrases of the type *you and I* and *my wife and I* are often used hypercorrectly as the object of prepositions.

    This food is for John and *I*

If we subtract *John* from the double object we are left with an unacceptable *for I*. The use of *John* with the first person pronoun obscures the need to say *for me*. Some speakers, unsure whether to say *I* or *me* here, resort to the form 'for John and myself', using the reflexive pronoun quite inappropriately. This is a case of jumping out of the frying pan into the fire: the evasive *myself* is worse than the hypercorrect *I*.

In the 16th and 17th centuries, when the well-bred spoke as they pleased and used pronouns according to personal whim, the phrase *between you and I* was a regular idiom, as it still is in the United States today. Thus, in American usage, it is not primarily a hypercorrect form since it is used even by well-educated speakers. *Between you and I* is an inherited idiom that has successfully resisted schoolmastering or, more likely, schoolmarming. The fact remains, however, that the phrase, regardless of its origin, is something of a linguistic sore thumb. It is unsatisfactory because it clashes with forms such as *between us* (not *we*) and *between them* (not *they*). English prepositions take the object case of pronouns, whether used alone, with a noun, or with another pronoun, as in *for (his son and) him* or *like (you and) me*. Thus *we* is nobbish, not to say snobbish, in such statements as:

This was a raw deal for *we* students

The fault comes from altering non-standard '*Us students* had a raw deal' to the standard subject form *We students* and then hypercorrectly reversing the process. The combination *for we*, with or without a noun in apposition (like *students*), is unacceptable. Likewise nobbish is *he who* after a preposition. A well-known building society recently advertised its services with a picture of an angler, below which it put this hypercorrected version of an old saying:

Everything comes to *he* who waits

If he waits long enough it will come not to *he* but to *him*.

Further nobbishness is sometimes found after the preposition *but* (meaning 'except').

No one but *he* knew about it

The hypercorrective tendency is doubtless reinforced here by the apparent incongruity of saying *him knew*, but the subject of *know* is, of course, *no one*. This difficulty disappears if the sentence is rearranged so that the problematic phrase follows the verb, i.e. 'No one knew about it but him'.

The nob's adverbs

As there are nob's pronouns, so there are nob's adverbs. Since the late 18th century, through the efforts of tidy-minded precriptivists, the suffix *-ly* has been tacked on to more and more adverbs, especially in American English (at least that of the genteel variety). This form of hypercorrection springs from the mistaken notion that adverbs related to adjectives must end in *-ly*, so as to distinguish the two forms, e.g. *swiftly* and *swift*.

From earliest times, however, English has had two types of adverbs derived from adjectives. The first type was formed by adding the suffix *-lice* (= *-like*), which was gradually whittled down to *-ly*; thus the adjective *glaed* ('glad') gave the adverb *glaedlice*, now *gladly*. The second type was formed by adding the suffix *-e*, an unstressed vowel which fell silent in the 15th century; in this way the adjective *deop* ('deep') gave the adverb *deope*, which became *deep*. Adverbs of the second type thus eventually had the same form as adjectives. These so-called flat adverbs were in regular use until the prescriptivists bore down on them. For example, until well into the 18th century it was normal to say 'The sun shone bright', whereas *shone brightly* is more usual today.

Flat adverbs survive in set expressions such as *buy cheap, cost dear, bow low, dig deep, hold tight, stand firm, rest easy, sitting pretty, writ large*, and in compounds with participles, such as *clear-cut, deep-seated, full-grown, high-flown, slow-moving* and *tight-fitting*. Some adverbs historically had two forms; such is the case with *slowly*, the descendant of *slawlice*, and *slow*, the descendant of *slawe*. Thus both *slowly* and *slow* are adverbs, the choice of one or other depending on custom and context. The phrase *go slow* is hallowed by long usage, so it is appropriate to use *slow* with similar verbs, e.g. *drive slow*, but contrary to idiom to say *drink slow* or *think slow*.

Thus, outside established idioms, the flat adverbs are not normally used. Though we *fight fair* and *play fair*, we do not *judge fair* but *judge fairly*. We speak of *new-born babies* but *newly married couples*, of *high-born people* but *highly placed officials*. Sometimes we have free choice, as with *talk loud* and *talk loudly*, *soft-spoken* and *softly spoken*. But sometimes the two forms are not synonymous. *Sleep easy* is not the same as *sleep easily*, nor is *high-rated* the same as *highly rated*.

Adverbs for adjectives

The rejection of non-standard sentences like 'He comes here regular' (for *regularly*), 'I beat him easy' (for *easily*) and 'She doesn't talk proper' (for *properly*) leads to such hypercorrect utterances as 'I feel *badly* about it'. Idiomatically, one *feels bad* or *feels good* about something, the adjective forms *bad* and *good* being used for the complement of verbs of sensation or perception. The proper analogy is not with *feel strongly* (expressing manner) but with *feel sad* (expressing state). Compare 'She smiles *sweetly*' and 'She smells *sweet*'.

Elsewhere too the adverb in *-ly* is often used where the adjective is more idiomatic.

> She stared *bewilderedly*

Better here is *bewildered*, relating to *she*, or the adverbial *in bewilderment*.

Compare:

> (1) This cannot be done single-handedly
> (2) He rescued the victims single-handedly

In (1) the adverb *single-handedly* qualifies *done*, there being no doer expressed. In (2), where the doer is mentioned, the adverb form is hypercorrect; the appropriate form is the adjective *single-handed*, referring to the subject *he*.

Very often nowadays an adverb in *-ly* is used with *more, most* or *equally* in parenthetic phrases, where the adjective form is perfectly acceptable.

> He is clever and, *more importantly,* he is honest

Much neater and more succinct is *more important*, an elliptical form of *what is more important*, just as *better still* and *best of all* are shortenings of *what is better still* and *what is best of all*. Similarly, in enumerations the adverbs *first, second, third, ... last* are still preferred by many writers to the longer forms in *-ly*, most of which came into use only in the early modern period. Both forms are acceptable, but they are not mixed in good style. Consistency requires matching forms; either *first, second, ...* and *last* or *firstly, secondly ...* and *lastly*.

Hypercorrect 'whom'

The pronoun *who* is a rogue among relatives, causing more grief and mischief than any other word in the English language. It is the only relative pronoun that is inflected and it differs from the personal pronouns in preceding the verb that governs it. Since there is widespread confusion between the different forms of personal pronouns, especially *I* and *me*, it is not suprising that *who* and *whom* should often be confounded too. In spoken English the subject form *who* had supplanted *whom* as the object form in questions by the 16th century. Since that time *whom* as a relative has only been kept alive, chiefly in written English, by the Latinate tradition that nurtured the old prescriptivists.

Today most native speakers never use the word *whom*, either in speech or writing, and they regard its use as pedantic. 'To whom did you speak?' is English on stilts; the natural turn of phrase is 'Who did you speak to?' with a perfectly acceptable final preposition. *Whom*-avoidance is possible in all constructions. The interrogative *whom*, where used without a preposition, is avoided by saying 'Who did you see?' for 'Whom did you see?' The relative *whom* can be avoided by saying 'He is the man (that) I saw' for 'He is the man whom I saw', 'She has four sisters, two (of them) married' for 'She has four sisters, two of whom are married' and 'He is a fine magician, who knows as many tricks as anyone' for 'He is a fine magician, than whom no one knows more tricks'.

The preservation of the object form *whom* in educated usage has inevitably led to its being used hypercorrectly, i.e. as subject. The commonest type of hypercorrect *whom* occurs where it is immediately followed by a subject and verb.

He is the man *whom* we know will lead us

The relative, which is the subject of *will lead*, is taken to be the object of *we know*, by false analogy with 'He is the man whom we know' and 'He is the man whom we expect to lead us', where *whom* is the object of *we know* and *we expect* respectively.

Like us, our ancestors had trouble with *whom*. The translators of the Bible used it as a complement of the verb *to be*, despite the fact that 'It is he' (not *him*) was then the norm. Thus Tyndale (1526) wrote: 'Whom do men saye that I the son of man am?' (Matthew 16:13). And Shakespeare wrote: 'Young Ferdinand, – whom they suppose is drown'd' (*The Tempest, c.* 1610), a cross between *who, they suppose, is drowned*, where *they suppose* is parenthetic, and *whom they suppose to be drowned*, where *they suppose* governs *whom*.

Edward Sapir, in his book *Language* (1921), wrote of *whom* as a word which would eventually disappear from English speech. He pointed out that *who* is increasingly invariable because it belongs to the same category as the other relative pronouns, *which, what* and *that*, and resembles the interrogative adverbs *how, when* and *where*, all of which have but one form. Moreover, since it normally comes before the verb, i.e. in the subject position, *who* sounds natural. For all that, *whom* is used – and misused – probably as much today as when Sapir wrote. The pseudo-genteel *whom*, as in 'Whom shall I say is calling?' 'Whom is calling?' and 'Whom is this speaking?' still flourishes telephonically in secretarial parlance, where *whom* is treated as the polite form of *who*.

'Who' and 'who(so)ever' after prepositions

Sometimes *whom* is used hypercorrectly for *who* because it is taken to be the object of a preposition.

> We have no doubt about *whom* is to blame

The appropriate form here is *who*, which is the subject of *is*, not the object of the word *about*. The object of *about* is the unexpressed antecedent *him*, i.e. *about (him) who is to blame*, another way of saying *about the one/the person who is to blame*.

Similarly with *who(so)ever*:

> Give it to *whomever* needs it
> He cannot be prevented by *whomsoever* it may be

Here again the relative pronouns have been mistakenly seen as the object of a preposition. The true object becomes apparent when the ellipsis is supplied, i.e. *to [him] whoever needs it* and *by [him] whosoever it may be*. The difficulty can be avoided by using the more modern turns of phrase *to anyone who needs it* and *by anyone at all*.

In all these cases the antecedent *he*, in the appropriate form, is suppressed, leaving just *who* as the subject or *whom* as the object of the following verb. Parallel examples are '[He] who dares wins', 'To [him] whom it may concern' and Charles Kingsley's well-known line 'Be good, sweet maid, and let [him] who will be clever' (*A Farewell to C.E.G.*, 1856).

Gentrified 'as' and 'as with'

In non-standard English the word *like*, traditionally used as a preposition at the head of a noun phrase, serves as a conjunction, introducing an adverbial clause of manner or comparison.

> Do it *like* I do
> He is ill, *like* I said
> Leave the bathroom *like* you found it

In such cases, i.e. when a verb follows, *as* is standard usage, not *like*. The confusion is understandable since both words are used in making comparisons. *Like*-phrases are synonymous with *as*-phrases that include a verb.

He teaches, like his wife (= as his wife does)

There is a radical difference, however, when the *as*-phrase is verbless. Compare:

(3) He spoke like a politician
(4) He spoke as a politician

The *like* in (3) expresses similarity (the speaker is not a politician); the *as* in (4) expresses identity (the speaker is a politician).

Similarly, *like* is used in comparisons of the speculative type.

He looked *like* he had seen a ghost

This use of *like* comes from confusing two synonymous modes of expression:

It looked like rain
It looked as if it would rain

The preposition *like* is then substituted for the conjunction *as if*, giving:

It looked *like* it would rain

A similar result is achieved by transference:

(5) He looks like a man who is in trouble
(6) He looks *like* he is in trouble

The resemblance to some hypothetical other person in (5) is transferred to the subject himself in (6).

Strong attacks have been made on the use of *like* for *as* and *as if*. In America the expression 'Tell it like it is' has been severely condemned and there was an outcry from purists when an advertisement proclaimed that 'Winston tastes good like a cigarette should'. Over-zealous attempts to avoid such uses of *like* have led to the opposite fault, the gentrification of *as*.

The rocket speeds *as* the wind
The adults are behaving *as* children
As all politicians, he loves to air his views

Fear of misusing *like* leads to the use of a gentrified *as* where *like* is the appropriate word. The same fear explains the use of *as with* where *like* is appropriate.

As with most artists, he worked long hours

The construction *as with* is used in indirect comparisons, e.g. 'As with most artists, his work came first'. But here we have a direct comparison, hence the word *like* is appropriate.

Pseudo-subjunctive 'were'

The subjunctive is a form of the verb used in non-factual or uncertain statements. In its earlier stages English made regular use of the subjunctive but nowadays it is restricted to fossilized phrases such as 'so *be* it', 'as it *were*', '*come* what may' and 'God *help* you', and to expressions of necessity, desirability and the like, as in 'It is essential that he *attend*'.

The use of the subjunctive *were* is still common in *if*-clauses, for example 'If I *were* you I would go', although the non-subjunctive *was* is equally acceptable. This use of *were* in contrary-to-fact statements leads to the false inference that it may be used in all *if*-clauses, including those that express a realized or realizable condition. Its use is thus hypercorrectly extended to factual statements, in the belief that *were*, not *was*, goes with *if*. Compare:

(7) If he were at home on Sunday, he would receive us
(8) If he *were* at home on Sundays, he would (always) receive us

(7) poses a hypothetical situation which may or may not arise on one future occasion; here *would* is conditional and the subjunctive *were* is used appropriately. By contrast, (8) speaks of real events that occurred in the past; here *would* is not conditional but habitual, hence the word *was* is required. Similarly, compare:

(9) If ever he were ill, he would not show it
(10) If he *were* ill yesterday, he did not show it

In (9) there is a hypothetical condition relating to the present-future, whereas in (10) there is a real condition that relates to a past possibility. In the latter case the writer has succumbed to what Fowler called 'the glamour of the word *were*', but glamour is no substitute for grammar.

The subjunctive *were* may be used after *if* or *whether* in indirect questions.

He asked if I were at home
I wondered whether it were true

This use, justified by the uncertainty about the facts that is inherent in questions, was common in earlier English, where it was modelled on Latin usage. Today, however, this use of *were* is so uncommon that, though correct, it gives the impression of being hypercorrect, i.e. of being used by false analogy with hypothetical *if*-clauses. For this reason *was* is to be preferred.

Further examples

That mistake has cost them dearly.
He has invited Bill and I to dinner.
He retrieved the stolen jewels single-handedly.

10. Hypercorrection

Let you and I go and sit by ourselves.
They told everyone but John and I.
She waxed lyrically about the beauty of the island.
Whom do you think is responsible for this damage?
Let we in Britain do all we can to help the Third World.
As his father before him, James failed to achieve his ambition.
Women's breasts bulk largely in men's sexual fantasies.
She was quite charming to whomever had aroused her interest.
If I were working, I would often lock the door.
Somebody told me your name, but I forget whom.
The world is subject to the will of he who created it.
People like you and I are not affected by this change.
Will you tell me whom ought to be notified?
We met he and his wife at the club last night.
That is the boy whom we thought was not playing.
As with many intellectuals he loved humanity but disliked people.
We must support the leader, whomsoever he may be.
As for my mother and I, we are taking it easily.
First and foremostly, I must speak of the frustrations of we women.
He asked both of us, my brother and I, to give evidence.
Power generally changes he who possesses it into a different person.
Such writers have more widely ranging minds than most other people.

11. False Agreement

Collective nouns

As a rule verbs agree in number and person with their subject. In the present tense all verbs, apart from modals and the irregular verb *to be*, have the ending *-s* in the third person singular and no ending in the other forms. Thus we say 'The boy sings' but 'The boys sing'. There are many cases, however, where a singular subject may be followed by a verb in the singular or the plural. Collective nouns denoting small or informal groups, such as *couple, class, family* and *team,* may take a singular or plural verb. Thus we may say either:

> The band was/were playing
> Is/are the team winning?
> The class has/have behaved badly

In practice formal agreement, in the singular, is used when the collective is thought of as a group or unit, and notional agreement, in the plural, when it is seen as individuals. Compare the following pairs.

> The jury has given its verdict
> The jury were arguing for hours
> The crowd is moving slowly
> The crowd are getting restless
> The staff was reduced
> The staff were disgruntled

At this point we enter an area of divided usage. The British take notional (i.e. plural) agreement much further than Americans do. In British usage nouns denoting large organizations, official bodies, the names of firms and sports teams may take a singular or plural verb, and the plural is generally preferred.

> The navy does/do not want this ship
> The government is/are in trouble
> The Mafia refuses/refuse to talk
> Fiat has/have opened a new factory
> Manchester United tops/top the league

In such sentences as these only a singular verb is used in American English.

11. False Agreement

A common fault to avoid is mixed agreement, i.e. the use of both singular and plural forms referring to the same subject.

>The board has decided they must make changes

The verb *has* treats *board* as a collective singular, but the pronoun *they* treats it as a collective plural. To be consistent, one should say either *has* and *it* or *have* and *they*.

Mixed agreement can switch from singular to plural or vice versa.

>The IRA says they planted the bomb
>The IRA say it planted the bomb

Both variants can be heard and both are slovenly; *says* should be followed by *it*, and *say* by *they*.

Plural and compound subjects

Plural nouns denoting a single unit or entity are followed by a singular verb.

>The United States has protested
>*The Times* was in financial trouble
>Ten years is a long time
>Fifteen cents buys very little

Likewise compound subjects linked by *and*, if they refer to a single thing or idea, take a singular verb.

>The Stars and Stripes (the flag) has been lowered
>Fish and chips (the dish) is a nourishing meal
>*Romeo and Juliet* (the play) was being performed

A singular subject linked to another by *with*, *along with* or *together with* does not form a compound subject. The second noun is not part of the subject, but dependent on it, hence the verb goes in the singular, e.g.

>The President, with his entourage, has arrived in the capital

Names of illnesses ending in *-s,* such as *shingles*, are usually treated as singular, but may take plural agreement too.

>Measles is (are) very catching
>Mumps was (were) diagnosed

A few other nouns that are singular in meaning but end in a plural *-s* may also take a verb of either number.

>The headquarters was/were in Berlin
>The works is/are situated in Detroit

But the name of games in *-s*, such as *billiards*, are treated as singulars.

>Dominoes is his favourite game

With this last compare 'The dominoes are in the box', where *dominoes* refers to the individual pieces, not to the game itself.

Plural anomalies

Nouns of number, when used with numerals, remain unchanged in the plural, e.g. *two dozen, five score, six hundred* and *twenty million*. The measure nouns *foot* and *stone* may stand in the plural or remain unchanged after numerals. We can equally well say 'He is six feet tall' or 'He is six foot tall' and likewise 'He weighs ten stones' or 'He weighs ten stone'. This unchanged plural has a long history and it is still widely used in non-standard English with other nouns of measure, names of time periods and units of currency, e.g. *ten ton, six pound, five mile, eight year, four month, twenty cent*. These all have a plural in *-s* in standard usage, except where they form part of a hyphenated combination, as in *a ten-ton lorry, a six-pound weight, a five-mile walk, an eight-year-old boy, a four-month holiday* and *a twenty-cent surcharge*. Forms such as *a two-weeks-old baby* and *a ten-years lease*, with an *-s,* are hypercorrect.

Nouns in *-ics* are treated sometimes as singulars and sometimes as plurals. Those which denote a subject of study, such as *physics*, or a sphere of activity, such as *athletics*, are treated as singulars, and those which are used in some different sense, like *acrobatics* (display of acrobatic skill), are treated as plurals. Many such nouns are ambivalent, taking a singular or plural verb depending on the sense. Compare the following sentence pairs.

> Politics is the art of the possible
> His politics (political beliefs) have changed

> Economics is taught in this school
> The economics (economic foundations) of this industry are shaky

> Acoustics is the science of sound
> The acoustics (acoustic properties) of this hall are good

> Statistics is a dry subject
> The statistics (figures) tell a different story

A special problem is posed by loan-words, especially Latin and Greek nouns with plurals in *-a*. Borrowings such as *agenda* (from *agendum,* 'a thing to be done') and *opera* (from *opus,* 'a work') are established as singulars and have English plurals in *-s*. The Latin neuter plurals *insignia* and *regalia* also have plurals in *-s*, at least in American English. The words *data* and *media*, though in origin the Latin plurals of *datum* and *medium*, may take plural agreement but are nowadays mostly treated as collective singulars, equivalent to 'a body of facts' and 'all the means of mass communication lumped together', so that it is acceptable to say *this data* and *the media is* ...

Other plural nouns such as *bacteria* (from *bacterium*), *criteria* (from *criterion*), *phenomena* (from *phenomenon*) and *strata* (from *stratum*) are quite often taken for singulars and given new plural forms in -*s*. These ambivalent forms will most probably settle down in this newer pattern of singular -*a*, plural -*as* (e.g. *stratas*), regardless of objections by purists.

The source-language plural of borrowed nouns is retained in formal or scholarly usage, but the plural in -*s* is preferred in everyday parlance. Thus we have alternative plurals such as *automaton: automata* and *automatons, curriculum: curricula* and *curriculums, formula: formulae* and *formulas, narcissus: narcissi* and *narcissuses, sanatorium: sanatoria* and *sanatoriums*. Sometimes the two plurals have different meanings. Thus *stigma* in the medical and botanical senses has the plural *stigmata*, but when it means 'a mark of social disapproval' it has the plural *stigmas*. Similarly, when *forum* refers to a market-place in ancient Rome it has the plural *fora*, but otherwise *forums*. In view of the tendency to abandon the Greco-Latin plurals it is advisable, when in doubt, to use the English plural form. The field of foreign plurals is strewn with traps for the unwary; only ignoramuses say *ignorami*.

Attraction

A verb is sometimes made to agree not with its subject but, by attraction, with another noun that is nearer.

(1) The last round of the races *are* now being held
(2) The minister, as well as his advisers, *have* seen this
(3) Foreign firms, rather than American industry, *is* getting the orders

In (1) and (2) we see the pull of the plural (*races* and *advisers*) and in (3) the pull of the singular (*industry*). The real subject *round* in (1) requires *is*, *minister* in (2) requires *has*, and *firms* in (3) requires *are*.

Agreement by attraction is acceptable, however, when the subject has a dependent genitive noun in the plural (*of -s*). Compare:

(4) A pile of chairs is (are) blocking the doorway
(5) A gang of youths were (was) playing ball

In (4) singular agreement is more likely with *chairs*, which are inanimate and may be seen as a mass, while in (5) plural agreement is more likely with *youths*, who are animate and can be seen as individuals. Once again, as with collective nouns, sense often prevails over form in the matter of agreement.

It should be noted that whereas *a number of* takes a plural verb, *the number of* takes a singular. Compare:

(6) A number of pupils are missing
(7) The number of pupils is small

In (6) *number* is part of a composite plural subject, equivalent in meaning to 'some' and therefore takes a plural verb. In (7) it stands as the subject in its own right, signifying 'the numerical total' and thus takes a singular verb. A similar distinction in the form of agreement is made with the words *range*, *series*, *set*, *total* and *variety*, depending on whether they are used with an indefinite or a definite article. Thus we say 'A wide range of goods are available' but 'The range of goods is limited'.

When the verb *to be* is followed by two or more singular subjects it usually agrees with the first only, by attraction to the nearest element.

> Here is the doctor and his wife
> There was frost, snow and ice on the ground

In colloquial speech *here's*, *there's* and *where's*, like *it's*, are treated as invariable introductory formulas. Just as we say 'It's my friends', we also say 'Here's your friends' and 'Where's your friends?' But this use of *is* for *are* before a plural subject is non-standard and not appropriate in serious writing. It is unacceptable, for example, to write 'There *is* not the facilities for dealing with them'. This is a case of false agreement, where *are* is required.

When the verb *to be* stands in a *what*-clause before a plural complement, it may be put in the singular or the plural.

> What we need is/are bigger subsidies

Traditional grammarians argued that since *what* means 'that which' the verb here should be singular and not be attracted to the following plural noun. But the word *what* may equally well mean 'those which', as in the sentence 'I went to buy some cakes but what I found were stale'. The plural agreement in the *what*-clauses is not necessarily caused by attraction, as it is in the following:

> The only protection we have *are* the dogs

The plural form *are* would be required if the sentence were reversed to read 'The dogs are the only protection we have', but in the sentence as it stands the subject is the singular noun *protection*, therefore the verb form should be *is*.

'Each', 'either', 'neither' and 'none'

The word *each*, used alone, or with a singular noun, or with a dependent genitive noun in the plural, takes a singular verb.

> Each (parent) has a part to play
> Each of the parents has a part to play

But when *each* is used with a plural pronoun or noun the verb agrees with the plural word.

> You/The parents each have a part to play

The words *either* and *neither*, like *each*, take a singular verb when they are used alone or with a singular noun.

11. False Agreement

Either (method) works well
Neither (method) is suitable

But with a dependent genitive they may take a verb in the singular (agreeing with their singular form) or in the plural (by attraction to the following noun).

Either of the readings makes/make sense
Neither of the readings satisfies/satisfy me

According to traditional grammar the correlatives *neither ... nor*, like *either ... or*, should take a singular verb, but nowadays a plural verb is normal and acceptable with the negative pair. Compare:

Either he or his wife is lying
Neither he nor his wife are (is) here

The plural form is found in the writings of good authors in the past. The rationale for its use is that the underlying sense is 'He is not here and his wife is not here', i.e. cumulative rather than alternative. When *either ... or* and *neither ... nor* are used with mixed singular and plural subjects the verb agrees with the nearest subject.

(N)either you (n)or he is right
(N)either he (n)or you are right

When the pronoun *none* refers to an uncountable noun it means 'no part' and takes a singular verb. When it refers to a countable noun it means 'not any of a group' and may take a singular or plural verb, the latter being more common.

None of the sugar is left
None of the cakes are (is) left

Similarly with pronouns.

None of it is right
None of them are (is) right

The old rule that *none* must take a singular verb strikes most people nowadays as pedantic, and the use of the plural has established itself in the teeth of fierce pedagogical resistance.

'One' in subjects

The expressions *many a one* and *more than one*, though notionally plural, have verbal agreement in the singular, by attraction to the word *one*.

Many a one (many a person) has said that
More than one (person) was involved

When the subject is the number *one* with a dependent genitive a singular verb is used.

> One of the airmen was rescued

Expressions of the type *one in four -s*, *one in every five -s*, traditionally used with a singular verb, nowadays often take a verb in the plural, legitimately so since the underlying sense is plural.

> One in every three marriages ends/end in divorce

But when *one* goes with a singular noun the verb is always singular.

> One worker in eight is self-employed

The construction *one of ... who/that* takes a following verb in the plural.

> He is one of those who are (not *is*) never satisfied
> This is one of the best films that have (not *has*) ever been made

False agreement is very common in this type of sentence. The pull of the singular *one* is so strong that many people would use singular verbs here, though the verbs clearly refer to the plural antecedents *those* and *films* respectively. False agreement of this kind sometimes extends from the verb to a following pronoun.

> He is one of the few journalists who *makes his* readers think

Just as *makes* needs changing to *make*, so *his* needs to be replaced by *their*.

Naturally, when the true subject is *one*, a singular verb is used. Compare:

> (8) He is one of those students who take drugs
> (9) He is the only one of those students who takes drugs

In (8) *who* refers to *those students*, while in (9) it refers to *the only one*.

Epicene pronouns

It is often stated, as a matter of regret, that English lacks epicene (common gender) pronouns in the third person singular, i.e. words to express the ideas *he or she* and *his or her*. But this is not so; the pronouns *they* and *their* have long been so used when they refer to an indefinite pronoun such as *anyone, everyone, neither, no one* and *somebody*. For example:

> Everyone likes to do as they please
> Has anyone lost their gloves?
> Nobody helped you, did they?

This use of *they* and *their* avoids the clumsiness of the alternative forms *he or she pleases* and *his or her gloves* as well as the male primacy implicit in the traditional masculine generic forms *he pleases* and *his gloves*.

It may be objected that the indefinite pronouns, which are singular in form, should not be followed by the plural pronouns *they* and *their*.

11. False Agreement

But there is no reason why we should not regard the personal pronouns, in this use, as being epicene singular i.e. as having the alternative senses *he or she* and *his or her*. There is a notable precedent for such an extension in the meaning of a pronoun, namely the word *you*. *You*, originally the object form of *ye*, gradually became interchangeable with it, then ousted it, took over the functions of *thou* and *thee*, and finally assumed the role of indefinite universal pronoun, largely replacing the word *one* in this sense. The pronouns *they* and *their* have been singularly bisexual for some 700 years. Shakespeare and the Bible, as in so many other cases, furnish suitable examples.

> ... God send everyone their heart's desire! (*Much Ado About Nothing, c.* 1598)
> ... let each esteem other better than themselves (Philippians 2:3)

The epicene use of *they* and *their* in reference to indefinite pronouns thus has a long history and defensible grounds for acceptance. Very questionable, by contrast, is the increasingly common practice of using *they* and *their* with a singular noun of common gender, such as *teacher*, *parent* or *person*.

> Each adult will get their own card
> Every taxpayer should invest if they can
> When a person is afraid they tend to exaggerate

Generalizations like these are better expressed in the plural, i.e. by saying *all adults*, *all taxpayers* and *people are*.

Faulty pronoun use

It is an easy slip to use a pronoun, especially *it* or *they*, without ensuring that it has an appropriate noun antecedent.

> (10) He volunteered to go but *it* was refused
> (11) When divorce laws are liberalized *they* rise sharply

Because of the absent antecedents, *it* in (10) and *they* in (11) are unrelated and thus left dangling. Vague pronouns will not do. What a pronoun refers to should be made explicit and not merely implied. The word *it* in (10) should be replaced by *his offer*, and *they* in (11) by *divorces*, since *divorce laws* are not what rise sharply.

An introductory pronoun sometimes lacks an antecedent in the previous sentence.

> Italy is in a financial crisis. *They* will have to devalue the lira

They is intended to refer not to the actual antecedent *Italy* but to the absent antecedent *the Italian government*.

Another fault in pronoun use is 'change of standpoint', i.e. switching from one pronoun to another in reference to the same person or thing. The commonest type of switch is from indefinite *one* to indefinite *you*.

If one wants attention, *you* must shout

To be consistent, we should say either *one wants* and *one must* or *you want* and *you must*. In American English the indefinite *one* is generally followed by *he* or *his*, retaining older British usage.

One must try not to offend his friends
One often thinks he knows best

The difficulty here is that the pronoun *one* is of common gender, but these days *he* and *his* are not often thought to refer to both sexes, as they once were. To avoid giving offence to women it is thus better to use *one's* in reference to *one* or, since *one* and *one's* sound stilted to modern ears, *you* and *your* instead.

Switching sometimes occurs with other pronouns.

(14) It was a fine ship, loved by all *her* crew
(15) When we looked closer, *you* could see traces of mould

A ship may be referred to as *it* or *she*, but not by both pronouns in the same sentence, as in (14). Similarly, the *we* who looked closer in (15) should remain *we* and not be switched to *you*.

Pronoun anomalies

The colloquial expression *these/those kind of things* appears to flout the rules of agreement since the plural demonstrative *these* or *those* qualifies the singular noun *kind*. Henry Sweet regarded this construction as a blend of two forms, *these things* and *this kind of things* (plural) and Henry Fowler saw it as 'a sort of inchoate compound, equivalent to *those-like*, on the analogy of *suchlike*'. But most modern grammarians treat it as a case of plural attraction. According to H. Poutsma, 'the subservient nature of *kind* or *sort*, as compared with that of the following noun, causes the plural of the demonstrative pronouns to be used instead of the grammatically correct singular in such word-groups as *these (those) kind (sort) of apples*' (*A Grammar of Late Modern English*, 1914-29).

The true explanation, buried in history, is much more complicated. Old English had the construction *alles cynnes deor*, in which *all* had the singular sense 'every' and *cynn* (literally *kin*) meant 'kind', the whole phrase signifying 'of every kind animals'. In the medieval period this construction underwent a twofold reinterpretation. First the reduction and finally the loss of the genitive ending *-es* obscured the grammatical relationship between the elements in what was *al kin deer*, with *kin* often replaced by *kind*. Following this a form such as *alle kinde* (or *alkinde*) *fisshis* was taken to consist of a head noun phrase *all kind* and a dependent genitive *fishes* and not vice versa, as before. After this reversal of roles *all kind* was construed not as 'every kind' but as 'all kinds' i.e. *kind* was taken to be an uninflected plural like *sheep* and *swine*. To make the dependency clearer the word *of* was at first occasionally and then regularly placed before the second noun, so that *kind of*, like *alkin(d)* before it, came to be treated in effect as a composite adjective. The word *manner*, borrowed from French, functioned likewise, in phrases such as *all manner (of) things*. After this the words *kind* and *manner*, perceived as uninflected plurals, were used with other determiners, for example in the phrases *two kind of*, *several kind of*, *three manner of* and *many manner of*. Finally, in the modern period, the words *sort* and *type* were assimilated to the pattern of *kind*, being used as uninflected plurals after *these* and *those*.

The expressions *all manner of* and *these (those) kind of* are thus relics of an old construction, in which the words *manner* and *kind* are now seen as singular forms. But whereas *all* readily combines with a singular, as in the phrases *for all time* and *with all speed*, the demonstratives *these* and *those* clash with a following singular noun. For this reason *all manner of men* sounds elegantly archaic, but *those kind of things* seems crudely illiterate and should be avoided in writing. Acceptable alternatives are *that kind of thing*, *things of that kind* and, if there is more than one kind, *those kinds of things*.

Further examples

They are a dangerous insect.
This bacteria thrives in such conditions.
The value of its contents are not yet known.
A pupil may be punished if they are late.
Soon nobody will understand each other at all.
A number of files has gone missing.
This is one of the largest eels that has ever been caught.
The high-jumper has just cleared six foot one inches.
I don't like to see an accident because they upset me.
One should begin early, since you are at your best then.
My reading and research has led me to reject the idea.
The upper class was the minority, but they wielded all the power.
Everyone, even his mother and father, have condemned his action.
The public don't seem to have made up its mind.
What criteria is used in deciding such matters?
There's your stockings, staring you in the face.
Every one of these hospitals have their own power supply.
The 18th century could appeal to Latin grammar, as they often did.
The head, along with his deputies, oppose this move.
Sometimes male control breaks down and he rapes the woman.
We can all admire his novels, whatever one's doubts about his morals.
No sex education class should ignore the moral dimension, nor do they.
He is one of those people who considers himself entitled to privileges.
This is another of those long list of false promises made by the opposition.

He was noted as a disciplinarian, though this was exercised with good humour.

12. False Attachment

The rule of attachment

Introductory modifying phrases are understood to refer to the subject of the clause to which they are attached.

> Anxious to get away early, he looked at his watch
> After ten hours without food, they were miserable

The adjective phrase *Anxious to get away early* refers to the subject *he*, and the adverb phrase *After ten hours without food* refers to the subject *they*.

It is a common fault to attach such phrases to an inappropriate subject.

> Anxious to get away early, the letter had to wait
> After ten hours without food, the flight was cancelled

The qualifying phrases anticipate an animate subject like *he* or *they*; a letter cannot be anxious, nor can a flight spend ten hours without food. Both sentences are faulty because of 'absent agents' — not missing spies but grammatical subjects whose presence is required. The subjects can be supplied, with some rewording where necessary, either in the first part of the sentence:

> As he was anxious to get away early, the letter had to wait
> After they had gone ten hours without food, the flight was cancelled

or in the clause that follows:

> Anxious to get away early, he decided that the letter had to wait
> After ten hours without food, they heard that the flight had been cancelled

False apposition

When a noun phrase is misattached to a following clause, the result is false apposition.

> An only son, his mother died when he was a child

It is obviously not the mother who is an only son, hence the sentence needs amending to read 'An only son, he lost his mother when he was a child' or 'He was an only son, whose mother died when he was a child'.

Similarly flawed are:

A man of integrity, his promises were always kept
A native of the isles, Gaelic is her mother tongue

The appositive phrases need to be attached to the real subjects *he* and *she*, not the bogus subjects *his promises* and *Gaelic*. Amend to read:

A man of integrity, he always kept his promises
A native of the isles, she speaks Gaelic as her mother tongue

False apposition is often found with *as*-phrases. Compare:

(1) As a soldier, he is mainly concerned with discipline
(2) As a soldier, his main concern is with discipline
(3) As a soldier, discipline is his main concern

(1) and (2) are well-formed sentences, but (3) is a nonsense because it describes discipline as a soldier. Version (2) is acceptable because the point of attachment is not *concern*, but *his* (= *of him*), i.e. 'The main concern of him, as a soldier, is discipline'.

As a nation, I do not think we are prudes

Can one person (*I*) be a nation? This smacks of Louis XIV's boastful claim to statehood, 'L'état, c'est moi'. Amend, by shifting the *as*-phrase, to read, 'I do not think we as a nation are prudes'.

As a student of craft, it was interesting to visit your shop

Here the *as*-phrase does not relate to any element in the following clause. It is attached not to a real subject but to *it*, the dummy subject of an impersonal expression. Instead of *it was interesting* we should say *I was interested*; alternatively we may say 'It was interesting for me, as a student of craft, to visit your shop'.

As a valued client, we are offering you a discount

Generous, but ungrammatical. Here we have not only misattachment but also misagreement; singular *client* is equated with plural *we*. Both faults can be rectified by attaching the *as*-phrase to *you*, placed after *a discount* and preceded by *to*, so as to read *to you as a valued client*.

Common misattachments

Expressions of age are often misattached.

At 70 years of age, his music is played throughout the world

It is the composer, not his music, that is 70 years old. Replace *At* by *Now he is*.

At 18 months, his mother was told he was deaf

12. False Attachment

There are no 18-month-old mothers. Replace *At* by *When he was*.

Phrases beginning with *as well as*, *besides*, and *instead of* are also commonly misattached.

> As well as cars, boys are interested in trains

Cars belong to the same class as trains, not boys. The initial phrase should either bring up the rear or be followed by *trains interest boys*.

> Besides catching flu, my ankle was sprained

Ankles do not catch flu; say *I sprained my ankle*.

> Instead of three pumps, the water is controlled by one

To avoid the non-matching forms *pumps* and *water*, rephrase in one of the two following ways:

> The water is controlled by one pump instead of three
> Instead of three pumps, one is used to control the water

Phrases that start with *as such* and *such as* are sometimes misattached at the beginning and end of a sentence respectively.

> The papers are incomplete. As such we must treat them with caution

It is not we but the papers that are *such*, i.e. *incomplete*. Amend to read 'As such they must be treated with caution'.

> Some countries have no navy, such as Austria

The phrase *such as Austria* should follow *countries*, since Austria is not a navy but a country.

An infinitive phrase is quite often misattached.

> To really understand gorillas, they must be seen in their habitat

This may be amended in two ways.

> To really understand gorillas, you must see them in their habitat
> To be really understood, gorillas must be seen in their habitat

Misrelated participles

Introductory participle phrases follow the attachment rule, i.e. they are normally taken to refer to the subject of the clause to which they are attached.

> Waiting for his wife, he grew impatient
> Abandoned by her husband, she took to drink

The rule still applies when the participle is preceded by a conjunction or preposition.

> While dancing, she sprained her foot
> On opening the box, I discovered a will

A participle phrase may follow the clause to which it is attached and still refer to the subject. The following sentences mean the same.

(1) Lying on the beach, he caught sunstroke
(2) He caught sunstroke, lying on the beach

But a following participle phrase, if it is not adverbial but adjectival, refers to the object of the preceding clause. Compare:

(3) Lying on the beach, he saw a naked girl
(4) He saw a naked girl lying on the beach

In (3) *lying* refers to the subject *he* and has the adverbial sense 'while (he was) lying'. In (4) *lying* qualifies the object, *a naked girl*, and has the adjectival sense 'who was lying'.

In practice the attachment rule is often breached with participles, even by good writers. This faulty construction, one of the commonest in the language, is most accurately described as a misrelated participle. The terms 'dangling' or 'floating' participle, which are often used, are misnomers since such a participle neither dangles nor floats; on the contrary it is attached, but to the wrong word. Compare:

(5) Running to catch a bus, he dropped his glasses
(6) Running to catch a bus, his glasses fell off

In (5) *running* relates to the following subject *he*. In (6) *running* is misattached to *his glasses*, so that, taken literally, this means the glasses were running. Thus (6) should be expanded to include the real subject, by saying 'As he was running'.

Participial absurdities

The flawed nature of the misrelated participle construction is illustrated by the literally absurd zoological specimens given below.

(7) Reading *The Times*, the cat began to miaow

Even top cats cannot read the top newspaper.

(8) After unlocking the cage, the rats sprang out

Rodents can pick bones but they can't pick locks.

(9) Having packed our bags, the horses were brought to the porch

This gives a whole new meaning to the word 'pack-horse'.

(10) Smiling to reassure it, the tiger suddenly pounced on her

Then presumably, as in the well-known limerick, the smile was on the face of the tiger.

In all these sentences the participles are attached to animals instead of the unmentioned humans. Accuracy of expression requires the inclusion of a real subject, as follows: (7) 'As *I* was reading ...'; (8) 'After *he* unlocked the cage'; (9) 'After *we* had packed ...'; (10) '*she* was suddenly pounced on by the tiger'. In the unreconstructed sentence (10) the tiger is smiling to reassure it (the tiger). This exemplifies the worst kind of misrelated participle, one which produces a self-contradictory statement, Other examples of this type are:

> Summoning an ambulance, the dead man was taken to the mortuary

Dead men tell no tales and ring no bells. Amend to read: *After they had summoned* ...

> Talking to Bill, he was very frank with me

Apparently *he* (Bill) was talking frankly to Bill, i.e. to himself. The actual subject of *talking*, the interlocutor (*me*), needs to be expressed in the first part. Add an introductory *When I was*.

> Having given them freedom, they abused it

Here *they*, the subject of *abused*, is also the subject of *having given*. This creates an impossible situation in which those who have been given their freedom are at the same time those who gave it them. A suitable correction is to substitute *Having been given* for *Having given them*.

> While waiting at the station, the train pulled out

This defies that laws of physics as well as the rules of grammar. Between *While* and *waiting* insert *I was*, *we were*, *you were*, etc., as appropriate.

Common participial misconstructions

Participle phrases beginning with *based on* and *born in* are often misrelated.

> Based on the latest survey, the prospects look dim

It is not the prospects that are based on the survey, but the statement about them. Rephrase the first part to read *According to estimates based on the latest survey* or simply *According to the latest survey*.

> Born in London, Max's first instrument was the flute

It is Max, not his first instrument, that was born in London. In addition, the sentence contains a non sequitur, suggesting as it does that if Max had been born elsewhere he might have taken up some other musical instrument first. This turn of phrase, in which two unconnected pieces of information are jammed together in such a way as to appear linked, is a journalistic device, one often found in obituaries. The defect can be remedied either by using a connective:

> Max was born in London and his first instrument was the flute

or by incorporating one of the facts in a relative clause:

> Max, who was born in London, took up the flute as his first instrument

Participle phrases beginning with *far from*, *instead of* and *rather than* are often misattached.

> Far from reducing the interest rate, it should be raised

This may be reconstructed in either of two ways:

> Far from reducing the interest rate, they should raise it
> Far from being reduced, the interest rate should be raised

> Instead of giving all students a grant, over half of them get no support

The first part should be recast to read *Instead of a grant being given to all students*.

> Rather than easing the tax burden, the rate has been increased

Failure to ease the tax burden is the fault not of the rate, but of the government which fixes the rate. Enter the absent agent as the active subject:

> Rather than easing the tax burden, the government has increased the rate

The participle *being*, followed by an expression of time or weather, if often misattached in colloquial speech.

> Being Friday, he went to the bank

Say either *It being Friday* or, better, *As it was Friday*.

> Being a wet day, she took her umbrella

Here a third variant is possible: *The day being wet*. Like *It being a wet day*, this is an absolute participle construction, i.e. one with its own subject and juxtaposed to but not grammatically related to a main clause. Absolute constructions with *being* allow a dummy subject, as in '*It* being Friday, he went to the bank' and '*There* being no further business, the meeting closed'. But the combinations *being as* and *being that* are regarded as illiterate substitutes for the conjunction *since* or *seeing that*.

Absolute and loose participle phrases

Participles can be used as absolutes, i.e. independently of the subject, in adverbial commenting phrases.

> Strictly speaking, that is not relevant
> He is not, frankly speaking, a good teacher
> Putting it mildly, he is not co-operative

In these and similar expressions (*generally / personally / roughly speak-*

12. False Attachment

ing) the participle does not relate to the subject but forms part of a subjective comment by the speaker. Such absolute usage is readily granted acceptability.

A similar status, but one of more questionable validity, has been acquired by what are called loose participle constructions.

>Speaking of food, do you fancy a sandwich?

The participle phrase *Speaking of food* is here an elliptical form of *While we are speaking of food*. Similar expressions, mostly marking a change of topic or time focus, follow the same pattern. Usually an intermediate phrase has been dropped.

>Turning to your divorce, [I want to ask you] have you any regrets?
>Coming to the present, [we can see that] the picture is brighter
>Knowing him, [I can say that] this was no surprise
>Casting your mind back, [tell me] what were things like then?

Such omissions are quite admissible in casual speech, but in writing, especially in formal style, the missing links should be supplied in order to legitimize the use of the participles.

Loose participle constructions can sometimes be replaced, to advantage, by an absolute construction.

>Having said that, the risk of fire is still great

In place of the very common pseudo-absolute phrase *Having said that* we can always use the neater, more appropriate absolute phrase *That said*, a long-established elliptical form of *That having been said*.

>Taking all things into consideration, this was a good move

This would be accepted by most grammarians today because the reference is general and indefinite; *Taking* is equivalent to *If one takes*. Better that this pseudo-absolute phrase, however, is the real absolute participle phrase *All things considered*.

>Put another way, yours is not a test case

Preferable to the loose participle construction is the absolute infinitive phrase *To put it another way*.

In this area of grammar usage is divided and so too is opinion about the acceptability of loose participles. Through long use they have won general acceptance, but they are appropriate to informal style only. As there is always a more exact expression available, this will be preferred by careful speakers and writers.

Generalizing participle phrases

Participle phrases may be used with an impersonal expression if the sentence has a generalized meaning.

>On leaving, it is not necessary to lock the door

On leaving, there is no need to lock the door

The expressions *it is not necessary* and *there is no need* have the same meaning as the phrases *you do not need* and *one does not need*, so that there is a covert subject, the indefinite pronoun *you* or *one*, to which the participle phrase can attach itself. By contrast, participle phrases should not be attached to impersonal expressions relating to specific occasions.

Once embarked on this course, it was hard to stop
After buying the flat, there wasn't any money left

These sentences need to be personalized by bringing in the absent agents. Alter the second parts to read *I (he) found it hard to stop* and *I (we) hadn't any money left*.

Participle phrases of the type *by -ing* and *when -ing* may be unrelated to the subject if they form part of a statement applicable to anyone.

By adding salt, the flavour can be improved

The phrase *by adding* here implies an indefinite subject ('by *anyone* adding' or 'if *you* add'). The agent of the adding is not the same as the subject *flavour* but the same as the agent of the improving, namely the person cooking or eating the food. All the same, the sentence runs better the other way round: 'The flavour can be improved by adding salt'.
Compare:

(11) (By) using this technique, the process can be speeded up
(12) (By) using this technique, the engine soon stalled

In (11) the participle phrase, being part of a general statement, is acceptable. In (12) the same phrase is unacceptable because it forms part of a statement about a specific event. Here the participle relates to the subject and thus we are told that the engine used the technique. The participle phrase should be replaced in this case by *When this technique was used* or *When we used this technique*.

(13) When handling bees, gloves should be used
(14) When handling bees, it is wise to wear gloves

Both (13) and (14) are general statements in which the phrase *When handling bees* is an abbreviated form of the clause *When one is handling bees*.
Compare:

(15) When handling bees, use gloves
(16) When handling bees, his face got stung

In (15) all is well since *handling* relates to the covert subject *you*, which is normally omitted with the imperative. By contrast, (16) refers to a specific event. All is not well here because *handling* is misrelated to *his face*, so that the man's face appears to be handling bees. Instead of the participle phrase we need a full clause, *When he was handling bees*.

Participles converted

Participles that have been converted into prepositions and conjunctions are exempt from the rule of attachment since their reference is indefinite and they no longer require the peg of a noun or pronoun subject on which to hang. Of participial origin are the prepositions *assuming, barring, concerning, considering, (not) counting, excepting, excluding, failing, following, given, granted/granting, including, regarding, respecting* and the archaic *touching*. Compound prepositions in this class are *allowing for, beginning with, depending on, judging by/from, leaving aside, owing to* and *referring to*. The transition from participle to preposition is easily made.

(17) He wrote me a letter concerning my friend
(18) He wrote to me concerning my friend

In (17) *concerning* is an adjectival participle meaning *which concerns* and synonymous with the preposition *about*. In (18) *concerning* has no participial function and is now a preposition.

Other examples:

(19) Allowing for minor details, they are very similar
(20) Assuming fair weather, the ship will sail
(21) Barring accidents, the race will proceed
(22) Considering his age, he plays very well
(23) Failing an explanation, he will be penalized
(24) Given his attitude, an apology is not expected
(25) Judging by her looks, she is not at all pleased

These prepositions may be paraphrased as follows: (19) *Allowances being made for*; (20) *On the assumption that there is*; (21) *Unless there are any*; (22) *If one considers*; (23) *In the absence of*; (24) *In view of*; (25) *If one judges*.

Conjunctions of participial origin are *allowing, assuming, considering, given, granted, provided/providing, seeing* and *supposing*, all of which may be used with *that*, which adds a touch of formality.

(26) Assuming (that) it doesn't rain, the match will be played
(27) Considering (that) she is over eighty, she walks very well
(28) Granted (that) the car is old, I still want it
(29) I don't care where he goes, provided (that) he tells me first
(30) Supposing (that) she dies, what will you do then?

Here the conjunctions may be paraphrased as follows: (26) *On the assumption that*; (27) *When one considers that*; (28) *Though I grant you that*; (29) *so long as*; (30) *If (we suppose that)*. The conjunctions *granted (that)* and *provided (that)* are elliptical forms of the absolute phrases *it being granted that* and *it being provided that*.

Further examples

Now forty-three, this is her tenth novel.
Rose-coloured or not, I hate spectacles.
Opening the closet door, a skeleton fell out.
As well as having a pot belly, there isn't a hair on his head.
A devout Muslim, his concubines are numbered in hundreds.
Listening to the soft music, her eyes filled with tears.
Put another way, the statue seems indecent.
Being decrepit, he was able to buy the house cheap.
As a mother of eight, her ironing board is always up.
Set in a country house, the cast includes several well-known actors.
More corpulent than chubby now, his hair is flecked with grey.
Despite being eight months pregnant, her callous husband abandoned her.
Turning the corner, a bullet whizzed past his head.
Far from being grateful, the gift made him furious.
Of all political writers his outlook most resembles that of Shaw.
To enter for a prize, the coupon below must be filled in.
Once a busy cotton town, he found that few people now work in the mills.
Asked for details, it took them a week to reply.
Among other symptoms, she becomes very tired in the afternoon.
Having created a monster, it must be tamed.
By moving to a small town, my car insurance has been halved.
Walking through the square, a statue of Queen Victoria struck my eye.
These are complex problems and as such you must not expect easy answers.
After marrying Ann, she moved into my flat.
Personally responsible for France's baby boom, it shocked de Gaulle to discover the economic cost.

13. False Ellipsis

Acceptable ellipsis

Ellipsis, a common device in English, is the omission from a sentence of some word or words needed to complete the sense or the construction. The missing words may be found within the sentence:

He drinks and [he] smokes too much
He can [return] and should return
He wants to go home but he can't [go home]

or they may be deduced from the situational context:

[This is] very odd!
[Have you] got a light?

or from one's knowledge of grammar:

She will help you if [it is] necessary
I want a pen [that is] like [the one] you use

Certain types of locution, especially proverbial and aphoristic sayings, allow more drastic omissions.

[Whether there is] rain or no rain, we must go
[The] first [to] come [will be] first served
[That is] easier said than [it is] done
Once [you are] bitten, [you are] twice shy

In headlinese the articles and the verb *to be* are omitted.

[The] President [is] to meet [the] Queen

Omission of 'as' and 'than'

The common element may be dropped with the first of two words that take the same construction. Thus in comparisons it is acceptable to say:

(1) He is taller and thinner than you
(2) He is as tall and as thin as you

In (1) *than* has been dropped after *taller* and in (2) *as* has been dropped after *tall* because in each sentence the two comparisons are of the same kind: of superiority in (1) and of equality in (2). But with mixed comparisons this will not do because they involve different constructions, one with *than*, the other with *as*.

(3) He is taller but not as thin as you
(4) He is as tall if not taller than you

Here we have comparisons with incomplete first elements. In (3) *as* is made to serve two masters, the first falsely, the second justly. If we remove the second comparison *but not as thin* we are left with the ungrammatical statement 'He is taller ... as you'. Similarly *than* in (4) clashes with *as tall*. We can insert the missing *as* and *than* in these slipshod sentences but this results in rather clumsy expressions.

(5) He is taller than but not as thin as you
(6) He is as tall as if not taller than you

This clumsiness is easily avoided by separating the two comparative constructions.

(7) He is taller than you but not as thin
(8) He is as tall as you, if not taller

Now we have ellipses of *as you* in (7) and of *than you* in (8), but they are of words that would follow in the full expression, therefore the mixed forms do not jar.

Omission of prepositions

When two nouns which are used together take the same preposition, it is omissible with the first.

He has no need or desire to work

Both *need* and *desire* are construed with *to*. But it is not good English to say:

He has no desire or intention of working

The words *to work* should follow *desire* in order to avoid the false collocation 'He has no desire of working'.

Similarly acceptable, with adjectives and verbs, are:

He is eager and ready to work
We hope and strive for agreement

But unacceptable are:

He is hostile but dependent on his father
She is both repelled and attracted to the man

These would be better expressed by completing the first construction and using a pronoun in the second, thus:

He is hostile towards his father but dependent on him
She is both repelled by the man and attracted to him

13. False Ellipsis

Sometimes a preposition needs repeating in order to prevent misunderstanding. Compare:

(9) Sir John was a great lover of antiques and old books
(10) Sir John was a great lover and keen collector of antiques

In (9) the second *of* may safely be omitted before *old books*, but in (10), to avoid the suggestion that Sir John was something of a Don Juan, a second *of* is needed after *lover*.

Omission of verbs

The infinitive may be dropped if any form of the same verb occurs earlier in the sentence.

They are staying but we can't [stay]
She has never flown and never will [fly]
He still stammers as he used to [stammer]
It took longer than I thought it would [take]

It is also colloquially acceptable, but not appropriate in written English, to omit a participle in the same way, i.e. when it is preceded by any form of the same verb.

I wanted to play and I am [playing]
You could do it better than you are [doing] at present
He doesn't smoke and never has [smoked]
John may be complaining but Jane hasn't [complained]

In all other cases a verb may be omitted only if the identical form occurs elsewhere in the same sentence, e.g.

We can [play] and will play
She was [suffering] and still is suffering
I have resigned and he has [resigned] too

Thus it will not do to say:

(11) This method has and is proving useful
(12) Animals have and still do inhabit these caves

Here each verb requires full expression. In (11) the present participle *proving* will not serve both tense forms; the past participle *proved* is needed after *has*. Similarly in (12) the auxiliary *have* cannot be completed by the infinitive form *inhabit*, but requires the past participle *inhabited*.

A change of voice from active to passive, or vice versa, likewise precludes ellipsis.

(13) He manages the firm efficiently, as it was before
(14) They should be supervised so far as we can

The active verb *manages* in (13) will not serve in the second part, which needs the passive participle *managed* after *was*. In (14) the second part needs to be completed both with the active verb *supervise* and the pronoun *them*, since *they* are now the object.

Ellipsis is not admissible when two auxiliaries require different parts of the main verb. The sequence *can ... -ing* often offends in this way.

> Different conclusions can, and indeed are, being drawn

Remove the matter between commas and you are left with the ungrammatical *can being drawn*; the auxiliary *can* requires *be*, not *being*. Compare the following ellipses, the first valid, the second false.

> (15) This has not been and will not be done
> (16) This has not and will not be done

In both versions the missing *done* is supplied at the end, but in (16) the *been* missing after *has not* is not recoverable and thus needs to be included.

Abbreviated clauses

Dependent clauses in which the subject and the verb *to be* have been omitted are called abbreviated clauses. Such elliptical clauses are acceptable so long as the missing subject is the same as that of the main clause.

> If [you are] in doubt, you must ask
> Once [we were] indoors we felt safe
> The plums, when [they are] ripe, are delicious
> He broke a leg when [he was] skiing
> She is never angry unless [she is] provoked

An abbreviated clause is unacceptable if its subject is not that of the main clause, since this results in false attachment. Compare:

> (17) Though good at sums, he could not solve the problem
> (18) Though good at sums, the problem defeated him

In (17) the omission of *he was* is valid because *he* is the subject of the whole statement. In (18) the ellipsis is false because the subject is *the problem*. Here we need the full expression *Though he was good at sums*.

> (19) Once in power, he forgot all his promises
> (20) Once in power, all his promises were forgotten

It is all too easy to slip from well-constructed sentence (19) to the jerry-built sentence (20), which has the same meaning, but an absent agent (*he*).

Similar examples:

> (21) If drunk, the police will arrest them
> (22) When ten years old, my father bought me a bike

(23) While in prison, a burglar raided his flat
(24) However painful, we should practise what we preach

Here the ellipses have produced some rather absurd attachments. The sub-clauses are attached to *the police, my father, a burglar* and *we*, which are not the words they refer to. The real subjects should be made explicit by adding *they are* (21), *I was* (22), *he was* (23) and *it is* (24).

Sometimes the subject of a false ellipsis is found in the previous clause or sentence.

> There is a good case against him and, if proved, he could face dismissal

If the case is proved we are meant to understand. But the *if*-clause is not subordinate to the previous clause; *and* joins coordinates, marking the transition from one to the other. Therefore the *if*-clause must go with the second coordinate and take its subject from that, giving *if he could be proved*, which is absurd. As the ellipsis cannot be supplied from the proper clause, we need to expand *if proved* to *if it is proved*. Similarly:

> Permission has been sought. As soon as received, the work will begin

The two parts of the second sentence do not cohere. It is not the work that is to be received, but the permission, inadmissibly stolen from the previous sentence. Coherence requires us to say *As soon as it is received*.

Absent connectives

In idiomatic English wide use is made of contact clauses, i.e. dependent clauses added to a main clause without a connecting word. This is accepted practice if the clause can be joined by the conjunction *that*:

> He said [that] he was ill

or by a relative pronoun, *that, which* or *whom*, expressing the direct object:

> This is the key [that/which] I need
> This is the boy [that/whom] I chose

In non-standard English the subject relative pronoun is also omitted:

> There's a man outside [that/who] wants to see you

Sometimes the absence of the conjunction *that* can result in a loss of clarity.

> He proved the belief I had assumed to be true was false

This is a garden-path sentence, which leads the reader at first to suppose that *the belief* is the direct object of *proved*. It becomes clear if *that* is inserted between these words.

> The girl said yesterday she was a virgin

We are not sure from this statement whether the girl has subsequently lost her virginity. If she has, insert *that* before *yesterday*; if not, insert *that* after *yesterday*.

The word *that* may be dropped from the cleft construction (*it is ... that*) when the intermediate word is the object of the following verb.

> It's water [that] I want
> That's all [that] I want

It may also be omitted after *so*, used with an adjective or adverb.

> It's so small [that] we can't see it
> He sang so badly [that] I left the hall

But its omission after *so* in clauses of purpose is undesirable.

> He did it repeatedly, so I would get angry

This colloquial use of *so* for *so that* comes of confusing *so*, which expresses result, with *so that*, which expresses purpose. Purpose is, of course, anticipated result, hence the confusion. However, it is helpful to distinguish purpose from result, as follows.

> He shouted, so that everyone could hear
> He shouted, so everyone could hear

The connective *when* is sometimes an absentee.

> There are times I'd like to kill her

We need the connective *when* here after *times*. Its omission can be explained by false analogy with such sentences as 'There are people [whom] I'd like to kill' and 'There are things [that] I'd never do', in which the relative may be dropped.

Occasionally a whole connective phrase is falsely omitted.

> The ground was very uneven, caused by subsidence

The word *caused*, which obviously does not refer to *ground*, is left hanging in mid-air. It needs to be brought down to earth by being bodied out with the words *which was* or *this being*.

> Asked which issue was most important, unemployment came top with 40%

This sentence calls for radical repair. We should either extend it by starting *When they (the respondents) were asked ...* or change the second clause to read *40% of respondents put unemployment first*.

Instructionese and advertese

Violent contractions are typical of instructionese, the language used in giving directions for the proper handling of goods and equipment. Here are some examples, followed by their expanded forms.

13. False Ellipsis

Once opened, treat as fresh milk
Once this carton is opened, treat the contents as fresh milk

When prepared, eat at once
When this food is prepared, eat it at once

If undelivered, return to sender
If this parcel is undelivered, return it to the sender

Here the elliptical structures have been stretched beyond their grammatical limits, for the truncated phrases at the beginning refer to unnamed containers or contents, while what follows refers to the person handling them.

Similar disjointed grammar is sometimes found in advertisers' language, or advertese. One television commercial for a new model of car ran as follows.

Once driven, forever smitten

This is clearly patterned on such sayings as 'Once seen, never forgotten', but whereas *seen* and *forgotten* refer to the same thing, *driven* refers to the car but *smitten* refers to the driver who tries it out. The result of putting two subjects where only one will fit is syntactical dislocation. The English language has a genius for compression, but here it is taken too far.

Further examples

His first book was written aged twenty.
He was as strong or stronger than his opponent.
They will punish him, as he ought to be.
Safely ashore, work began on treating the sick.
She never has and never will admit it.
I paid him at once, so he wouldn't complain.
Once published, everyone will be reading his book.
When annoyed, his eyebrows would twitch alarmingly.
He had little aptitude or interest in study.
If encouraged, we can expect good work from her.
She has and still is improving slowly.
Though very ill, the drugs cured him quite quickly.
We can and are doing a great deal to help them.
Such language is appropriate and typical of religious rites.
America is and will continue to resist this policy.
This method is not to be recommended, unless under stress.
Although the latest model, she did not like the car.
This did not add but detracted from his merits.
When wet outside, wipe your feet on entering.
The board's advice is to accept, but, if heeded, disaster could follow.
However beautiful to the eye, not everyone finds Concorde pleasant to the ears.

The Republicans must do more than they have to meet this challenge.
People stay in one place too long, made worse by our housing policy.
A journey can be agony if confined for hours with a screaming baby.
These bonds can be purchased separately or together. Bought together, you will make a big saving.

14. False Comparison

Elliptical comparisons

Ellipsis of the verb often occurs in the second part of a comparison. This is acceptable if the omitted words occur in the first part.

> She eats less than a sparrow [eats]
> He has a hide like a rhinoceros [has]
> He is chosen more often than his brother [is chosen]

The linking verbs *be*, *feel*, *look* and *seem* may be omitted, together with their subject, even where there is a tense change in the comparison.

> It is as warm here as [it is] upstairs
> There were more rooms than [there were] at home
> You are later today than [you were] yesterday
> It feels cooler now than [it felt] this afternoon
> He looks fitter now than [he looked] last week
> It will seem funnier in the film than [it seems] in the book

The dropping of a preposition can produce a false comparison.

> The air here is cleaner than London

In a valid comparison like is compared with like, but here a comparison is made between two unlike things: air and London. By adding *in* to *London* we make the comparison a valid one, between *here* and *in London*.

Compare:

> (1) Today the price of gold is higher than yesterday
> (2) Today the price of gold is higher than silver

In (1) there is a valid comparison between the price of gold today and the price of gold yesterday. In (2) there is a false comparison between the abstract *price* and the concrete *silver*. To make a match we need to say *higher than that* (i.e. the price) *of silver*.

Similar false comparisons:

> (3) Her behaviour was like an alley-cat
> (4) The habits of the badger are different from the beaver
> (5) Compared with Britain, crop yields in Russia are low

Sound comparisons can be made by inserting *that / those of* or a possessive *'s*, giving in (3) *that of an alley-cat* or *an alley-cat's*; in (4) *those of the beaver* or *the beaver's*; and in (5) *those of Britain* or *Britain's*.

Elliptical comparisons involving animate beings are sometimes ambiguous.

> She loves the cat more than her husband

Expansion is needed here to make clear whether the husband is a subject or an object. Depending on what is meant, say either 'She loves the cat more than her husband does' or 'She loves the cat more than she does her husband'.

Like-phrases and *unlike*-phrases

False comparison often arises from an inappropriate use of *like* or *unlike*. Compare:

> (6) Like a child, he gazed in wonder
> (7) *Like* a child, his anger sprang from fear

A man may be likened to a child, as in (6), but anger cannot be likened to a child, as it is in (7). The appropriate construction in (7) is not the direct comparison *like a child* but the indirect comparison *as with a child*, an elliptical form of *as is the case with a child*.

> *Like* any winner's dressing room, the champagne flowed freely

There is no similarity between a dressing room and champagne. Here again an indirect comparison is required, in the form *As in any winner's dressing room*.

Unlike suffers from the same kind of mishandling.

> *Unlike* Europe, the Industrial Revolution came to America suddenly

Here misplacement has produced unequal yokefellows, *Europe* and *the Industrial Revolution*. The sentence needs re-ordering to read 'In America, unlike Europe, the Industrial Revolution came suddenly'.

> *Unlike* his brother, it was not important for him to win

This needs rephrasing to read either 'For him, unlike his brother, it was not important to win' or 'It was not important for him to win, as it was for his brother'.

It should be noted that there is no negative equivalent of *as in*; the construction *unlike in* is not acceptable since *unlike*, in the same way as *like*, requires a noun or pronoun object.

> *Unlike in* France, we drive on the left

The prepositional phrase *in France* cannot be the object of *unlike*. This jerry-built sentence needs reconstructing to read either 'Unlike the

French, we drive on the left' or 'In Britain, unlike France, we drive on the left'. What has happened, evidently, is that with the increasing use of *like* as a conjunction, *like in* has come to be used in place of *as in*, and this has given rise to the negative *unlike in*. The acceptable forms are:

In Britain, as in France …
In Britain, like France …
In Britain, unlike France …

The use of *unlike* as a conjunction can and should be avoided.

We must be prepared, *unlike we were* before the last war

For *unlike we were* read *as we were not*.

Inclusive exclusion

Sam Goldwyn, it is said, once expressed his disagreement with a decision of his fellow film-makers by reaching for his hat and uttering the immortal words: 'Gentlemen, include me out'. This much-quoted Goldwynism, like the Irishman's enquiry about 'the entrance out', embodies a contradiction of the kind quite often found in casual – but not good – English. In this type of expression something is both excluded from and at the same time included in a group of things with which it is being compared.

Tokyo is more densely populated than any city in the world

Since *any city in the world* includes Tokyo, this is tantamount to saying that Tokyo is more densely populated than Tokyo, which is self-contradictory. The sentence may be restored to reason by saying not *any* but *any other*.

He did more than anyone of his time to keep the peace

What we need is not *anyone*, which includes the subject, but *anyone else*.

Equally illogical is the confusion of superlative and comparative expressions in the so-called 'blended genitive', a mixture of the genitive and some other construction.

Germany has the lowest inflation rate of any country

The superlative expresses the idea of one or more members of a group outdoing the others in some way; its second term must therefore be put in the plural. Now the pronoun *any* is not a plural, but distributive singular, hence what we need here is not *any country* but *all countries*. Alternatively we can use the comparative with *other*: 'Germany has a lower inflation rate than any other country'.

Just as the word *other* is sometimes missing where it is needed, so is it used where it is not needed. Its use with a blended genitive, for example, only increases the illogicality.

John won in the fastest time of any other runner

Now we have not only the illogical *any* instead of *all*, but an illogical *other* too. In superlative expressions the group needs to be complete, but *any other runner* excludes John. He must therefore be included in the group of which he is fastest by saying *of all the runners*. Plainly the superlative construction has here again been influenced by the equivalent comparative expression (*in a faster time than any other runner*).

An illogical exclusion can occur even when the second term of a comparison, after a superlative, is in the plural, as it should be.

Jane is the sexiest of all her sisters

The group *all her sisters* excludes Jane, but she belongs to the group of which she is the most sexy. To make a complete group, including her, we must say 'Jane is the sexiest of all the sisters'. Alternatively we can use the comparative construction, which properly excludes her from the group, i.e. 'Jane is sexier than all her sisters'.

Blended genitives were used by many of our best writers in the past. Chaucer, for example, wrote: 'A thief of venysoun ... kan kepe a forest best of any man' (*The Physician's Tale*, c. 1386). Shakespeare wrote: 'York is most unmeet [=unsuitable] of any man' (*Henry VI, Part 2*, c. 1590). And Milton, in Book IV of *Paradise Lost* (1667), described the mythical mother of mankind as 'the fairest of her daughters Eve', but even in myth a mother cannot be counted among her own daughters and female descendants.

The blended construction *of all other(s)* was also used in older English. Both in *Sir Gawain and the Green Knight* (c. 1380) and in Sir Thomas Malory's *Morte d'Arthur* (1485) the lady of a castle is praised as being 'the fairest of all other' (*other* being an old plural). This medieval construction has died out, except where the superlative *most* has been suppressed.

This method [most] of all others ought to be rejected

The use of *others* is censurable here because it excludes *this method* from the class to which it belongs (all the methods) and makes the expression self-contradictory. The contradiction is removed quite simply by saying not *of all others* but *above all (others)*.

Illogical expressions like those instanced above had their idiomatic analogues in Greek and Latin, upon which they were most probably modelled, but they are no longer countenanced in good English today. In the interests of accurate expressions *any* should not be used where *all* is required in a comparison, and *other* should be inserted or omitted as logic dictates.

False 'than'

Apart from comparative adjectives and adverbs only the words *different(ly)*, *else(where)* and *other(wise)* are in standard use before *than*. Sometimes *than* is misused with the verb *prefer*. We can say:

14. False Comparison

I like to skate but I prefer to ski

But we do not use *prefer* with two infinitives because of the clash of adjacent *to*'s that this causes. We would not say:

I prefer to ski *to to* skate

Instead we say:

I prefer to ski rather than (to) skate

This is common usage but tautological, since *rather* is used together with *prefer*, which means 'choose rather'. For this reason we should not say 'I rather prefer to ski' but either 'I would rather ski' or 'I prefer to ski'. Nor should we say 'I prefer roast potatoes rather than boiled' but 'I prefer roast potatoes to boiled'. The sentence given above is thus better expressed by substituting *would* for *prefer to*:

I would rather ski than skate

or by using *-ing* forms instead of infinitives:

I prefer skiing to skating

It is not acceptable to say either of the following:

I prefer to ski than (to) skate
I prefer skiing than skating

Nor should *than* be used with *preferable*.

I think skiing is preferable *than* skating

The analogy here with *better than* is obvious, but the accepted form is *preferable to*, following the pattern of *prefer A to B*.

Occasionally the words *inferior* and *superior* are falsely construed with *than*. But although both words, like *junior* and *senior*, are comparatives in Latin, from which they are borrowed, they are followed in English by *to*.

He is a man of greatly inferior abilities *than* his father

Here even the substitution of *to* for *than* still leaves an unsatisfactory sentence in which the father is falsely compared with his son's abilities. It would be better to say 'He is a man whose abilities are greatly inferior to his father's' or to paraphrase and say 'He is a man much less able than his father'.

Further examples

Texas is larger than any state in the Union.
You should enjoy it more than last year.
The handwriting is like a doddering man of ninety.
His drawings are as good as any professional cartoonist.
Unlike pliers, the jaws of pincers are rounded.

Consumers prefer to cut their borrowing than to spend.
America has the highest crime rate of any country in the world.
She is the best dancer of all her friends.
His medieval characters speak just like today.
The weather in Spain is warmer than Britain.
Personal choice is preferable than censorship.
Our interest rates are high compared with Japan.
More than any writer, Joyce's works express Celtic attitudes.
This has produced the highest growth of any similar fund.
Like any wedding, the bride was the centre of attention.
Sex is more earthy in *Lady Chatterley's Lover* than in anything Lawrence wrote.
The language here is not smutty, unlike in many modern plays.
In comparison with many animals, human eyes have a very limited range.
Rather like rape fantasies, women enjoy denying responsibility for their own desires.
Our standards of hygiene are on a par with the rest of world.
In contrast with the earlier novels, a single theme is pursued in this one.
Racism today differs from the thirties.
The charges on this investment are less than unit trusts.
He is a leader far superior than Bill Clinton.
His latest thriller had the best review of all his other works.

15. False Negation

Multiple negation

In some languages, like Greek, two or more negatives have a cumulative effect, reinforcing each other; in other languages, such as Latin, they cancel each other. Until late in the 17th century English had cumulative negation. But several generations of English teachers, besotted with the 'perfection' of Latin, gradually succeeded in imposing its logical, cancelling type of negation on their own tongue, though cumulative negation persists to this day in non-standard speech. This is perhaps the most remarkable instance of educated or learned usage triumphing over the vernacular. Thus today a single negative word suffices to express negation in standard English, and statements containing two negatives have an affirmative meaning. Take the sentence:

He doesn't know nothing

In standard English this means 'He does know something' or 'He is not totally ignorant', but in non-standard English it means the opposite, 'He doesn't know anything' or 'He is totally ignorant'. Similarly, in the standard language

He can't not understand = He must understand
He wouldn't never wear a tie = He would sometimes wear a tie
It is impossible not to agree with that = One must agree with that
There was no one that did not weep = Everyone wept
Not many people have nothing to offer = Most people have something to offer

Likewise the expression *not for nothing* means 'with good reason' in standard English, but in non-standard English it means 'in no circumstances'.

The cancelling principle also operates in double negatives of the type *not un-* and *not without* .... Thus *not impossible* means 'just possible', *not bad* means 'moderately good' and *not without loss* means 'with some (but not great) loss'. The affirmative meaning of these expressions is reduced in force and is thus not an exact synonym of the straightforward affirmative forms *possible*, *good*, and *with loss*.

Acceptable multiple negation

Multiple negation is still found in the standard language, but only in the following types of sentence.

(a) A negative clause followed by a negated verb of thinking or supposing.

>He's not here, I don't think
>That's not likely, I don't suppose

Here the second part can be seen as a compressed form of the longer expressions 'I don't think he's here' and 'I don't suppose that's likely'.

(b) A negative clause followed by a negative modifying phrase.

>He doesn't drink, not even at Christmas
>You didn't fool me, not for one minute

Here the second part can be interpreted as elliptical for 'not even at Christmas does he drink' and 'not for one minute did you fool me'.

(c) A negative clause following a negated verb of surprise or wonder.

>It wouldn't surprise me if it didn't snow

This type is a crossed construction, blending *wouldn't surprise ... if ... did* and *would surprise ... if ... didn't*.

In all the sentences above the two negatives, if taken logically, cancel each other and yield a sense opposite to that which is intended, but here idiom overrules logic. Nevertheless, the same sentences could be expressed just as idiomatically, and more clearly in the case of type (c), without the second negative.

Negative transference

The negative *not* sometimes deserts the word it properly qualifies and goes next to the verb. This negative transference occurs when the pronoun subjects *all* and *every(one)* are placed first for emphasis.

>(1) All is not well
>(2) All men are not fools
>(3) Every story is not true
>(4) Everyone is not a good listener

We understand (1) as meaning not that everything is in a bad state, but only that some things are, and take (2) to mean that not all men are fools, rather than that all men are sensible. Similarly in (3) *Every story is not* means *Not every story is* and in (4) *Everyone is not* means *Not everyone is*.

With the construction *not ... but* the negative is also often displaced.

>(5) He did not die in York but in Leeds
>(6) It was not the fault of the girls but of the boys

The negative applies, strictly speaking, to *in York* in (5) and to *of the girls* in (6). A similar displacement often occurs with *not only ... but also*.

(7) They not only invited us but also the Browns

The phrase *not only* properly goes with *us*, not with *invited*.

Certain verbs, such as *believe, expect, seem, suppose* and *think* are often used with a negative although the negation applies to what follows, usually in a sub-clause.

(8) I don't believe (that) he knows her
(9) We didn't expect (that) he'd pay for us
(10) These figures do not seem to be correct

These would be more accurately expressed as (8) 'I believe he doesn't know her'; (9) 'We expected he wouldn't pay for us', and (10) 'These figures seem not to be correct'. The common expression 'I don't think so' similarly contains a displaced negative and is thus synonymous with 'I think not'.

These illogical positionings of the negative, however, are firmly rooted in idiom and rarely give any trouble, except to linguistic fusspots.

'Neither', 'nor' and 'not'

Correlative negatives are expressed by *neither ... nor* or by *not ... or*.

He is neither mean nor petty
He is not mean or petty

Neither calls for *nor*, as *either* calls for *or*. Though the correlatives *neither ... or* were commonly used in the past, they are condemned in present-day usage. Thus it is now unacceptable to say:

He is neither mean *or* petty

In the past, when double negation was normal, *not ... nor* and *never ... nor* were used in the same clause, but this usage is avoided nowadays. It is thus not now standard practice to say:

He is not mean *nor* petty

Today *nor* may follow another negative word such as *not* or *never*, but only in a fresh clause and with inversion.

He is not mean, nor is he petty
He is never mean, nor is he (ever) petty

It should be noted that although *not* is normally followed by *or*, in certain cases it must be followed by *nor*. Compare:

(11) The fault does not lie with the father or with the mother
(12) The fault lies not with the father, nor with the mother

In (11) the force of the negative phrase *does not lie* carries over to the second part, applying to both father and mother, hence there is no need to repeat the negative and *or* is sufficient. In (12) it is the positive verb *lies* that runs through the rest of the sentence. The word *not* is here attached not to the verb but to *the father*, hence the negative force is cut off and needs to be restored by using *nor*.

It is quite acceptable, and often very effective, to use *nor* (= 'and ... not') at the beginning of a clause or sentence, even after an affirmative statement.

> He promised to help, nor did he fail to do so
> TV dominates family life. Nor is it only children who are its addicts

Underreaching and overreaching negatives

In compound sentences, i.e. those containing more than one main clause, the force of a negative in the first clause may not extend to the second clause when it should or, conversely, it may extend to the second clause when it should not.

When two negatives are intended, the negative in the first clause may be so placed that it cannot carry over into the second, where it is also needed.

> There is not one manager that has not bought shares and is profiting from them.

As it stands, this sentence says that not one manager is profiting from his shares, i.e. the opposite of the intended meaning. To make matters right another *not* is needed before *profiting*. It would make easier reading, however, to cut out the mutually cancelling negatives in the first clause and say 'Each of the managers has bought shares'.

> They are more anxious not to flout convention than to break the law

Here again the negative does not reach into the second part of the sentence, though it is obviously intended to do so. An extra *not* is required after *than* in order to avoid saying that these people are anxious to break the law.

> There was often no meat or much bread

The second part reads affirmatively, as meaning that there was often much bread. The intended negative sense may be conveyed by saying *and not much bread either*. Alternatively the negative can be removed altogether and the same idea expressed by saying 'There was seldom any meat or much bread'.

In a similar way a negative in the first clause may be inadvertently carried over into the second.

> The minister's speeches do not seem compassionate and to reek of hypocrisy

The wording leads to the logical inference that the minister's speeches do not reek of hypocrisy. To indicate the contrary we may delete the *to* and thereby sever the link with *do not seem*, but then *seem* does not carry over. The exact sense is given by inserting a second *seem* before *to reek*.

> It is not expected that the talk will last long, but will cover essentials

This can be altered to give the desired meaning by moving the *not* to stand before *last*, or by inserting *it* after *but*.

It is often for want of a simple pronoun that the second part of a sentence falsely acquires a negative sense.

> No children are allowed in the bar but may use the annexe

The subject *no children* erroneously carries over to *may use the annexe*. The notice should include *they* before *may*, or the negative in the first part may be expressed as *Children are not allowed*.

> None of the staff expected the attack and had taken no protective measures

The negative *none* may be neutralized by inserting *they* before *had taken*, or the negative may be expressed as *The staff did not expect*.

> He must not be allowed to shirk his duty but tackle the problem

To prevent the negative from invading the second clause an affirmative *must* should be placed after *but*.

When inversion follows an initial negative expression the negative may again contaminate the following clause.

> In neither case was this due to mechanical failure but to human error

To prevent the second part from reading negatively we need to add *in each case* after *but*.

Redundant negatives

The word *not* sometimes illicitly accompanies words that are negative in import though positive in form, for example verbs such as *deny, doubt, fail, forbid, miss, prevent* and *refrain*.

> He asked me to refrain from *not* smoking

The logical sense of this is that he asked me to smoke. To convey the intended sense we should say either 'He asked me to refrain from smoking' or 'He asked me not to smoke'. Other examples of a hidden negative used with a redundant *not* are:

> He misses *not* hearing the news
> What he forgets is *not* to turn the light out
> She tried to prevent the baby from *not* crying

The word *unless* (= 'if ... not') is sometimes given a redundant *not*.

He could be in trouble unless he does*n't* agree

And the near-negative words *barely*, *hardly* and *scarcely* are sometimes combined contradictorily with the full negative *not* in non-standard usage, as they were in older English.

He has*n't* barely any clothes to wear
She did*n't* hardly notice me
There is*n't* scarcely any food left

In a similar way these near-negatives are sometimes falsely combined with the negative preposition *without*.

It was almost flat, with*out* hardly any bumps
With*out* scarcely a sound he entered the room

A redundant *not* sometimes occurs with the word *but*, used in the sense 'only'.

It will not take but a minute

This is an obvious confusion of 'This will not take a minute' (i.e. but less) with 'This will take but a minute' (i.e. no more). Either *not* or *but* must go.

An extra negative is likewise expressed when *not* combines with *but that*.

Who knows but that he might not succeed?

This comes of confusing the two constructions *but that ... might* and *that ... might not*. Here again either *not* or *but* should be deleted.

The verbs *to doubt* and *to deny*, when used negatively, are occasionally followed by a superfluous *not*. This old construction is almost certainly derived from French, where an expletive *ne* is used after the verbs *douter* and *nier* if they are negated.

I do not doubt (deny) that he may not succeed

This sentence can easily cause confusion since most people would now interpret it as meaning 'I am certain (admit) that he may not succeed'. If the opposite sense is intended the second *not* should be omitted.

A pile-up of negative words or words of negative force can obscure meaning.

We must not assume that there are no circumstances in which a strike may not be justified

This would be clearer if worded positively to read: 'We must assume that there are some circumstances in which a strike may be justified.'

15. False Negation

Further examples

That is neither funny or true.
That won't do him no harm neither.
He couldn't have done that, not nohow.
Never before nor since have I been so fit.
We miss her not coming round on Sundays.
He is not monarch, dictator, nor head of state.
He forbade his son not to play rock music.
No one does nothing for no one no more.
She wouldn't expose herself for love nor money.
Without scarcely a glance at him, she left the room.
He was out and his wife was not at home neither.
None of the papers were sold and were left in the archive.
This school was no better nor worse than the others.
It was so cold that we couldn't hardly move.
Unless we aren't careful, there could be trouble.
You can hardly fail to be unaware of the difficulties.
He spoke as if he knew nothing of it, which indeed he didn't.
There are no lights in the attic, nor none in the cellar.
We didn't want either a cat or a dog, nor any other kind of pet.
I learnt nothing to make me doubt that he was not justly convicted.
We are not in a position, no more than the Americans, to stop this.
Foreigners cannot work without a permit, neither here nor in France.
I wouldn't want to be a teacher without not knowing my students.
There is nothing that we as a country, nor Europe, nor the West, can do about this.
I do not think that his case has been proved and should therefore be rejected.

16. Crossed Constructions

Blends

Blending is the process whereby elements of two words or constructions are fused, and blend is the name of any form so produced. Blending has made a modest but useful contribution to our vocabulary. Thackeray, in *The History of Pendennis* (1849-50), introduced 'the famous university of Oxbridge' and this blend, revived or re-coined about a century later, is now frequently used to designate 'Oxford University or Cambridge University or both'. In Lewis Carroll's *Through the Looking-Glass* (1872) the nonsense verse *Jabberwocky* includes several 'portmanteau words' as he called them, lexical blends such as *slithy* (from *slimy* and *lithe*), *chortle* (from *chuckle* and *snort*) and *galumph* (from *gallop* and *triumph*), the last two of which are still sometimes used.

Some blends are jocular combinations of near-synonyms, such as *insinuendo* (from *insinuation* and *innuendo*), but most of them denote a compound idea, such as *smog* (from *smoke* or *fog*) and *camcorder* (from *camera* and *recorder*). Sometimes children create blends like *rememory* (from *remember* and *memory*), and adults produce illiterate blends like *doubtlessly* (from *doubtless* and *undoubtedly*) and *modern-day* (from *modern* and *present-day*).

Syntactical blends, or crossed constructions, arise from the simultaneous recollection of two different ways of saying the same thing. Thus *let us* and *shall we* produced the non-standard form *shall us*. A few such blends have become accepted idioms. The expression *I had better*, first attested in the 15th century, came from blending *I were better* (earlier *me were better*) and *I had liefer* (= *I would hold dearer*) is sanctioned by long use. Likewise well entrenched in idiom is the blended expression *to be friends with*, recorded since the late 16th century. 'He and I are friends' merged with 'I am friendly with him' to give 'I am friends with him', a grammatical oddity in having a singular subject and a plural predicate. Another well-established blend is the expression *cannot help but*. 'I cannot help but do it' is a cross between 'I cannot but do it', where *but* means *not*, and 'I cannot help doing it', where *help* means *prevent myself*. The earliest example of its use occurs in Keats: 'So fond, so beauteous was his bedfellow,/He could not help but kiss her' (*Endymion*, bk. IV, 1818). Recognition is now also granted to the colloquial *blame on*, as in 'He blamed it on me', a blend of 'He blamed me for it' and 'He put the blame on me'. Likewise approved is the idiom *so far from*, as in the sentence 'So far from mocking my work, he praised it', where *far from* would suffice, but is mixed with the longer construction 'He was so far from mocking my work that he praised it'.

Tautological blends

Among the commonest crossed constructions are blends which embody a double expression of some kind.

Cause: The cause of the accident was due to fog

A confusion between 'The cause of the accident was fog' and 'The accident was due to fog'.

Manner: He showed us the way how to mend it

Either *the way* or *how*, but not both.

Origin: The only source of money is from the public

Either delete *from* or recast to read 'Money can only come from the public'.

Purpose: The purpose of the fund is for famine relief

Delete either *The purpose of* or *for*.

Reason: The reason he lies is because he is afraid

Either substitute *that* for *because* or shorten to 'He lies because he is afraid'.

Result: The outcome of the strike will lead to job losses

Either delete *The outcome of* or substitute *be* for *lead to*.

Confusion with the cleft construction (*it is ... that*) is common in expressions of place and time.

It was in Africa where he died

Either substitute *that* for *where* or say 'Africa is where he died'.

It was in 1990 when he died

Either substitute *that* for *when* or say '1990 is when he died'.
Compare:

(1) It was winter when he died
(2) It was in winter that he died

In both (1) and (2) we are told when the person died, but the cleft construction in (2) is more pointed, being used in a context of clarification or correction.

Verb harmonization

A notable feature of modern English is the tendency to harmonize the verbs in a sentence by making one match the form of another. A very common mixed construction of this type is the double perfect, used in hypothetical statements. This combination has a legitimate use where the second perfect form is anterior to the first.

I would have been proud to have made it

Here *have made* is prior *to have been proud*, but in most such sentences the second perfect does not express anteriority but is a matching form introduced under the influence of the first perfect.

He would have liked to have played

What is meant is either 'He would have liked (then) to play (then)' or 'He would like (now) to have played (then)'. Only one of the verbs should be in the perfect ('have') form.

Similarly faulty is the double conditional.

It would be France that would be the loser

We do not need two *would*'s. Say either 'It is France that would be the loser' or 'It would be France that was the loser'.

I should have thought it would have been wiser to have waited

This sentence has three *haves* where only one is needed and one conditional *would* too many. Say either 'I should have thought it was wiser to wait' or 'I think it would have been wiser to wait'.

Verb harmonization is found with the verb *to be* even where no blending is involved.

All that he has done *has been* to complain
The most likely outcome *will be* that he will resign
What would be fairer *would be* a retrial

The italicized forms should be replaced in each case by a simple *is*.

Object swapping

Verbs with similar meanings sometimes borrow each other's constructions and in so doing switch the roles of direct and indirect object. The verbs *inspire*, *instil*, *inculcate* and *infuse*, which have similar meanings, are prime examples of object swapping. The verb *inspire* allows two constructions.

(3) This sight inspired awe in the spectators
(4) This sight inspired the spectators with awe

Awe is the direct object in (3) but the indirect object, when combined with *with*, in (4). Conversely, *the spectators*, who are the indirect object

16. Crossed Constructions

(with *in*) in (3) are the direct object in (4). By analogy with *inspire* the other verbs, which are constructed with an indirect object after *in(to)*, sometimes take an indirect object after *with*.

His words instilled them *with* fear

You do not instil people with some emotion, but instil it in them or imbue them with it (thus 'imbued with fear in them' is equally bad).

He tried to inculcate them with his own beliefs

This is accepted American usage, but the British form is *inculcate into* or (rarely) *upon*, i.e. 'He tried to inculcate his own beliefs into (upon) them'. Care should be taken not to express this the wrong way round by saying 'inculcate them into his beliefs'.

He infused his team with confidence

Although some dictionaries allow *infuse with* it is generally considered better to say 'He infused confidence into his team'. One can infuse or instil qualities, feelings or beliefs into people, or one can inbue or inspire people with these things.

A similar crossing of constructions occurs with the verb pairs *afflict-inflict* and *fob-foist*. The verb *inflict*, because of its close resemblance to *afflict*, is especially liable to this type of confusion.

He inflicted the pupils with new punishments

This should read either 'He inflicted new punishments on the pupils' or 'He afflicted the pupils with new punishments'. *Inflict with* is a cross between *inflict (up)on* and *afflict with*.

He foisted them off with shoddy goods

Here one should say 'He foisted shoddy goods on them', 'He fobbed them off with shoddy goods' or 'He fobbed shoddy goods off on them'. *Foist off with* is a faulty construction formed on the analogy of *fob off with*.

The construction of the verb *comprise* is quite often altered to that of *compose* or *consist*, not surprisingly since all three words express a relationship between a whole and its parts.

The area is comprised of three states

Comprised of is always wrong; say either *is composed of* or *comprises*. The verb *to comprise*, which means 'embrace', takes a direct object. The whole comprises, consists of or is composed of its parts. It is thus equally bad to say 'Three states comprise this area' since the parts cannot embrace the whole; here use *compose* or *constitute*.

The verb *to attribute* is sometimes wrongly attached to the subject instead of the object.

She was attributed with psychic powers

This is false attribution and should be amended to read 'Psychic powers were attributed to her'. Alternatively one can say 'She was credited with psychic powers'; *credit with* may well be the source of this faulty construction.

The verb *to pose* occasionally takes the construction of *to present*.

The blockade posed them with great problems

Either put *presented* for *posed* or say 'posed great problems for them'.

Miscellaneous blends

Besides the kinds of blend described above a number of other crossed constructions are found, most of them being mixed correlatives. For example *other*, after *any* or *no*, is often used without *than*.

In any other age but ours this would have been forbidden

Either 'any other age than' or 'any age but'.

He offered no other excuse except lack of time

Either 'no other excuse than' or 'no excuse except'.

A correlative conjunction *as*, in second position, is sometimes replaced by *but, that* or *than*.

It was not so much a discussion but a quarrel

Either 'not so much a discussion as' or 'not a discussion but'.

I followed the same path that you took

Either 'the same path as' or 'the path that'.

Nearly four times as many boys were affected than girls

Either 'four times as many boys ... as girls' or 'four times more boys ... than girls'.

The correlatives *as ... as* are sometimes mixed with the superlatives *best* and *least*.

You must make the change as best as you can

Either 'as well as you can' or 'as best you can'.

They troubled him as least as possible

Either 'as little as possible' or 'the least possible'.

Constructions are sometimes exchanged between *hardly* ... and *no sooner* ....

> Hardly had I left the room than a shot rang out
> No sooner had the clock chimed when the lights went out

Hardly, like *barely* and *scarcely*, goes with *when* or *before*, whereas *no sooner* goes with *than*.

Inclusive expressions with *both* and alternative expressions with *between* are often confused with synonymous forms.

16. Crossed Constructions

This will affect both teacher as well as students

The correlative *both* goes with *and*, not *as well as*. Without *both*, however, *as well as* is acceptable.

He had to choose between a divorce or a miserable marriage

Either 'between ... and', or 'either ... or'.

The expression *(just) because ... does not mean* is a common confusion.

Just because he's deaf doesn't mean he's daft

Just because he's deaf is an adverbial clause of reason, but the verb form *doesn't mean* requires a noun or noun phrase as its subject. Either say 'The fact that he's deaf' or rephrase the second part to read 'you need not think that he's daft'.

The combination *ago since* is another confused construction.

It is ten days ago since he died

We should say either 'It is ten days since' or, changing to the past tense, 'It was ten days ago that'. The adverb *ago* reckons from the present to the past, whereas the conjunction *since* looks forward from the past to the present; thus the two cannot logically be reconciled.

A few compound conjunctions and prepositions are crossed in construction. *Inasmuch that* is a blend of *inasmuch as* and *in that*, *so as that* is a blend of *so that* and *so as to*, and *up until* is a blend of *up to* and *until*. Respects and regards have become hopelessly muddled. The form *in respect to* crosses *in respect of* and *with respect to*. The form *as regards to* is an absurd mixture of *with regard to* and *as regards*, in which the plural noun *regards* has been confused with the singular verb *regards*. The forms *in regards to* and *with regards to* are similarly muddled barbarisms and should be replaced by the singular *in regard to* and *with regard to*. It is often better, however, to use a simple preposition instead of one of these compound forms. For example:

> They were very protective as regards (*say* towards) their children
> He expressed concern in regard to (*say* about) our safety
> There were no problems with regard to (*say* with) supplies

Further examples

Beer prices will soon cost £2 a pint.
It is here where he wishes to be buried.
What I would expect would be an apology.
Just because it's new doesn't mean it's better.
The faculty is comprised of ten departments.
Customers are sometimes foisted off with feeble excuses.
He was feared both by his allies as well as his enemies.
I would really have liked to have been a musician.

It is not long ago since children were sent down the mines.
She wouldn't have expected him to have understood.
The subject of next Friday's talk is about beekeeping.
I had to choose between an abortion or an unwanted baby.
It was at midnight when the bomb went off.
They failed to imbue in their children a respect for others.
Three times as many of these drugs were seized than last year.
The mistake was not so much over-eating but under-exercising.
The source of this pollution originated from the chemical plant.
She had no sooner stepped in the bath when the phone rang.
We could not reach any other conclusion but that he was insane.
The cause of her breakdown was because of this other woman.
He never thought of anyone else but himself.
He had scarcely got through the door than the thief pounced on him.
The significance of this change means that permits are no longer needed.
It is possible that investors may have been influenced by the Chancellor's statement.
The effect of this ruling will serve to make tenants resentful.

17. Broken Constructions

Grammatical dislocation

To breakdowns of sentence structure the Greeks gave the name *anacoluthia*, meaning 'want of sequence'. Such breakdowns occur when a speaker or writer begins a sentence and either breaks off or completes it with an incongruous construction. Incomplete or 'stop-short' sentences are characteristic of colloquial speech.

> Well, I'll be –
> He just can't, you know –
> I think she's, oh –

The unspoken words can generally be inferred from the context or the speaker's gestures and facial expressions. In print unfinished statements rarely occur, except as a device used in advertisements to avoid explicit comparisons. Thus 'Fizzo is more refreshing' does not say than what, but implies 'than all other soft drinks'.

Besides leaving sentences uncompleted, people often start to say something in one way, then decide to put it differently or remember something else and change tack, or are distracted and digress from their original path. Such false starts and deviations abound in ordinary conversation.

> She wasn't really – I thought she looked worried
> As I was saying – oh, look at the time!
> He came to me and – you've dropped your glove
> I was going to – would you like to join us?

Syntactical non sequiturs

Sentences made up of incongruous parts are common in both speech and writing.

> That man who came today, I've seen him somewhere before

The subject of the first part (*that man*), lacking a predicate, is a dangling subject, so called because it is left in the air; in reality it is the object of the second part, whose subject is *I*. Grammatical coherence requires us to delete *him* and the comma, or to put the real subject first and say 'I've seen that man who came today somewhere before'.

> I'm at a meeting that I don't know when it will end

In the sub-clause the word *it* is a shadow pronoun which duplicates the relative pronoun *that*, referring to the antecedent *meeting*. The second part of the sentence needs reorganizing to read either 'and I don't know when it will end' or 'which will end I don't know when'.

> Even now it is not fully realized the importance of fibre in our diet

Here we have a typical case of changing grammatical horses in midstream. The words 'it is not fully realized' in the first part require completing with 'how important fibre is in our diet'. We may keep *the importance* only if we re-order the sentence to read 'Even now the importance of fibre in our diet is not fully realized'.

> The need is for prices to be fixed and retailers are allowed bigger profit margins

The phrase 'for prices to be fixed' should be followed by a matching construction '(for) retailers to be allowed', with a passive infinitive, and not by the present passive form *are allowed*. The sentence is improved by the use of matching active verb forms, i.e. *to fix prices* and *to allow retailers*.

Ronald Reagan, before he became President, made the following disjointed statement. 'If what I understand, if it is true, that I was told what I understood, yes, I thought that made sense.' What he presumably meant to say was 'If I correctly understood what I was told, I thought it made sense'.

Broken questions

Sometimes sentences contain an interrogative element that is not grammatically related to what comes before.

> You must see that if you don't stay here, what will happen to you?

The construction 'You must see that' needs to be completed not by a question like 'what will happen to you?' but by a statement such as 'anything could happen to you'.

> This word is so expressive that how could we do without it?

The construction *so ... that* should introduce not a direct question but a dependent clause of consequence, i.e. 'that we could not do without it'. Alternatively the word *that* may be dropped and a semicolon used in its place.

> We must tighten the regulations, because otherwise how can we control the epidemic?

The word *because* should introduce an explanation, but here it introduces a question, which explains nothing. Change *how can we control*

17. Broken Constructions

to *we cannot control*, or keep the question and suppress the word *because*.

Sometimes, in defiance of idiom, a question is given a false tag.

> It shows that he was brave, wasn't he?

The tag *wasn't he?*, relating to *he was brave*, is used here instead of the proper tag *doesn't it?*, relating to *it shows*.

> He's one of those who air opinions about everything, doesn't he?

The proper tag is *isn't he?*, relating to *He's*.

> You haven't any cinemas in your town, do you?

The words *you haven't* require the tag *have you?* The tag *do you?* would be right if the sentence started *You don't have*, in the American fashion, now increasingly used by British speakers.

Sometimes *ought* has both a false tag and a false auxiliary.

> He didn't ought to have done it, had he?
> He hadn't ought to do it, did he?

Both the British *didn't ought* and the American *hadn't ought* are non-standard and even if they were standard the tags would still be wrong; *had he?* should go with *he hadn't* and *did he?* with *he didn't*. Acceptable ways of saying this are: 'He oughtn't to have done it, ought he?' and 'He shouldn't have done it, should he?'

Mixed voices

The verb *to do* is often used a pro-verb, i.e. in place of a previously used verb, to avoid repetition. Sometimes it is mistakenly used in the active voice with an antecedent verb in the passive, thereby creating a discontinuity.

> I've heard brasserie confused with brassière, which is easy to do

The two parts of the sentence do not hang together, since *do* cannot represent the active verb *confuse* supplied from the passive *confused*. The second part should therefore read 'which is easily done'.

> It may be said, as the bishop does, that morals have declined

The active *does* cannot stand proxy for the passive *be said*. We need either 'as it is by the bishop' or 'as the bishop says'.

> These facts should not be ignored, as the editor has done

Either repeat the verb and say 'has ignored them' or use the passive form 'as has been done by the editor'.

The phrase *to do so* frequently offends by having a passive antecedent.

> These people cannot be expelled, even if we wanted to do so

The words *to do so*, which fail to accord with *be expelled*, should be replaced by 'them to be (expelled)'.

> This problem can be solved, if we have the will to do so

To do what? Not 'to be solved it', but 'to solve it', which is the only coherent way to finish the sentence.

> As the engine needed renewal, I decided this was a good time to do so

Here the fault is compounded by making the pro-verb *do* refer not to a verb (*renewing*) but to the related noun (*renewal*). The final *to do so* needs to be replaced by *for it* (renewal).

> I was told the money must be paid, but refused to do so

The all-purpose *to do so* should be replaced here by the explicit verb form *to pay* or by the noun *payment*.

One-legged constructions

One leg of a comparative construction is sometimes paired with an incompatible limb.

> The more you relax, it makes it easier

The (= by how much) *more* is the first part of a correlative comparative construction, which requires a parallel form *the* (= by so much) *easier*, not just *easier* alone. The sentence should thus be reconstructed to read 'The more you relax, the easier it makes it' or 'the easier it becomes'.

> The faster he moves, he's wasting energy

Here the construction is even worse, as there is no comparative word at all in the second part, which needs altering to read 'the more energy he wastes'.

> But the closer we look, we find that this is rarely so

Here too the second part lacks a comparative element. In this case we do not need correlatives and can simply say 'But if we look closer'.

> The more uncertainty there is, then confidence will diminish

Here *the more* qualifies the word *uncertainty*, hence the answering construction in the second part should be 'the less confidence there will be'. Alternatively the first part may be reordered to read 'If there is greater uncertainty'.

As there are one-legged comparatives, so there are one-legged conditionals.

> If I could point out one snag, the records have been lost

The fact that the records are lost is not conditional upon the speaker's reference to it as a snag. The *if*-clause is a polite pseudo-conditional, better expressed in the form 'I would point out one snag', with a semicolon replacing the comma.

If I may make a suggestion, let us film that again

Here too the condition is not related to the statement in the main clause. The sentence should be rephrased to read 'I would suggest that we film that again'.

The only way to achieve success is if more time is allowed

An *if*-clause should correlate with a main clause expressing result or consequence, not method, as here. Restructure the sentence to read either 'The only way to achieve success is to allow more time' or 'Success will be achieved only if more time is allowed'.

If Asia has many starving people, Africa has even more

This is another non sequitur. The word *if* is badly chosen, because the truth of the second part is in no way conditional on the truth of the first part. The *if* should be replaced here either by the contrastive *while* or by the concessive *although*.

False sequence of tenses

In conditional statements and indirect speech the form of the verb in the sub-clause is determined by that of the main verb. Sometimes the sequence is broken, producing a grammatical non sequitur. Compare:

(1) If I go there again, I know what I *would* do
(2) If I went there again, I know what I *will* do

Two kinds of conditional statements are muddled here. There is a switch from real to hypothetical in (1) and from hypothetical to real in (2). The sequence of tenses requires *will* in (1) and *would* in (2).

Even if he does complain, he wouldn't mention you

Here again the verb forms of real and hypothetical conditions are confused. Say either *he does* and *he won't*, or *he did* and he *wouldn't*.

If they have found the key, they would try to escape

Have found should be followed by *will try*; *would try* goes with *had found*.

He would have come if he knew you were coming

The contrary-to-fact conditional, relating to the past, requires the sequence *would have come ... if he had known*. The form *if he knew* goes with *he would come* to express a speculative future.

Sometimes *may* is misused for *might* in a main clause linked to a contrary-to-fact conditional.

If he hadn't dropped down, he may have been killed

The sense demands *might*, not *may*, because the man was not killed. *May have* expresses a possibility that may or may not have been realized; *might have* expresses a possibility that has not been realized.

In indirect or reported speech the pronouns of direct speech often need to be altered and the tenses to be back-shifted. Thus the sentence 'John said that he was ill' reports the spoken words 'I am ill' by changing *I* to *he* and *am* to *was*. Grammatical sequence is broken when what is intended as indirect speech is given in the form of direct speech. Such mixing of forms was normal in Old and Middle English, but it will not pass muster in the standard language today.

I told the President that we respect you

The *you* here refers to the President. Therefore, in indirect speech, *we respect you* should become *we respected him*, or *respect him*, since back-shifting is optional if the reported statement is still true at the time of reporting.

False inversion

In non-standard English the inversion characteristic of direct questions is often transferred to indirect questions, where it is not appropriate.

He asked who was my new client

This reports the direct question 'Who is your new client?' by altering *is* to *was* and *your* to *my*, but fails to reposition the verb after the subject so as to read 'who my new client was'.

We must consider what drug abuse is and what harm does it do

The sub-clause 'what drug abuse is' has the word order of an indirect question, as it should, but 'what harm does it do' has the inverted order and use of *do* found in a direct question. The second sub-clause should read 'what harm it does'.

I wonder how could I have forgotten it

The words 'how could I' need reordering to read 'how I could'.

Question forms such as 'Do you know who ...?' and 'Could you say when ...?' have inversion in the main clause but not in what follows.

Do you know what time does the office close?

The second part, which is indirect, should be couched in the form 'what time the office closes'. This type of lapse is common because the word order is sound if the clause sequence is reversed, i.e. 'What time does the office close, do you know?'

She asked herself was it her own fault

In direct speech she asked herself: 'Is it my own fault?' In indirect speech this should be expressed with a conjunction and without inversion, so as to read 'She asked herself if/whether it was her own fault'.

Logical gaps

When the middle part of a statement is omitted, as it often is in conversational English, the broken construction produces a non sequitur. A logical gap of this kind frequently occurs in sentences beginning with an *if*-clause or a *when*-clause.

> If you like old films, there's one on TV every afternoon

Clearly, the showing of old films on TV takes place whether the interlocutor likes them or not. The speaker is merely passing on information which may be useful to the other person. The missing link, which restores a connection between the two logically unrelated clauses, is some form of words like 'you may be interested to know that'.

Similar examples, with the gaps supplied, are:

> If you're going to Blackpool, [remember that] it's crowded in July
> When you think about it, [you will agree that] this is a scandal
> When you look back, [you can see that] our decline began long ago

A logical gap commonly occurs also between a participle phrase and main clause.

> Knowing John, he'll take the easy way out

Obviously the knowing is being done by the speaker, not by the subject *he*, to which the word *knowing* relates grammatically. In writing the main clause should be introduced by the words *I think (that)*.

Comparable examples of this type are:

> Being very hungry, [I thought that] the pie smelled delicious
> Speaking off the record, [I would say that] he should be locked up
> Having met her, [I believe that] the answer must be 'No'

In all these sentences the participles in *-ing* relate to the speakers, who coyly – but ungrammatically – efface themselves.

A special kind of logical gap is that produced when a noun is defined by a *when*-clause or a *where*-clause.

> Panic is when you lose your nerve

This wording, typical of the colloquial language, is both clumsy and ungrammatical. A noun can be properly defined only in terms of another noun or a noun phrase. In formal writing the above definition should be amended to read 'Panic is the state resulting from a loss of nerve'.

> Etching is where you cut lines on a copper plate

Amend this to read 'Etching is the action of cutting lines on a copper plate'.

Sentence fragments

Skilful fiction writers know how to use very short sentences, sometimes of one word, in order to create a dramatic effect.

> His expression told her all. Bankruptcy. Disaster. Ruin.

This is a graphic way of saying 'His expression told her all; that he faced bankruptcy, disaster and ruin'. The separation of the nouns and the suppression of the connectives is only justified in such contexts, however. It serves no good purpose elsewhere, as in the following example.

> She was in pain. The pain of isolation. Very hard to bear.

Here the second and third 'sentences' are mere fragments consisting of a noun phrase and an adjective phrase. The three parts, which all relate to the pain suffered, should be integrated to read 'She was in pain — the pain of isolation, which is very hard to bear'.

Sentence fragments are sometimes resorted to by journalists of the tabloid variety, seeking to add punch to their flagging style.

> The Royal Family has huge assets. Vast wealth, palaces and castles. With no tax to pay. Which gives them every advantage in life.

Such prose is like a piece of bad knitting, with holes and dropped stitches. It is used in advertese as well as journalese. A copywriter, praising the virtues of some ointment, wrote:

> It gently massages your limbs. Soothing many aches and pains. Reducing the effects of fatigue.

The two *-ing* phrases are real dangling participles. They should be attached to the main clause by using commas in place of stops.

> All you need is a little help. The sort which you can only get from life assurance. And which Universal Life, in particular, is well equipped to give.

Such copy offers little assurance to the literate. Will people who handle the language so badly manage your money any better? Chopped-up sentences? Avoid them. Because they aren't easier to read. Or understand. They are jerky. Breaking the flow of thought. Which annoys the reader. Who is no fool. And make the writer seem a dimwit. See what I mean?

Further examples

The days spent at home, I make good use of them.
This is the mower that you said you'd show me how it works.
The fact that I did it all alone, I really am proud.
I'm longing for a child and my husband does too.

17. Broken Constructions

Frustration is when you can't get your own way.
He ought to pay for the damage, didn't he?
The problem cannot be ignored, however much we try to do so.
The more we learn about Aids, we might be able to conquer it.
I have several interests, like I go to the races a lot.
If you'll allow me to interrupt, the house isn't sold yet.
On a personal note, this is a rather special day.
Were he still willing to see me, my door will be open to him.
He may ask what guarantee is there that he will be paid.
He submitted an entry which, if it had won, he would not have needed to work.
One way of winning votes is if you offer tax cuts.
If the test is successful, it would make scientific history.
The change is so quick that who is to know what the result will be?
He asked himself was he the cause of her unhappiness.
It cannot be assumed, as the author does, that this is true.
He wants to know has the postman been yet.
Had they acted sooner, more lives may have been saved.
For those of you who wrote earlier, you will be aware that we have staffing problems.
If my father's people were labourers, my mother's were shopkeepers.
If the manager will not improve the service, the stronger the action I shall take.
Child-minders should not be hounded, which is what this judgement does.

18. Word Confusion

Malapropisms

The erroneous use of one word for another that resembles it in sound or spelling is called a malapropism. The term derives from Mrs Malaprop, a character in Sheridan's play *The Rivals* (1775). When taxed with using words she does not understand, the lady protests: 'Sure, if I *reprehend* anything in this world, it is the use of my *oracular* tongue, and a nice *derangement* of *epitaphs*!' – blunders for *comprehend, vernacular, arrangement* and *epithets*. Her phrase 'the very *pineapple* (for *pinnacle*) of perfection' is on a par with today's 'casting *nasturtiums* (for *aspersions*)'. Mrs Malaprop, the matron saint of all word-muddlers, had predecessors as well as followers.

Several of Shakespeare's plebeian characters come out with malapropian illiteracies. In *The Two Gentlemen of Verona* (c. 1594) Launce says 'I have received my *proportion* like the *Prodigious* Son', meaning *portion* and *Prodigal*. In *Much Ado about Nothing* (c. 1599) Dogberry, a constable, says '*comprehended* two *auspicious* persons' for *apprehended* and *suspicious*, and in *The Merry Wives of Windsor* (c.1598) he observes that 'comparisons are *odorous*', meaning *odious*. In *Henry IV, Part 2*, (c. 1597) Mistress Quickly, an inveterate malapropist, talks of *canaries* when she means *quandaries* and calls Falstaff a *honeysuckle* (for *homicidal*) villain. Later writers also put malapropisms into the mouths of the unlearned. One such character is Mrs Slipslop in Fielding's *Joseph Andrews* (1742). Another is Winifred Jenkins in Smollett's *Humphry Clinker* (1771), who tells a friend in a letter that her mistress 'was taken with the *asterisks* (*hysterics*)' and that the doctor 'had *subscribed* a *repository* (*prescribed* a *suppository*) for the dog'.

Mrs Malaprop was an ignorant woman with absurd pretentions to polite learning, but her confusions are too frequent and sometimes too far-fetched to be plausible. Yet, though overdone, they bespeak a common human tendency to take similarities for identities. It is safe to say that if two words or phrases resemble each other in any way they will be muddled sooner or later. English offers great scope for such blundering because most of its learned words, being drawn from Latin and Greek, are opaque to the majority of English-speaking people, who have not had a classical education. Thus the word *prodigy* is easily mistaken for its sound-alike *progeny*, and the now fashionable *parameter* is confused with the more familiar *perimeter*. The phrase *on behalf of* is quite often used these days in place of the similar-sounding *on the part of*, and a valuable distinction is in danger of being blurred. A protest on behalf of pensioners is made for their sake by others, but a protest on the part of pensioners is one made by pensioners themselves.

Sometimes borrowings, especially from French, are confused with native words or with other borrowings. A businessman once told how his mistress moved into his home and they set up a *menagerie (ménage) à trois*. A jockey once boasted that he had a good *repartee (rapport)* with his horse; no doubt it came straight from the horse's mouth. And a journalist described some woman as an excellent *flamingo (flamenco)* dancer. Foreign phrases and names also lend themselves to confusion. A backward art student owned to having mistaken a painting by *Cannelloni (Canaletto)* for a *Rio Tinto (Tintoretto)*. One word may be metamorphosed into two, turning *intricacies* into *inky traces*, for example. And occasionally a phrase is "malapropped" by shifting the word boundaries, as when a student wrote that Eugene O'Neill had won a *Pullet Surprise (Pulitzer Prize)* and a schoolboy wrote of the need to be careful when handling a *Bun St Bernard (Bunsen burner)*.

Confusable adjectives and adverbs

Some pairs of adjectives, mostly of Latin origin, are frequently confused. *Ambiguous*, 'allowing of more than one interpretation', is used instead of *ambivalent*, 'emotionally conflicting', as in the sentence 'His attitude to the French is *ambiguous*'. Both *derisive* and *derisory* mean 'mocking' (e.g. of laughter or remarks), but only *derisory* means 'worthy of ridicule'. Yet we hear talk of employers offering a 'derisive' pay increase, as though they intended to mock their workers. The words *effective*, *effectual*, *efficacious* and *efficient* are easily confused, since they all refer to what has an effect. *Effective* is used of people or actions that are highly successful; *effectual* of actions that produce the desired effect; *efficacious* of remedies that work; and *efficient* of people or systems that achieve results with the best use of resources. Thus an efficient doctor prescribing efficacious medicines is effective in action and his actions are effectual in achieving their purpose.

Emotional, 'of the emotions' or 'liable to emotion' is sometimes used for *emotive*, 'tending to arouse emotions'. An emotional speech vents the speaker's feelings, whereas an emotive speech seeks to stir the audience's feelings. *Historical* means 'relating to history', while *historic* means 'important in history', though in the world of finance it is proper to speak of historic or historical costs. *Masterful* denotes 'acting like a master', 'commanding', but *masterly* denotes 'worthy of a master', 'very skilful'. Sometimes *masterful* is used in phrases like *a masterful speech*, which would have been acceptable in older English, but today *masterly* is the appropriate form. *Practicable* and *practical* are easily confused. What is practicable can be done, regardless of whether it is sensible or efficient, but what is practical is only sensibly done. Thus it is practicable to hike in one's slippers, but hardly practical. *Sensual*, signifying something gross, should be distinguished from *sensuous*, signifying something refined. *Sensual* refers to gratification of the physical senses, especially during sexual activity (*sensual pleasures*), whereas *sensuous* refers to satisfaction of any of the senses, especially the aesthetic sense (*sensuous music* or *colours*).

Other adjectives sometimes confused are:

ceremonial: 'pertaining to a ceremony'; *ceremonious*: 'observing ceremony'
credible: 'believable', 'trustworthy'; *creditable*: 'deserving credit'
definite: 'precise', 'specific'; *definitive*: 'serving to define/settle'
equable: 'even-tempered', 'placid'; *equitable*: 'even-handed', 'fair'
fortuitous: 'accidental', 'casual'; *fortunate*: 'favourable', 'lucky'
ingenious: 'clever at contriving'; *ingenuous*: 'artless', 'innocent'
intense: 'violent', 'extreme'; *intensive*: 'highly concentrated'
judicial: 'relating to a judge or court'; *judicious*: 'well-judged'
triumphal: 'marking a triumph'; *triumphant*: 'victorious'
unexceptionable: 'beyond criticism'; *unexceptional*: 'ordinary'
venal: 'corruptible', 'mercenary'; *venial*: 'pardonable'

Some pairs are more commonly confused in their adverb forms:

alternately: 'taking turns'; *alternatively*: 'by way of another choice'
decidedly: 'undeniably', 'unmistakably'; *decisively*: 'resolutely'
purposely: 'intentionally'; *purposefully*: 'with determination'
regretfully: 'with regret'; *regrettably*: 'to my/our regret'

Confusable verbs

The use of *deprecate* for *depreciate* is widespread, even among good writers. *Deprecate*, which means 'deplore', 'express disapproval of', refers to actions or behaviour, while *depreciate*, which means 'undervalue' or 'disparage', may refer to people or their efforts. We can thus depreciate but not deprecate a person, yet the words *self-deprecation* and *self-deprecatory*, though manifest absurdities, are regularly used instead of the appropriate forms *self-depreciation* and *self-depreciatory*.

The verb *flaunt*, 'display ostentatiously', is often used instead of *flout*, 'treat (authorities, rules, etc.) with contempt'. The difference in meaning is exemplified by the sentence: 'The Serbs are flouting sanctions and flaunting their ability to do so'. The verb *instigate*, meaning 'incite to some (usually wrongful) action' is often used for *initiate* or *institute*. One may instigate a plot or legal proceedings, but one does not instigate a reform or a new system. *Mitigate* for *militate* has long been a common malapropism, as in the statement 'Heavy drinking *mitigated* against his chances of promotion'. *Mitigate*, which is used without *against*, means 'moderate', 'soften the force of'; *militate against* means 'provide a reason against', 'tell against'. The verb *perpetuate*, 'preserve indefinitely' quite often usurps the rights of the verb *perpetrate*, 'commit' (a misdeed), as in the sentence 'He *perpetuated* one of the greatest hoaxes of all time'.

Other verbs sometimes confused are:

activate: 'set in motion'; *actuate*: 'motivate'
adapt: 'make suitable', 'modify'; *adopt*: 'assume', 'take up'
affect: 'concern', 'influence'; *effect*: 'accomplish', 'bring about'
appraise: 'assess the value of'; *apprise*: 'inform', 'notify'
ravage: 'devastate', 'plunder'; *ravish*: 'abduct', 'rape'

Confusable nouns

The words *admission* and *admittance*, though both related to the verb *admit*, are not synonymous. Only *admission* is used in the sense of 'confession', but both are used to mean 'permission to enter', though in rather different ways. *Admittance* is used in a purely physical sense, as in the notice 'No admittance'. *Admission* is used in a more abstract sense, where physical entrance and access to facilities are combined, for example when one is admitted as a member of some club; also for the cost of entrance ('Admission 50p').

There is understandable confusion between *credence*, 'belief or trust', *credibility*, 'believability or trustworthiness', and *credulity*, 'readiness to believe'. Thus one could say of journalists that if they are to retain any credibility they should not give credence to rumours that strain most people's credulity. Likewise the words *expectancy* and *expectation* are not interchangeable. *Expectancy* means 'a state of expecting something desirable', i.e. pleasurable anticipation, as when an audience waits to hear a master musician perform. *Expectation* is 'a state of expecting something, whether it is desirable or not'; for example, one may be left a bequest, contrary to one's expectation, or may receive a legacy that exceeds one's expectations. But the phrase *life expectancy* is now used instead of the earlier *expectation of life* to mean 'the number of years a person can expect to live'.

The words *observance* and *observation* relate to the two different senses of the verb *observe*. *Observance* is the observing of some ceremony, custom or law. By contrast, *observation* is observing in the sense of 'watching and noting' or of 'remark'. One would say 'We must enforce observance of the highway code', but 'His writing is the product of imagination rather than careful observation'. Another confusion, increasingly common nowadays, is the use of *testament* for *testimony*. A *testament* is a will or covenant, i.e. a solemn document, whereas *testimony* is anything that serves as evidence or proof, whether documentary or otherwise. Thus we should say 'This performance was a testimony (not *testament*) to his remarkable stamina'.

Other nouns sometimes confused are:

assignation: 'agreement to meet'; *assignment*: 'task assigned to one'
delusion: 'false or deranged belief'; *illusion*: 'deceptive appearance'

hesitancy: 'tendency to hesitate'; *hesitation*: 'act of hesitating'
informant: 'supplier of information'; *informer*: 'one who informs police'
perspicacity: 'perceptiveness'; *perspicuity*: 'clarity of expression'
sewage: 'waste matter drained by sewers; *sewerage*: 'sewer system'
summary: 'brief account', 'abstract'; *summation*: 'calculation of total'

Sesquipedalian substitutes

'When a man has anything of his own to say,' wrote Dickens, 'and is really in earnest that it should be understood, he does not usually make cavalry regiments of his sentences, and seek abroad for sesquipedalian words' (*Household Words*, vol. 18, 1858). Sesquipedalian words, from Horace's *sesquipedalia verba*, literally 'words a foot and a half long', appeal to writers who wish to impress their readers by seeming learned. Mediocre academics and copycat journalists love to use polysyllabic words and phrases where simple and shorter ones would do as well or better. From their pens flow such elegancies as *underprivileged* for *poor*, *correctional facilities* for *prisons* and *pedagogical strategies* for *teaching methods*. But a rat's tail is not ennobled by being described as its 'caudal appendage'.

The lure of the long word is especially great when there is a shorter word related to or resembling it. Many writers seize upon the longer word and, ignoring semantic distinctions, treat it as a grander-sounding synonym of the shorter one. Thus *advancement*, which means 'promotion', is sometimes used for *advance*, which means 'progress'. The advance of science is the way it is advancing, whereas the advancement of science is action taken to advance it. Hence it is inaccurate to say 'Only by compromise will any *advancement* be made'; the appropriate word here is *advance*.

The word *method* is in some danger today of being annihilated by its fashionable big brother *methodology*, which is 'the science of method' or 'a body of methods used in some field of study'. *Methodology* belongs to the world of scholarship and research and even there it is often used when *method* or *methods* would suffice. To talk of 'the methodology of basket-weaving', however, is sheer pomposity. *Motive* is not grand enough for some people either; they prefer the longer *motivation*, which sounds more imposing and learned. *Motivation* is a term used by psychologists for 'that which makes us act' or 'the condition of being motivated'; the layman does better to say *motive* for the first sense and *interest* for the second. And in plain English 'What was his motivation?' is 'What made him do it?'

As *motivation* has been taken over from psychology, so has *objective* been borrowed from military terminology, being used where the simpler *object* would suffice. An *objective*, short for *objective point*, is the place towards which a military advance is directed; it thus denotes something concrete, whereas *object*, meaning 'aim' or 'purpose' is abstract. We should leave motivations to the psychologists and objectives to the generals.

Trade unions no longer have flesh-and-blood leaders and members, but impersonal abstractions, *the leadership* and *the membership*. The *-ship* words have good uses; *leadership* is 'the ability to lead' and *membership* is 'the state of being a member' or 'the number of members'. To say *the leadership* for *the leaders* or *the membership* for *the members* is like saying *the ownership* for *the owners*, *the scholarship* for *the scholars* or *the sponsorship* for *the sponsors*. The captains of industry are no better than the trade unionists, for they refer to themselves as *the management* instead of *the managers* and speak of *the competition* when they mean *our competitors*. In a similar way one's opponents, in both sport and politics, are dehumanized into *the opposition*.

The word *proposition*, which has precise meanings in logic and mathematics, has become a maid-of-all-work in the 20th century, serving as a substitute for *affair, matter, problem, task, prospect, job* or any thing, person or situation considered as something to be coped with. It can mean 'suggestion', 'plan' or 'offer', although in these senses *proposal* is better. But in men's relations with women there is a sharp distinction between the two words; a *proposal* is an offer of permanent marital union, while a *proposition* is an invitation to a temporary sexual union.

Pseudo-synonyms

The itch for polysyllables makes many writers prefer the longer of two words which come from the same root and leads to the creation of pseudo-synonyms. Thus the word *productivity*, defined as 'the degree of productive efficiency' is often used as a grander synonym for *production*, which means 'output' or 'what is produced'. The word *documentation*, meaning 'the provision of documents', has all but displaced the humbler *documents*. In political comment the word *expansionism*, meaning 'a policy of expansion' is sometimes used where 'an act of expansion' is meant. The Royal Family is sometimes said to be subjected to unprecedented *intrusiveness* ('the fact of being intrusive') instead of *intrusion*.

Some nouns in *-age, -ing, -ism* and *-tion* are mistakenly used for shorter nouns to which they are related. Examples are given below, with only the longer forms defined:

(*leak*) *leakage*: 'leaking', 'what leaks out'
(*link*) *linkage*: 'system of links', 'the fact of being linked'
(*use*) *usage*: 'customary practice', 'treatment'
(*waste*) *wastage*: 'loss by leaking or decay'
(*fund*) *funding*: 'provision of funds', 'financial backing'
(*group*) *grouping*: 'placing in groups'
(*list*) *listing*: 'compilation of a list'
(*sample*) *sampling*: 'testing by taking samples'
(*intervention*) *interventionism*: 'policy of political intervention'

(*isolation*) *isolationism*: 'policy of avoiding foreign entanglements'
(*parallel*) *parallelism*: 'balanced construction'
(*argument*) *argumentation*: 'use of arguments', 'methodical reasoning'
(*cause*) *causation*: 'operation of cause and effect'
(*class*) *classification*: 'arrangement in classes'
(*experiment*) *experimentation*: 'act of experimenting'
(*formula*) *formulation*: 'expression in systematic form'
(*identity*) *identification*: 'identifying or being identified'
(*protest*) *protestation*: 'declaration on oath', 'affirmation'
(*visit*) *visitation*: 'formal or official visit'

Big words, especially ponderous Latinisms, are the stock-in-trade of those who seek to dress up banalities as profundities. People who run to long words confuse mass with force and length with erudition.

Semantic reversal

When two verbs have a converse relationship, one of them sometimes assumes the function of the other. Thus *to learn* ('acquire skill or knowledge') and *to teach* ('impart skill or knowledge') are opposites, yet *learn* is often said for *teach* in non-standard English, especially in the expression 'I'll learn you'. Learning points to the learner, hence 'He learns us history' points the wrong way, to the teacher. The use of *learn* for *teach*, found in both Chaucer and Shakespeare, was once acceptable, but purists of the 18th century fought and won the battle to preserve the distinction between the two verbs. Using *learn* for *teach* is now regarded as illiterate, like using *lend* for *borrow*, as in the request 'Can I *lend* your pencil?' or using *export* for *import*, as in the statement 'American dealers are keen to *export* the new car from Japan'.

A very common semantic reversal is the use of *infer* ('deduce') for *imply* ('express indirectly'). It is true that *infer* was so used in the 16th to 18th centuries by reputable writers, but the two verbs have since become clearly differentiated. The distinction between them was neatly illustrated by A.P. Herbert as follows. 'If you see a man staggering along the road you may *infer* that he is drunk, without saying a word; but if you say "Had one too many?" you do not *infer* but *imply* that he is drunk' (*What a Word!*, 1935). An equally common reversal is the use of *substitute* ('put in the place of') for *replace* ('take the place of'). To say that B is substituted for A is the same as saying that A is replaced by B. Hence the construction *substituted by*, as in 'paper was *substituted by* plastic' is false, being a confused mixture of 'paper was replaced by plastic' and 'plastic was substituted for paper'. Equally bad is to say 'plastic *substituted for* (instead of *was substituted for*) paper'. The verb *substitute* has become a two-edged sword that can cut both ways; it needs to be refashioned so as to possess but a single blade. Too many of us replace *replace* by *substitute* or, to put it another way, substitute *substitute* for *replace*. The distinction is not a difficult one to make, yet many intelligent people fail to master it.

Mixed metaphors

Metaphor is a figure of speech in which one thing is identified with another, which it resembles in some way. If we say 'He is a tiger when roused' we mean that he is fierce and formidable, not that he is transmogrified into a tiger. The word *tiger* is being used here in a metaphorical, not literal sense. Language is strongly tinctured with metaphors, most of which have become detached from their primary or literal sense. When speaking of the *bed* of a river, for example, or the *key* to success, or the *hands* of clock, we do not think of a bed, key or hands in their primary sense.

When multiplied, metaphors can easily produce two or more conflicting images. If one says 'This book contains plenty of meat and it needs much chewing' the figurative use of *chewing* ('pondering') is in keeping with the metaphorical *meat* ('substance'). But if one says 'This book contains plenty of meat and it needs a lot of spadework', the image of a spade clashes with that of the meat; we do not eat meat with a spade. Such metaphorical confusions are common with parts of the body. Seeking to ease the distress of bereavement a man once remarked: 'The hand that rocked the cradle has kicked the bucket'. Impossible postures, too, are sometimes conjured up by mixed metaphors. A cautious statesman was once said to be 'sitting on the fence with one ear to the ground'. Some ear! Mixed imagery also begets hybrid monsters like those bovine gallinaceans, 'the sacred cows that have come home to roost'. Biological fact was ignored too by the scientist who announced the discovery of 'a virgin field pregnant with possibilities'.

Perhaps the most famous multiple mixed metaphor is that attributed to Sir Boyle Roche, an 18th-century parliamentarian, who is reported to have said: 'Mr Speaker, I smell a rat; I see him forming in the air and darkening the sky; but I'll nip him in the bud'. In the 19th century another MP memorably remarked: 'The well is running dry, and they thought that by putting in the pruning-knife they could bring more grist to the mill'. And in our own time a triple mixture of gaming and sports terms was produced by a football manager who said: 'We threw the dice into the ring and came up trumps'.

People who seek to add colour and life to their speech are in danger of coining figurative expressions in which images are at war with each other. They can overlook the incongruity of such phrases as 'ironing out the bottlenecks', 'shoring up lame ducks', 'enforcing price ceilings to the hilt' or 'breaking the back of the inflationary spiral'. Terms relating to quite different activities are thrown together in unholy union. Take the statement: 'While the Chinese were stoking up the Cold War, the Russians were playing it pianissimo'. Are we in the boiler-house or the concert hall? Or again: 'The minister was batting on a sticky wicket and had finally scored an own goal'. Was he on a cricket ground or a football pitch? And again: 'He threw in the towel just as his opponent was beating a retreat'. Was this man in the boxing ring or on the battlefield? And where was the man who 'stirred up a hornet's nest and ended up with egg on his face' – in a garden or a kitchen?

Politicians have probably produced the richest crop of mixed metaphors. 'We shall sail forth,' said one, 'riding roughshod over the backwoodsmen, to establish a new Jerusalem in England's green and pleasant land', mixing maritime and equestrian imagery, then confusing Blake's *Jerusalem* with the new Jerusalem spoken of in the Bible (Revelations 21:2). The Labour minister Ernest Bevin, referring to the Council of Europe, once said: 'If you open that Pandora's box you never know what Trojan horses will jump out'. Prominent figures in the artistic world have created some bizarre confusions too. A theatrical director once told an interviewer: 'The writer gives you a trampoline; you need an actor with a good comic instinct to mime it, deepen the texture, and a director to pull the plug out when it gets too much'. How do you mime a trampoline, or deepen its texture, and where is its plug?

Sam Goldwyn, the famous film producer, is said to have remarked: 'These directors are always biting the hand that lays the golden eggs'. This is the realm of mixed metaphors that are also mixed idioms. Other Goldwynisms that belong to the same category are 'keeping a stiff upper chin', a conflation of 'keeping a stiff upper lip' and 'keeping one's chin up', and 'taking the bull by the teeth', a blend of 'taking the bull by the horns' and 'taking the bit between one's teeth'.

It is perfectly acceptable to use a series of different metaphors, so long as they are kept distinct, or to sustain a metaphor so long as harmonious images are employed, but the handling of such complex forms requires verbal skills of a high order. Generally speaking, metaphors should not be crowded on one object and they are best kept simple and short.

Further examples

The nursing service is creaking at the seams.
He belonged, on his own admittance, to the criminal class.
She returned with a triumphal look on her face.
This dictionary is the fruition of ten years' labour.
These graffiti fall into definitive classifications.
If they were infected with Aids I would shun them like a bargepole.
Casanova deflowered many young virgins with the greatest felicity.
He objected that his boss was taking a sledgehammer to crack a molehill.
The duchess stepped forward and prostituted herself before the king.
Christians have all too often flaunted the teachings of Jesus.
For their own sakes the men and women intimates must be kept apart.

18. Word Confusion

If this proposal were pushed through it would be the thin end of a white elephant.

Some people substitute the term 'venereal disease' by the euphemism 'social disease'.

Her lustful desires were a fragment of his overheated imagination.

After he had examined me the doctor said I had acute vagina.

He was a wonderful lover who knew all her erroneous zones.

I was struck by her bony hands and emancipated breasts.

They all rushed to their own destruction, like the Gabardine swine.

The aim is to root out the stigma that dogs women alcoholics.

Fetchingly attired in next to nothing, she was the sinecure of all eyes.

The third type of trousers is knickerbockers, the crowning glory of the male toilet.

I have other irons in the fire but I'm keeping them close to my chest.

Adolescence is the stage of life after childhood and before adultery.

That was a definition of character when he called me a twit with more tit than wit.

Miss Bosomworth gave a bravado performance and her *London Derrière* was much admired.

19. Miscoupling

Gradability and secondary grading

Most adjectives and adverbs are gradable, that is to say modifiable by degree words (*slightly odd*, *very neat*, *extremely well*) and susceptible of comparison (*bigger*, *less sad*, *more cheerfully*). But some adjectives and adverbs, because of their meaning, are not gradable. It makes no sense, for example, to say *very medical*, *more atomic*, *most jointly* or *rather initially*. We speak of *nuclear physics*, but we cannot intensify or compare the expression by saying *more* (or *very*) *nuclear physics*. Similarly, we speak of an *economic crisis*, but nobody talks of a *very* (or *most*) *economic crisis*. If we say 'This crisis is more economic than political' we mean 'economic rather than political' and are using *more* to express a correction, not a comparison. And if we say 'This is very much an economic question' we are using *very much* not to qualify *economic* but as a sentence modifier, meaning 'emphatically'. In a similar way the words *very* and *too* are used colloquially to convey subjective emphasis or strong agreement in the phrases *very true* and *too right*. Adjectives which are non-gradable in their primary senses can be gradable in secondary ones. This is true of adjectives denoting nationality, for instance. One Frenchman cannot be literally more French (i.e. possess greater French nationality) than another. But if we take *French* in a different sense, to mean 'possessing qualities or traits considered typical of the French people', then we can reasonably say 'Simone is very French'. In a similar way it is quite acceptable to say 'Brendan is thoroughly Irish' and 'Boris is more English than the English'.

Other non-gradable adjectives, besides those of nationality, can become gradable when used in a secondary or derived sense. For example, the word *original*, in the sense 'primary', 'not copied', admits of no degrees. A manuscript can be *original*, but not *more* (or *very*) *original*. But when *original* means 'novel in style or character' it may be compared or intensified, so that we may speak of a *more* (or *highly*) *original poem*. Similarly the word *dead* becomes a degree adjective when it is used figuratively to mean 'lacking activity or vitality'. Thus we may say 'This is a rather dead town' or 'That was the deadest party I have ever been to'. In its literal sense, of course, *dead* is non-gradable, like the word *pregnant*. There are no degrees of death or pregnancy. A person is either dead or alive, just as a woman is either pregnant or not pregnant;

there are no intermediate states. One cannot be *a little dead* or *a bit pregnant*. It is colloquially acceptable, however, to use both words with *very*, here used to express not degree but duration. Thus *very dead* means 'dead a long time' and *very pregnant* means 'heavily pregnant', 'in an advanced stage of pregnancy'.

Elatives

Adjectives are elative if they express a high degree of the attribute or quality denoted. Such adjectives are *abominable* ('greatly detestable'), *colossal* ('exceptionally large'), *exorbitant* ('grossly excessive'), *hideous* ('horribly ugly'), *magnificent* ('very grand'), *minute* ('exceedingly small'), *prolific* ('highly productive'), *ravenous* ('intensely hungry'), *splendid* ('extremely fine'), and *succulent* ('most juicy'). Adverbs too are elative if they are intensifiers like *agonizingly* ('very painfully'), *amazingly* ('very surprisingly'), *atrociously* ('very badly'), *enormously* ('very greatly') and *vehemently* ('very forcibly').

Because of their extreme meaning elative adjectives admit of comparison but leave scarcely any room for modification by adverbs. Thus, of several delicious (i.e. very tasty) dishes one may be more delicious or less delicious than the others. It is also acceptable to say *extremely delicious* ('tasty in the highest degree'), but it is poor style to say either *very delicious*, which means no more than 'delicious', or *rather delicious*, which has the self-contradictory meaning 'rather very tasty'. Like *delicious*, the word *excellent* may be compared but can rarely be modified. One thing can clearly excel more, or less, than another, so we can properly say 'His work last year was excellent and it is even more excellent this year'. And the combination *most excellent* is good usage if it is superlative, as in the sentence 'That was the most excellent meal I have ever eaten', but not when it is elative, as when people say 'That was a most excellent meal'. In the latter case *most* means 'very', but *very excellent* is a tautology meaning no more than 'excellent'.

The word *disastrous* rarely attracts intensifiers (or boosters) such as *very* or *extremely*, but is sometimes modified by attenuators (or downtoners) like *a bit*, *slightly* and *rather*. 'The experiment was *rather disastrous*', we hear people say. But *disastrous* is too strong to be tamed by a feeble modifier like *rather*. The phrase *rather disastrous*, if taken literally, means 'somewhat very unsuccessful', which is nonsensical, and if taken ironically, i.e. as an understatement, means 'very disastrous', which is tautological. 'Her performance was *slightly disastrous*', even if said with tongue in cheek, is no better, for it means merely 'less than successful'.

As these examples show, elatives do not sit well, stylistically speaking, with either boosters or downtoners. In most cases they are neither boosted by boosters nor toned down by downtoners. Such expressions as *a bit drastic, a little astonishing, faintly repulsive, fairly extreme, pretty appalling, slightly horrific, somewhat overwhelming, rather devastating* and *very splendid* should be 'gently stamped out'.

Absolutes

Adjectives are absolute if they express a maximum of some attribute or quality, i.e. a *ne plus ultra*. Absolute adjectives are not, properly speaking, capable of being compared or of being modified, except by such words as *almost, nearly, possibly* and *probably*. The word *absolute* is itself absolute, as are other adjectives such as *equal, eternal, final, ideal, infinite, mortal, permanent, sufficient, total* and the adverbs derived from them. There are no degrees of absoluteness, equality, eternity, finality, ideality, infinity, mortality, permanence, sufficiency or totality. The class of absolutes also includes many adjectives of negative import such as *impossible, inaccessible, invisible, unbearable, uncontrollable, harmless* and *worthless*.

Consider the word *invisible*. Whereas there are degrees of visibility, there are no degrees of invisibility; visibility is relative, but invisibility is absolute. Similarly, while there are degrees of accessibility, controllability, fallibility and intelligibility, there are no degrees of inaccessibility, uncontrollability, infallibility or unintelligibility. Absolute terms, being 100-percent words, are non-gradable and uncomparable. A thing may be final, but it cannot be more final, i.e. exceed the ultimate limit, nor can it be less final or rather final, for then it would fall short of the ultimate limit. Likewise one blow cannot be more mortal than another, one vote cannot be more unanimous than another, and one consequence cannot be more inevitable than another.

Our reason tells us that one thing cannot be more, or less, equal than another; it can only be as equal as another, so to speak. True, in George Orwell's *Animal Farm* (1945), the boss pig declares: 'All animals are equal, but some animals are more equal than others'. This, though, is a deliberate perversion of logic used to expose political cant, in which authoritarianism masquerades as egalitarianism. In ordinary speech *more equal* is used to mean *more nearly equal*, as in the phrase 'a more equal distribution of wealth', but this can be expressed more precisely by substituting *equitable* for *equal*.

And what of truth? Strictly speaking, it is absolute, but, as a Greek philosopher wisely said: 'Pure truth hath no man seen, nor ever shall know'. It is impracticable to treat truth as a synonym of the pure or whole truth. We are compelled to allow degrees of truth. Thus in court witnesses are sworn to tell the truth, the whole truth and nothing but the truth, for they might otherwise be tempted to tell only part of the truth or to mingle truth with falsehood. A simple statement may be true or untrue, without qualification, but most matters are not so easily expounded. It is therefore reasonable to use such expressions as *absolutely true, broadly true, partly true, more or less true* and *it would be truer* (nearer to the truth) *to say* ...

Downgrading and upgrading

There has long been a tendency in English to downgrade absolutes, i.e. to treat them as elatives. The word *perfect* has been so treated since the time of Chaucer, especially by Elizabethan writers, who freely used the forms *perfecter*, *perfectest*, *most perfect* and similar hyperbolic forms such as *chiefest*, *extremest*, *most mortal* and *most supreme*. Since the 18th century scholars have condemned such usage, arguing that words like *perfect* can be neither compared nor intensified, since nothing can be more perfect than perfect. But *perfect* is a rather special case. Traditionally perfection has been seen as an unattainable state, something that in Christian eyes belongs to God alone, so the word *perfect* nearly always means 'approaching a state of perfection'. Hence *more perfect* signifies 'more nearly perfect' and it is in this sense that the phrase is used in the preamble to the US Constitution, where it speaks of 'a more perfect union'. Our disbelief in human perfection is so deep-rooted that we interpret the remark 'That woman is too perfect' as meaning that she must have hidden faults, that she is 'too good to be true'.

The absolute words *full(y)*, *complete(ly)* and *thorough(ly)* are often downgraded to near-absolutes. It is thus acceptable to say that a glass is *fuller* (more nearly full), that a report is *the most complete* (the most comprehensive) or that an investigation is *more thorough* (more exhaustive). It is equally acceptable to use these words with adverb modifiers, as in *describe very thoroughly* (in great detail), *a very full* (detailed) *statement* and *a fairly complete account* (one falling some way short of completeness). It is meaningless, however, to speak of 'a more complete silence' because silence does not admit of degrees, unlike darkness; there is no semi-silence, as there is semi-darkness.

The downgrading of the word *unique* has met with strong resistance. What is unique, in the original sense of the word, has no like or parallel; it is in a class by itself. No unique thing is more or less unique than any other unique thing. Consequently, while no one objects to phrases like *almost unique* and *possibly unique*, many reject such collocations as *absolutely unique* and *rather unique*, because an intensifier adds nothing to *unique* and an attenuator stands in contradiction to it. Since the early 19th century the word has been increasingly used to mean 'rare' or 'remarkable'. But we would do well to use it only as an absolute, for in this sense it is irreplaceable. There are plenty of adjectives, such as *distinctive*, *exceptional*, *original*, *uncommon* and *unusual*, as well as *rare* and *remarkable*, which can be used instead of the downgraded *unique*. There is no substitute for *unique* in the sense 'unlike any other'. In other words, *unique* is itself a unique word.

Absolute adjectives of negative import are not downgraded but upgraded, so as to acquire a positive sense. Examples of such upgrading are *harmless* (from 'causing no harm' to 'causing little harm'), *tasteless* (from 'having no taste' to 'having little taste'), *incredible* (from 'unbelievable' to 'hard to believe'), *uncontrollable* (from 'impossible to control' to 'difficult to control') and *unproductive* (from 'producing nothing' to 'producing little'). In this way the word *impossible*, when used as a shortened form of *impossible to deal with*, is readily upgraded to mean 'very difficult to deal with'. In this colloquial sense it is quite admissible to say 'Life is becoming more and more impossible' and 'She was particularly impossible yesterday'.

Odd couples

Voltaire once said that the adjective is the enemy of the noun. He might have added, with equal if not greater truth, that the adverb is often the enemy of the adjective. Many combinations of adverb and adjective are incongruous or incompatible. We must be careful, however to distinguish these from playful uses of language such as hyperbole, which exaggerates, understatement, which embodies ironic humour, and oxymoron, which presents a paradox.

Hyperbole: 'I was absolutely furious' (quite angry)
Understatement: 'Those hands are a bit grubby' (very dirty)
Oxymoron: 'He was cheerfully pessimistic' (outwardly cheerful, inwardly pessimistic)

But many clashes between adverb and adjective cannot be subsumed under any of these heads and are simply incongruities that will not bear examination.

To say 'The discrepancy is immensely slight' is not oxymoronic but plain moronic. The choice of adverb is a most unhappy one, for immensity and slightness do not mix. To refer to something as *slightly astonishing* is tantamount to saying that it is 'a little very surprising'. The expression *mildly grotesque*, sometimes used by literary critics, is a contradiction in terms, since the modifier *mildly* is at odds with the adjective *grotesque*, which means 'grossly distorted or exaggerated'.

The words *crucial*, *essential* and *major* are often used as synonyms of *important*, which blunts their meanings. The word *crucial* means 'critical' or 'decisive'. It therefore makes no sense to say *most crucial* or *very crucial*, since there can only be one crucial factor in any situation, the one which is most important. The word *essential*, which means 'indispensable' or 'all-important', should not be downgraded to mean merely 'important', nor unnecessarily modified by such intensifiers as *very* or *most*. Similarly the word *major* means not just 'important' but 'of more than ordinary importance', 'likely to have serious consequences'. It is much overused and often flanked by modifiers that have no business to be in attendance. We may speak of *a major* (= greater) *part*, as opposed to *a minor* (= smaller) *part*. We also speak of *a major change* and of *major surgery*, where no comparison is implied. But it is not good style to modify the word *major* and speak of *a rather major reform*, meaning 'a quite significant reform' or of *a very major work*, meaning 'a very important work'.

Apposite forms can always be found to replace incongruous attributions. A few examples of ill-assorted couples are given below, with suggested substitutes for the absolute adjectives.

> He has the most *insatiable* (voracious) appetite of them all
> Until more *infallible* (reliable) tests are devised, we must use caution
> I was told that this arrangement would be fairly *permanent* (long-lasting)
> Gesture is more *universal* (widespread) than speech
> The most *fatal* (dangerous) thing you can do is opt for a life of ease

Weakening intensifiers

Words used for reinforcement sometimes have the opposite effect. This is particularly so with the adverbial intensifier *very*, which quite often does not fortify the following adjective, but saps its strength. Phrases like *a very splendid film* and *a very lovely park* are weakened by the word *very*. *A very great man* sounds less great than one described simply as *a great man*. *Very* is such a facile means of emphasis that it can easily become a verbal tic. Take this extract from a parish magazine: 'None of us is very perfect, none of us is very Christian. We are all very subject to human errancy, very dead in spirit, very lost to grace.' The reverend gentleman who wrote these words was long on theology, but short on logic. There are no degrees of perfection or Christianity or subjection or death or loss. Human beings may be not nearly perfect, not genuinely Christian, permanently subject to errancy, long dead or hopelessly lost, but not *very* any of these things. The homily gains in both force and accuracy if all the *verys* are struck out, in accordance with the advice English teachers once used to give their pupils.

Just as it is wise to be sparing of *very*, lest it enfeeble what it is meant to fortify, so it is sound practice to avoid using the words *awfully*, *dreadfully*, *frightfully*, *terribly*, *terrifically* and *tremendously*, since they have lost most of their potency through overuse. Similarly, many adjectives preceded by *actually*, *definitely* and *really* would be strengthened by the removal of the qualifier. 'That's not actually true' sounds limp compared with the crisp 'That's not true'. 'He is definitely dangerous' sounds less threatening than 'He is dangerous'. And 'It's really scandalous' sounds less shocking than 'It's scandalous'. Like *very*, these emphatic words must be used with restraint to be effective. Excess in language, as in other things, over-reaches itself in the end.

Miscellaneous miscouplings

Although most miscoupling is found with adverbs and adjectives, other parts of speech can be involved too. Participles, like adjectives, can be attended by unsuitable adverb modifiers.

> The area was *slightly devastated*

Was it or was it not devastated, i.e. laid waste? If it was devastated, then it cannot have been slightly so; if it was damaged only slightly, then *devastated* is the wrong word.

Other verb forms too may be accompanied by inappropriate adverbs.

> These barriers *greatly minimized* the danger to children

A danger that had been somewhat maximized?

> Those pictures *rather appalled* me

A somewhat underwhelming experience.

> He raised his glass of wine and *sipped deeply*

A profoundly shallow accomplishment.

> He *literally glued* his ear to the ground

And figuratively came to a sticky end.

Pronouns and nouns sometimes have odd companions.

> They arrived *more or less promptly*

And left roughly when precisely?

> His efforts to save us proved *a bit of a disaster*

Or a fragment of a catastrophe.

> We do our best not to publish *inaccurate facts*

Or true fiction.

Such miscouplings are characteristic of loose speech but, being the product of woolly thinking, they are avoided by careful writers.

Further examples

My hotel bill was a bit exorbitant.
This is the most ideal spot for a picnic.
He is not so infallible as he once thought.
The insurance cover is extremely comprehensive.
We shall have to find a more permanent solution.
The action they took was a little drastic.
That was a somewhat calamitous performance.
The budget we have prepared is very adequate.
The Republicans won the election pretty overwhelmingly.
His control of the party is more absolute than that of his predecessor.
Problems do not arise where decisions are fairly unanimous.
Late nights do ruin the next day a little bit.
The risk of this happening is very minimal.
He has always been rather omnivorous.

19. Miscoupling

Public funds are no more inexhaustible than private ones.
This record is not quite as unique as it used to be.
His incompetence seems even more total now than it did before.
By the time I got back I was pretty exhausted.
He did it to the very utmost of his ability.
English is the most ubiquitous language in the world today.
However irresistible his charm, he will never be trusted by the voters.
Its varieties are so infinite that no rules can be given for its use.
The difficulties were far less insurmountable than we had imagined.
Parents have a very major role to play in educating their children.
As a teenager she was extremely prudish and very untouchable.

20. Misplacement

The rule of proximity

The English language, having only a few vestiges of case inflection, relies mainly on word order to indicate grammatical relations. In good English, placement, or the disposition of words, is as important as diction, or the choice of words. Under the heading, 'Wrong Placing of Words' William Cobbett wrote: 'Of all the faults to be found in writing this is one of the most common, and perhaps it leads to the greatest number of misconceptions' (*A Grammar of the English Language*, 1818).

It is a cardinal rule of good style in English that things belonging together should, wherever possible, go together. This principle was first propounded by Lord Kames, a Scottish rhetorician, who wrote: 'Words expressing things connected in the thought ought to be placed as near together as possible' (*Elements of Criticism*, 1762). The same idea was expressed somewhat later by another Scottish rhetorician, Hugh Blair, who wrote that 'the words or members most nearly related should be placed in the sentence as near to each other as possible, so as to make their mutual relations clearly appear' (*Lectures on Rhetoric*, 1783). What has been called 'Dr Blair's law of position', but would be more accurately described as 'Lord Kames's rule of proximity', is as valid today as when it was first formulated. For the sake of clarity, qualifying words and phrases should stand next to or near the words they refer to. Compare:

(1) He didn't deliberately move the pot
(2) He deliberately didn't move the pot

In (1) *deliberately* qualifies the negative *-n't*, i.e. his moving the pot was not intentional, but in (2) *deliberately* qualifies *didn't move*, i.e. his not moving the pot was intentional.

(3) In June I decided to retire
(4) I decided to retire in June

In (3) *in June* goes with *I decided*; in (4) it goes with *to retire*.

(5) The boys at the back must stand
(6) The boys must stand at the back

In (5) *at the back* refers to *the boys*; in (6) it refers to *stand*.

Parallel constructions

In the past grammarians and rhetoricians set great store by logical placement and balanced phrases. This led them to lay down the principle of parallel constructions, to be applied in any sentence containing correlative conjunctions, i.e. those used in pairs. Consider two versions of such a sentence.

(7) He neither had the gun nor the sword
(8) He had neither the gun nor the sword

Version (7) was considered illogical and slovenly because *neither* jumps the gun, so to speak. By contrast (8) was acceptable because the correlative *neither* goes with *the gun*, as *nor* goes with *the sword*. This is a sound enough argument, but it ignores other considerations. So long as the meaning is clear, there is no reason why rhythm and emphasis should be sacrificed on the altar of logical precision. Take two more pairs.

(9) He not only tells lies but bad lies
(10) He tells not only lies but bad lies

Version (9) violates the classical rule, yet it sounds much more natural than the logically expressed (10).

(11) He was either accused of being lazy or incompetent
(12) He was accused of being either lazy or incompetent

Here variant (12), which follows the rule, sounds better than (11), in which a wide gap separates *either* from *lazy*. Clearly, the parallel construction is better in some cases and the non-parallel one in others.

Adverb placement

Adverbs roam more freely than any other class of words in English, their placement being a matter partly of sense and partly of idiom. The anticipatory placing of the adverbs *just*, *merely* and *only*, though it runs counter to the intended sense, has been established idiomatic usage since the 17th century. These adverbs normally stand just before the verb, even when they qualify some word that follows it. Thus in the sentences 'This doesn't just affect us', 'I merely spoke of the cost' and 'He only likes plum jam' the displaced adverbs *just*, *merely* and *only* refer to *us*, *the cost* and *plum jam* respectively.

It is pedantic to insist, as some people still do, on logical placement in such cases since context and, in the spoken language, intonation and sentence stress help to make the meaning clear. But we should have a nice regard for the position of these adverbs when some special emphasis is required or where otherwise ambiguity would arise. Careful placement of other adverbs is sometimes necessary too, in order to avoid misunderstanding.

The girl learnt to type quickly

If it is rapid typing that the girl learnt, all is well, but if it is rapid learning that is meant, then *quickly* is out of place and should be moved to stand before *learnt*.

Sometimes an adverb or adverb phrase may be taken to refer to what precedes or what follows. Because it looks two ways at once it is called a 'squinting modifier' or 'squinter'.

Drinking normally doesn't upset me

The word *normally* may be taken with *drinking* or with *doesn't upset*. The squint can be cured by saying either 'Normally, drinking doesn't upset me' or 'Normal drinking doesn't upset me'.

She resolved once more to seduce him

Does *once more* go with *resolved* or *to seduce*? The ambiguity can be removed by shifting *once more* to the front or rear of the sentence.

He told me when we met we could discuss it

To make clear whether the adverbial clause *when we met* refers to what precedes or what follows it should be placed first or last. Alternatively the word *that* can be inserted after *me* or before *we*.

Back-to-frontery

A common type of misplacement is one in which a phrase is put at the wrong end of a sentence. This 'back-to-frontery' sometimes produces ludicrous results, as in the following sentences.

(13) Strapped to her thigh, the customs officer found a packet of heroin
(14) A teacher admitted indecently assaulting a pupil in court yesterday

Here are pretty cases of false attachment – both grammatical and anatomical. Sentences that conjure up a picture of a customs officer strapped to a woman's thigh or a teacher indecently assaulting a pupil in court are seriously flawed. If we are given the wrong mental image we can be sure the sentence is badly put together, for it is ill-constructed sentences that are most likely to be misconstrued. All that is needed to set matters right here is to shift the first phrase of (13) and the last phrase of (14) to the other end of the sentence, so that it is the heroin, not the officer, that was strapped to the woman's thigh, and the teacher's confession to assault, not the assault itself, that took place in court.

Misplacement can be a cause not only of absurdity but also of ambiguity, and sometimes both at once.

(15) Hiding in the shrubbery, the policeman spotted a youth
(16) Tucked under a rafter, he found a box of coins

(17) Plunging into the gorge, we saw the mighty waterfall

In (15) who is hiding in the shrubbery – the policeman or the youth? If the latter, then the participle phrase should come at the end. In (16) and (17) the participle phrase has been placed next to the subject (*he* and *we*), instead of the object (*box of coins* and *waterfall*), to which it refers. Back-to-frontery again.

Careless fronting can lead to false attachment. This is especially common with the construction *by* -*ing*.

By working shorter hours, we hope the staff will be more efficient

Since it is not *we* who are to work shorter hours, the initial phrase should be moved to the end.

Just as phrases are inappropriately put at the head of a sentence, so are they sometimes tacked on carelessly at the end of a sentence, when they do not refer to what immediately precedes them.

(18) He pointed to the woman with an umbrella
(19) They banned the journal to which I had contributed for several years

If the last phrase in each sentence is intended to refer to the words just before it, we cannot quarrel with the construction. If not, the phrases are misplaced and should come straight after *pointed* in (18) and *banned* in (19).

A participle phrase may likewise be misplaced after the main clause, sometimes with comic results, as in this example, taken from the magazine *Punch*.

You won't catch flu germs walking in the open air

Detached relative clauses

A relative clause may give rise to ambiguity if it is detached from its antecedent.

There was a man beating his wife, who was drunk

This is a typical example of ambiguity arising from the presence of two antecedents. If it is the wife who was drunk, the sentence stands as it is. If not, the words *who was drunk* need to be placed straight after *a man*.

This is a book about drug-taking, which has been much criticized

If it is the book and not drug-taking that has been subjected to criticism, then the relative clause (preferably reduced to *much criticized*) should stand after *book*.

A hamster is a domestic pet, smaller than a rabbit, which feeds on grains

As it is not the rabbit that feeds on grains, the *which*-clause should come directly after *hamster*.

Sometimes transposition of the clause will not remove the doubt.

> Problems in teenage marriages, which have been increasing lately, need more study

This requires recasting to show either that the problems have increased: 'Teenage marital problems, which have been increasing lately, need more study', or that teenage marriages have increased: 'Teenage marriages have been increasing lately and their problems need more study'.

Exiled phrases and participles

Sometimes a phrase is put in the main clause instead of the following sub-clause, where it logically belongs. The 'exiled phrase' is an increasingly common feature of written English.

> (18) In common with all our other products, we expect that this machine will sell well
> (19) After announcing a crisis, no one was surprised that the firm collapsed
> (20) Not content with killing the nurse, I understand that the robber killed her dog too

In (18) *we* are lumped together with our products; in (19) *no one* announces a crisis; and in (20) *I* was not content with killing the nurse. In each sentence the first phrase, which is banished to a remote place next to the pronoun subject, should be brought home and placed on either side of its proper neighbour, namely *this machine*, *the firm*, and *the robber*.

A participle may be similarly exiled.

> Unsupported, it is likely that the chairman will resign

The word *unsupported*, instead of hanging on to the dummy subject *it*, should go in the main clause, just before or after *the chairman*. Alternatively, the sentence may be recast in a terser form to read: 'Unsupported, the chairman is likely to resign'.

Misleading arrangement

The danger of misplacing a word is well demonstrated by the following notice, put up in a shop.

> No dissatisfied customer is ever allowed to leave these premises

The sinister suggestion of disgruntled customers being permanently incarcerated in the shop can easily be dispelled by putting *dissatisfied* at the end.

20. Misplacement

A misplaced phrase can likewise mislead.

> Customers complained about the toilet facilities as well as the staff

It is not clear whether the staff, like the customers, complained about the toilets or whether the staff, like the toilets, were complained about by the customers. If the former, then the phrase *as well as the staff* should go after *customers*; if the latter, it should stay where it is but be amended to read 'as well as *about* the staff'.

Further examples

The parachute failed completely to open.
The actress tried to kill herself for the third time.
At eighteen weeks I was told a baby would suck its thumb.
She admitted what she had done to the priest at confession.
We'll let you know whether we need you when the nurse arrives.
However old and gnarled, he would never cut down a tree.
Being a lawyer, we may assume that he knows some law.
I could see Concorde taking off through the restaurant window.
After the meeting the MP discussed the cost of living with several women.
Shimmering in the moonlight, I saw a beautiful big lake.
The figures below represent the British population, broken down by age and sex.
The exhibition features works by French painters, executed between 1850 and 1900.
The sperm bank contains samples from ten men frozen in a steel tank.
The lords of those days were continually stuffing themselves, as well as the ladies.
We observed the woman breast-feeding the child from a distance of three yards.
The blaze was put out before any damage could be done by the firemen.
Clinging firmly to your bosom, men will admire this alluring boa.
Previously issued in hard covers, you will be fascinated by this thriller.
She wore a rose in her bosom, which drooped as the evening wore on.
Although still on a ventilator, doctors said the girl was out of danger.
In this stubborn mood I knew that he was quite capable of refusing food.
Some paintings by women, well worthy of inspection, will be exhibited next month.
The frogs are in danger when crossing the road as motorists speed past to get to their breeding places.
There are two classrooms large enough to accommodate a hundred pupils, one above the other.
Jones, a bricklayer, cemented an amazing bond as he lay dying between his wife and his mistress.

21. Ambiguity

Ambiguous speech and writing

Ambiguity, or uncertainty of meaning, is sometimes a virtue, but more often a vice. When a poet combines words in such a way as to suggest multiple meanings, he is exploiting the elasticity of language for creative purposes. And when a comedian makes a pun or indulges in double entendre, he is using the same property of language for comic purposes. Most ambiguity, however, is not produced deliberately but comes from lack of care or from muddled thinking.

There are three main types of ambiguity: lexical, structural and syntactical, the last of which comes under the more general heading of misplacement. With all types of ambiguity a distinction needs to be made between speech and writing. What is ambiguous when spoken may not be so when written, and vice versa. Two quite distinct words may coincide in sound but not in spelling and this can lead to misunderstanding, though this is generally of a trivial kind. In spoken English we might well confuse *rite* with *right*, but we are hardly likely to confuse *beach* with *beech* or *rain* with *reign* in any context.

More often than not, something which is ambiguous when written may be spoken in two rather different ways, so that there is no possibility of confusion. The question 'Are they cooking apples?' when written could mean 'Are those people cooking some apples?' or 'Are those apples of the cooking variety?' But when the sentence is spoken, in the first case the word *apples* would be stressed, and in the second case the word *cooking*. Similarly the written sentence 'She wouldn't marry anyone' could mean 'She intends to remain single' or 'She will be very particular about whom she marries'. But when the sentence is spoken the first sense is conveyed by a falling tone on the last syllable of *anyone*, and the second sense by a drop in tone in both syllables. By contrast, the sentence 'Has the mail come?', ambiguous when spoken, becomes clear in print, where *the mail* (the post) is distinguished from *The Mail* (the newspaper).

Disambiguation

Most common words in English have more than one meaning and some of the commonest words have a great variety of meanings. 'I've done the lounge' may mean that the speaker has cleaned the lounge, painted it, rewired it, emptied it or stolen the valuables from it, depending on whether that person is a cleaner, a decorator, an electrician, a furniture remover or a burglar. Many words, too, have both concrete and abstract meanings. For example, the word *ceiling* in its primary sense denotes 'the upper inside surface of a room', and in its figurative sense 'an upper limit', especially a financial constraint. Literal and metaphorical meanings are not generally confusable, but sometimes the situational context fails to make clear which meaning is intended. If someone says 'John went into the church' it will be obvious from the context whether he entered a church building or became a priest. But if one says 'John loves the church', without further clarification, it could well remain uncertain whether he loves a particular church building or loves the church as an institution.

Where the context leaves room for misunderstanding it is easy in the spoken language to add some words of explanation. We sometimes, for example, explain a doubtful use of the word *funny* by saying whether we mean 'funny peculiar' or 'funny ha-ha', since the contexts in which the word occurs are similar for both senses. But a writer cannot correct a reader's misunderstanding, as a speaker can correct a listener's. When we write, therefore, we need to use greater care in framing our sentences than when we speak. The word *relations* in the following question is open to two interpretations.

What are John's relations like with Mary?

In speech the sentence can be disambiguated by adding 'How does he get on with her, I mean?' or 'How do they treat her?' according to sense. In writing more careful diction would remove the doubt. To give one sense *like* could be placed after *Mary*, and to give the other *relations* could be replaced by *relatives*.

Most ambiguities go unnoticed, since they are instantly resolved by contextual clues or by such features of speech as pause, stress and intonation. Normally, therefore, only one interpretation of a word or sentence is conveyed at any one time and communicative chaos is avoided.

Categorial confusion

English possesses remarkable flexibility in switching words, without alteration of form, from one speech category to another, an ease of conversion that can give rise to ambiguity. Nouns are able to turn into verbs, and verbs into nouns. The nouns *pepper* and *salt* have been converted into verbs, just as the verbs *hit* and *run* have been converted into nouns. Adjectives, such as *American*, *cordial*, *daily* and *private*, may also serve as nouns. Similarly, nouns take on the attributive functions of adjectives when they occur in block compounds such as *strawberry jam* and *blood money*. And a whole series of nouns can be used as premodifiers, producing an 'attributive queue', as in *data acquisition control system* and *giant car boot sale*. So varied and at times so complex are the relations between the elements of such compounds that they can easily bear more than one meaning. *A fire screen* may be 'a screen placed in front of a fire for safety' or 'a screen consisting of fire'. *Daffodil time* may be 'the time when daffodils bloom' or 'the time for giving daffodils as a present'. *Teacher guidance* may be 'guidance for teachers' or 'guidance by teachers'. *A child murderer* may be 'a murderer of children' or 'a child who has committed murder'. If I say 'Has the London train left yet?' it can only mean the train going to London, but if I say 'Has the London train arrived yet' it could refer to a train either going to or coming from London.

The block compound, because of its brevity, is a form much favoured by sub-editors. Whole stories can be compressed into headlines such as 'England team captain rumour', 'Beach murder trial court scene' and 'Speedboat death blaze rescue bid'. The scope for ambiguity in headlines is increased by the practice of omitting the articles and the verb *to be*. The condensed headline 'Policeman found drunk in shop window' leaves the reader in doubt as to whether the policeman found a drunk or was found drunk himself, because *found* could be active or passive and *drunk* could be an adjective or a noun. And the headline 'Birmingham tea breaks strike leader under fire' makes sense only if we know that there is a strike in Birmingham over tea breaks. Otherwise we may wonder how Birmingham tea could break a strike leader, or perhaps why tea breaks in Birmingham should strike a leader who is already in the unhappy position of being under a fire.

Pronoun ambiguities

One of the commonest types of ambiguity is unclear pronoun reference. A third-person pronoun with two or more antecedents may be taken to refer to either or any of them.

> John had offended his brother and he was obviously upset

We do not know who was upset, John or his brother; *he* could refer to either. If *he* is removed, it is clear that John was upset; if *and he* is replaced by *who*, it must be his brother who was upset.

> John said an old friend had hit his brother

We could take *his brother* to refer to the first antecedent, *John*, or the second antecedent, *an old friend*. If the first is meant, a passive construction can be used: 'John said his brother had been hit by an old friend'. If the second is intended, change *his brother* to *his own brother*.

21. Ambiguity

> Jane nursed her aged mother when she was dying from cancer

To make clear who was dying from cancer, say either 'When her aged mother was dying from cancer, Jane nursed her' or 'Jane nursed her aged mother though she herself was dying from cancer'.

The pronoun *it*, which has more potential referents than any other word in the English language, is especially prone to ambiguity.

> The government has mismanaged the economy and it will suffer as a consequence

Will the government suffer or the economy? If the first, say 'The government, having mismanaged the economy, will suffer ...' If the second, say *which will suffer* instead of *and it will suffer*.

The possibilities of misinterpreting the word *it* are increased by the fact that it also serves as a dummy subject.

> We didn't swim in the sea because it was too cold

Was the sea too cold or the weather? In place of *it* use either *the water* or *the weather* to make clear which is meant.

What the third-person pronoun refers to should be stated, not merely implied.

> After the divorce laws were liberalized they increased sharply

They refers grammatically to the plural antecedent *laws*, but is intended to refer to *divorces*, a noun premodifier expressed in the singular, as is usually the case in block compounds. Replace *they* by *divorces*.

The relative pronouns *which* and *who* are ambiguous if they have more than one antecedent. Occasionally there are as many as three referents to choose from.

> There is a library above the entrance to the museum, which is large and gloomy

The reader cannot be sure whether the museum library, the museum entrance or the museum itself is large and gloomy. If the first, say *There is a large gloomy library*; if the second, say *the museum entrance* instead of *the entrance to the museum*; if the third, say *the entrance to this large, gloomy museum*.

The pronoun *which* can refer to a specific antecedent or to the whole of the preceding clause, and this can lead to ambiguity.

> She kept bringing a little dog, which annoyed me

Is it the dog or the woman's constant bringing of the dog that annoyed the speaker? The first meaning can be expressed by saying *who* for *which*, and the second by saying *and that* instead of *which*.

Verb ambiguities

Auxiliary verbs often bear more than one interpretation. The verb *to be* may sometimes be taken in either of two modal senses or in either a modal or a non-modal sense.

    He is not to be put off

This may mean 'He cannot be put off' or 'He must not be put off'.

    She will not be beaten

This may mean 'She will win' or 'She is determined to win'.

    I asked him whether he would do it

Here *would* may mean 'was willing to' or 'intended to'.
    Most modal auxiliaries are susceptible to ambiguity.

    He can eat all the grapes

Can has two possible meanings, 'is able to' and 'is allowed to'.

    She could call tonight

She could call may mean 'It is possible that she will call' or 'It is convenient for her to call'.

    He could have gone to Russia

Could have gone means either 'may have gone' or 'had the opportunity to go but did not take it'.

    She may bring her boy-friend home

May could mean 'is allowed to' or 'will possibly'.

    He might earn fifty dollars in a day

Might means 'sometimes used to' or 'just possibly will'.

    He must be the leader

He must be can be taken to mean either 'It is necessary that he should be' or 'Presumably he is'.

    She should be in her office

Should be means either 'ought to be' or 'very probably is'.

Structural ambiguities

Ambiguity is found not only in the meaning of single words but in whole clauses and sentences. One and the same structure, for example, may sometimes be broken down into different constituent elements.

    We all admired that beautiful girl's dress

There is no way of telling whether *beautiful* refers to the girl or the

21. Ambiguity

dress. In the first interpretation *beautiful girl* is one constituent; in the second *girl's dress* is one constituent.

He needs some more suitable clothes

This may mean 'He needs some more clothes which are suitable' or 'He needs some clothes which are more suitable'. In the first case *more* is a quantifier; in the second it is a comparative. The constituents, enclosed in brackets, are *(some more) suitable clothes* and *some (more suitable) clothes* respectively.

Sometimes a preposition may be taken as part of a verb construction or as part of an adverb phrase.

He decided on the boat

This could mean 'He chose the boat' or 'He made his decision while on the boat'.

We sat there drinking in the moonlight

It is not sure whether the pleasure was in the spirit or of the spirit. Either 'We sat there drinking by the light of the moon' or 'We sat there contemplating the moonlight with rapture'.

The same surface structure may be derived from two different underlying structures and have two distinct meanings. This most often occurs with *-ing* forms, which may be adjectival participle, adverbial participle, gerund or adjective.

Kicking animals can be dangerous

This may mean 'Animals, when they kick, can be dangerous' or 'It can be dangerous to kick animals'.

He likes stimulating discussion

Here *stimulating* may mean either *to stimulate* or *which is stimulating*.

I like her singing

Here *her singing* may indicate the action of singing (= her to sing) or the manner of singing (= the way she sings).

I don't like that boy playing the drums

Does the speaker dislike the boy's drum-playing or the boy himself? It is not clear whether the participle *playing* is fused or not.

Verb forms in *-ed* can also be ambiguously participle or adjective.

John and Jane were married last year

This could mean that they got married last year or that they were still married last year.

Structural ambiguities can sometimes be easily resolved by more careful punctuation or spelling.

She eats simply in order to stay alive

The insertion of a comma after *simply* will show that it refers to what precedes; a comma placed before *simply* will indicate that it refers to what follows.

> We were much amused by the pickled herring merchant

Does the word *pickled* apply to the merchant or to the herrings he sells? The addition of a hyphen helps greatly here; *a pickled herring-merchant* is a drunken seller of herrings, whereas *a pickled-herring merchant* is one who sells pickled herrings. In such cases we may speak of a clarifying comma or a clarifying hyphen.

Negative ambiguities

Structural ambiguity can occur in negative sentences. The word *not*, when place before the verb, may refer to some other sentence element, and this can cause misunderstanding. The words *because* and *until* (*till*) are often ambiguous following a negative clause.

> Tom didn't marry her because he was poor.

It is unclear whether Tom did or did not marry, since *not* could modify *marry* or *because he was poor*. To elucidate, say either 'Because Tom was poor he didn't marry her' or 'It was not because Tom was poor that he married her'.

> John didn't sleep till mid-morning

Did John stay awake till mid-morning or did he wake up before then? This should be rephrased as either 'John didn't get to sleep till mid-morning' or 'John was awake before mid-morning'.

Not, followed by *one*, or *a single*, may be taken in two ways.

> I've not got one of those stamps

To make the meaning clear, say either *any of those stamps* or *just one of those stamps*.

> Don't rely on the advice of a single salesman

Clarify by saying *of just one salesman* or *of even one salesman* or, in this case, *of an unmarried salesman*.

A sentence containing *cannot* or *must not* followed by *too* plus an adverb may be read in two opposite ways.

> We can't punish them too severely

This could be interpreted as meaning either 'It would be wrong to inflict too severe a punishment on them' or 'No punishment we inflict on them could be too severe'.

When a negative clause is followed by an *as*-phrase or a *like*-phrase it is not always clear whether the negative carries over or not.

> The boy was not a thief, as his father said

Did the father say that his son was or was not a thief? This can be made clear by saying either 'The boy was not a thief, as his father said he was' or 'As his father said, the boy was not a thief'.

> He was no mathematician, like his brother

If the brother was no mathematician, say 'Like his brother, he was no mathematician'; if the brother was a mathematician, say 'Unlike his brother, he was no mathematician'.

Miscellaneous ambiguities

Possessive noun forms can often be understood in more than one way. *John's book* may be a book belonging to John, assigned to John, written by John or being read by John. *The creation of man* may be taken as a subjective genitive (what man has created) or an objective genitive (the creating of man by God).

> The criticism of the minister greatly embarrassed his colleagues

Who made the criticism, the minister or someone else? This can be clarified by saying either *The criticism made by the minister* or *The criticism made of the minister*.

The possessive adjective can likewise have a subjective or objective meaning.

> His exposure shocked his business partners

Here some extra words are needed to elucidate the meaning; either *His exposure of this scandal* (or whatever), or *His exposure by the media* (as a fraudster or whatever).

Linked genitives may create uncertainty about whether they refer to one or more than one thing or person. *The president's and the chairman's recommendations* may mean 'The joint recommendations of the president and the chairman' or 'the recommendations of the president and those of the chairman' and one of these longer forms should be used instead.

The same sort of ambiguity can arise with linked subjects or objects.

> Sir Edward, the Crown Prosecutor, and two other members objected

Are Sir Edward and the Crown Prosecutor the same person or two different persons? The first sense can be expressed by using brackets instead of commas: *Sir Edward (The Crown Prosecutor)*; the second by inserting the words *together with* before *the Crown Prosecutor* and placing the second comma after *members*.

> I turned for advice to my cousin and my best friend

The cousin and best friend could be taken as one person or two. If the cousin is also the best friend, say *who is my best friend*; if not, say *and to my best friend*.

When two nouns are used together and an adjective is placed before the first, there is always a risk of ambiguity.

>Old men and women were given free seats

If *old* applies to both men and women it should be repeated before *women*; if not, the phrase should be reversed to read *Women and old men*.

The phrases *as well as*, *if not*, and *so that* are sometimes ambiguous.

>The children endured this ordeal as well as the adults

The different meanings can be conveyed by saying *just as well as* (or *no less well than*) *the adults* or placing *as well as the adults* after *The children*.

>He wrote the best, if not the most exciting novel of the year

Was his novel the most exciting (as well as the best) or not? If it was not judged to be so, replace *if not* by *though not* or *even if not*; if it was judged to be possibly the most exciting too, replace *if not* by *perhaps even*.

>Someone took his trunks, so (that) he couldn't swim

So that may signify purpose or result, and *so* alone may signify result or, colloquially, purpose. To express purpose, say *so that he would not be able to swim*; to express result, say *so (that) he was not able to swim*.

Further examples

He's gone off fishing.
Is that your pudding?
What did you sell it for?
He's got a bloody cheek.
I thought you were a doctor.
We had our luggage taken.
I didn't believe them for a minute.
She sings as well as her sister.
My aunt couldn't bear children.
I wish I had a little girl like you.
Both the men and their wives were drunk.
I'll find out if my father is at home.
Is Henry applying for Yale or Harvard?
We must lose no time in answering such calls.
I do not believe that he eats snails, as you do.
They couldn't find a better man to do the job.
She changed her lovers as she changed her underwear.
He gave a brilliant lecture on Tolstoy's psychology.
A black cab driver was knifed outside the pub last night.
There is an acute shortage of American history teachers.

21. Ambiguity

The officers ordered the men to clean their quarters.
John phoned his brother an hour before he killed himself.
He has strong feelings regarding women's bare bosoms.
The parents of the bride and the groom were waiting for her.
Many men think their wives should wear their dresses longer.

22. Redundancy

Redundancy in speech and writing

Redundancy, or the use of unnecessary words, is not always to be condemned. It is a natural part of ordinary conversation, helping to keep up the flow and rhythm of thought. If redundancy and repetition were not a regular feature of informal speech, a mispronunciation by the speaker, a lapse of attention in the listener, or the intrusion of some noise could easily lead to a temporary breakdown in communication. When we are talking we have to improvise, we hesitate, make false starts, fumble for words, repeat ourselves, insert asides and leave sentences unfinished. Spontaneous discourse contains a good deal of redundant matter, including fillers such as *er, um, well, like, sort of*, lubricators such as *actually, I mean, you know*, and rhetorical questions such as *(all) right?, OK?* and *(y') know what I mean?* This is the stuff of normal conversational padding.

By contrast, the written language, except where it is used to mirror the spoken word, has no need of padding. Here redundancy serves no useful purpose because the reader, unlike the listener, can go back over what has been said. Indeed, superfluous words in writing are a hindrance, since they clutter the page and tend to confuse, distract or annoy the reader. They waste both time and paper. Written communication is most effective when it proceeds from the smallest number of words compatible with clarity. Hugh Blair made this a cardinal point of style when he wrote: 'The first rule which I shall give for promoting the strength of a sentence is to divest it of all redundant words' (*Lectures on Rhetoric*, 1783).

Pleonasm and tautology

There are two main kinds of redundancy: pleonasm and tautology. The first is an expression containing words which contribute nothing to the meaning, and the second is a repetition of the same idea in different words.

Pleonasms

When did they meet *up*?
Be more careful next time *round*

22. Redundancy

It is not clear at this moment *in time*
I couldn't make any sense *out* of it
This can be studied in any *given* situation
We must decide *as to* what should be done
I do not doubt *but* that he will come
We are reviewing the situation *on a* daily *basis*
More are sold here than in any other *single* country
He will change that, if *and when* he is elected
We won't move until *such time as* he gives the order
In *the course of* this article he made several errors

These sentences are pleonastic because the words in italics could be omitted without loss of meaning.

Tautologies

They *share* a *common* interest in music
They have a *mutual* dislike *of each other*
He was *forced* to sign the paper *against his will*
I've lived here *about* ten years *or so*
This place has a *unique* atmosphere *of its own*
These are *trivial* matters *of no importance*
She will *still*, of course, *continue to* need assistance
The *ordinary* man *in the street* is confused by all this
They are not *sufficiently* clever *enough* to catch him out
The discussions will be *confined to* labour relations *only*
If I were a millionaire, *which I am not*, I would buy a yacht
He *looked forward* to closer *future* co-operation with them

These sentences are tautological because each of them expresses the same idea twice in different ways. The italicized words which come second may be taken out, since they either repeat those which come first or are part of their meaning. Thus, *common* is implicit in *share*, for to share is to have or to use in common. *Of each other* merely repeats *mutual*, for a mutual dislike, by definition, is a dislike of each other. *Forced* means made to act *against one's will*, therefore we do not need this last phrase. Readers will readily detect for themselves the same type of flaw in the remaining sentences.

Types of tautology

Some tautological expressions, being established idioms, are acceptable. Such are the legal phrase *goods and chattels, rest, residue and remainder*, and *without let or hindrance*, and the everyday phrases *ways and means, by leaps and bounds, in any shape or form*, and *to all intents and purposes*. In such cases synonyms are used either to ensure comprehensiveness: *each* (individually) *and every* (collectively), or to add emphasis *the one* (single) *and only* (stressing uniqueness).

Much tautology, however, arises not from the use of synonyms but from the presence of one word or phrase whose meaning is incorporated in another one in the same sentence. The combination *but nor* has a sound use in qualifying one negative statement with another; by contrast the combination *and nor* is tautological, because *nor* by itself signifies 'and not'. In the phrase *out-of-date anachronism* the adjective is redundant because it forms part of the meaning of the noun. To speak of a *makeshift expedient* or a *temporary expedient* is to lapse into tautology, since expedients are by definition makeshift and temporary. To speak of *immigrants from other countries* is to use three words too many. In the sentence 'Tin is always scarce and there is never enough of it' there are seven wasted words after *scarce*. And even more words are squandered in the sentence 'Anthropology and linguistics were still in their infancy and their respective disciplines had only begun to develop'. As all the sense is expressed in the first part, we may lop off as an excrescence everything after *infancy*.

Abstract appendages

Abstract nouns are sometimes tacked on to another noun without adding to the sense. Words such as *condition*, *situation* and *state* are freely resorted to as appendages by people who mistakenly imagine that abstract terms add distinction or tone to their writing. But *in bad weather conditions* means no more than 'in bad weather', *in a crisis situation* means the same as 'in a crisis', and *in a state of coma* merely means 'in a coma'. Other abstract nouns are appended in the same way, nouns which have meaningful uses but are here pretentious verbiage. The italicized words in the examples below could be struck out to advantage.

> This was the subject of much research *activity*
> We had to accept the risk *factor*
> There was a rise in the price *level* of all goods
> This is the first stage in the freezing *process*
> We were both put on a diet *programme*
> The deal must be completed in a very short time *scale*
> The prestige *value* of this dialect has risen

Descriptive phrases containing an abstract noun also occur as unnecessary appendages. It is reasonable to say *ten metres in length*, distinguishing length from breadth, but the phrases *few in number, red in colour, small in size, stunted in growth* and *tubular in shape* all carry excess baggage since these adjectives relate only to number, colour, size, growth and shape. It would be just as absurd to say *hot in temperature, extreme in degree* or *worthless in value*.

The constructions *of a ... character* (or *nature*) and *in a ... condition* (or *state*) are generally used to eke out impoverished prose. *Acts of a hostile character* is a wordy way of saying *hostile acts*. 'The storms were of a violent nature' sounds less forceful than 'The storms were violent', 'She was in an agitated state' is a long-winded version of 'She was agitated', and 'The eggs are in a fresh condition' means no more than 'The eggs are fresh'.

Quiller-Couch made a strong attack on those who abuse the word *case*, and Fowler said of it that 'there is perhaps no single word so freely resorted to as a trouble-saver, and consequently responsible for so much flabby writing'. Yet plenty of people still use *case* needlessly, just 'in case'. The word has, of course, many legitimate uses, such as *a case of typhoid*, *cases of mistaken identity* and *in case of need*. But the sentence 'In the case of mammals this is unknown' does not need *the case of*, and *in most cases* could often be replaced by *mostly* or *usually*. A politician not long ago took the prize for *case*-abuse when he said in answer to an interviewer: 'In the case of my own case this has not been the case'.

As with cases, so with instances. It is usually possible to replace *in the first instance* by *first*, *in some instances* by *sometimes*, and *in this instance* by *here*. Less well advertised are the sins of the abstract phrase *in terms of*. It is often no more than a pretentious substitute for a simple preposition, e.g. 'He was not thinking in terms of a reward' (use *of*) and 'This makes no difference in terms of the total cost' (use *to*).

Redundant adjectives

In the expressions listed below the meaning of the adjective is embodied in that of the noun. They belong to the absurd, overgrown world of false lies and labyrinthine mazes.

absolute minimum	*grateful* thanks	*personal* belongings
added bonus	*grave* crisis	*positive* ideals
basic fundamentals	*hackneyed* cliché	*smug* complacency
conclusive proof	*important* essentials	*standard* norms
controversial issue	*indirect* allusion	*sweeping* generalization
essential prerequisite	*informal* chat	*sympathetic* compassion
exact replica	*joint* co-operation	*temporary* loan
false illusion	*keen* enthusiast	*total* annihilation
famous celebrity	*mutual* exchange	*true* facts
final completion	*necessary* requirement	*ultimate* conclusion
forward planning	*new* innovation	*unfilled* vacancy
free gift	*own* self-interest	*universal* panacea
general consensus	*past* history	

The word *single* is often used before a superlative adjective plus noun, as in *the single rarest jewel* and *the single most common cause*. But it is redundant here, since there can be only one rarest jewel or most common cause. It is acceptable, however, to speak of *the rarest single jewel* and *the most common single cause* because here *single* goes with the nouns *jewel* and *cause*, making an implicit contrast with a set of jewels and a complex of causes.

Redundant adverbs

These are found with words which embrace their meaning, with adjectives, verbs and other adverbs.

absolutely perfect	*first* begin	approach *nearer*
repeat *again*	*fully* sufficient	need not *necessarily*
or *alternatively*	but ... *however*	restrict to *only*
amply demonstrate	predict *in advance*	*over* again
besides ... *also*	must *inevitably*	may *perhaps*
prepare *beforehand*	*jointly* together	might *possibly*
carefully scrutinize	*just* exactly	could *potentially*
culpably to blame	*more* especially	*rather* prefer
adequate *enough*	increasingly *more*	more ... *rather* than
equally as	and ... *moreover*	*roughly* approximate
exactly identical	*mutually* interchangeable	so *therefore*
finally end		

Redundant particles

Adverbial particles added to a simple verb usually alter its meaning, giving a phrasal verb such as *eat up* (finish eating), *laugh off* (dismiss with a laugh) and *put up with* (tolerate). In pleonastic phrasal verbs the particles add nothing to the sense. Examples:

> debate *about*, discuss *about*, mention *about*, study *about*
> chase *after*, follow *after*
> erode *away*, file *away*, hide *away*
> recall *back*, reflect *back*, return *back*, revert *back*
> reduce *down*, swallow *down*
> add *in(to)*, examine *into*, penetrate *into*
> finish *off*, separate *off*, start *off*, trigger *off*
> continue *on*, elaborate *on*, forward *on*, linger *on*
> cancel *out*, drown *out*, protrude *out*, select *out*, try *out*
> collaborate *together*, join *together*, merge *together*
> block *up*, clutter *up*, connect *up*, divide *up*, seal *up*

Note, however, that *check up on, face up to, consult with* and *rest up*, which are sometimes objected to, are not synonymous with the corresponding simple verbs.

Redundant prepositions

A preposition sometimes pops up where it is not needed. The expression *for free*, in which *for* is borrowed from the synonymous *for nothing*, means no more than 'free (of charge)'. Other unnecessary prepositions occur in *at* about, where *at*, *from* henceforth, *in* between, from here on *in*, alongside *of*, inside *of*, off *of*, outside *of*, earlier *on*, later *on*, near *to* and full *up*.

Fore-and-aft prepositions are those put at the head of a *which*-clause and needlessly repeated at the end.

> This is a game of which he is very fond *of*

The redundancy comes of blending two constructions: *of which he is very fond* and *which he is very fond of*. This redundancy can also occur with a following pronoun, e.g.

> There were ten calls and of these we dealt with nine *of them*

The final *of them* can be discarded, being already expressed by *of these*.

In the combination *between ... and between* the second *between* is a gatecrasher. *For him and for her* means the same as *for him and her*, but *between him* and *between her* does not equal *between him and her*, since neither *between him* nor *between her* has any meaning on its own; *between* requires two singulars or a plural. For the same reason it is absurd to say 'There was a break between each act', meaning *between each act and the next* or *between acts*.

Other redundant function words

Besides prepositions, other function words (i.e. those which express a grammatical relationship) are sometimes used unnecessarily. A typical example of such redundancy is the 'shadow pronoun'.

> Here is the book which you asked me for *it*

The pronoun *it*, appropriate in a separate sentence, here simply duplicates *which*, referring to the book. When we have the substance we do not need the shadow.

In non-standard English *what* frequently inserts itself where it is not needed.

> She sang better than *what* he did

The *what* is brought in here by false analogy with such sentences as 'This is funnier than what he wrote', where *what* means 'that which'.

An adverbial *the* (= 'by that much') is sometimes placed before a single comparative inappropriately.

> His case would have been *the* stronger if he had produced witnesses

The purpose of a single adverbial *the* is to express not a condition but an added reason, e.g. 'His case was the stronger for his producing witnesses', implying that it was already strong for some other reason.

The infinitive marker *to* is sometimes an intruder.

What he must do is *to* work harder

Like most modal auxiliaries, *must* is used without *to*, e.g. 'He must work harder'. The *to* has been imported from similar expressions where it is necessary, such as 'He needs to work harder' and 'He ought to work harder'. Quite often needless repetition is also found in this construction, e.g. 'What he must do is *he must* work harder'.

Another common intruder is *have* after *had* in contrary-to-fact statements – a fault by no means confined to the illiterate.

I wish you hadn't *have* told me that

This unwanted *have* (pronounced *uv*) is evidently imported from modal verb combinations such as *would have* and *might have*, where it is used to indicate the past. But the auxiliary *had*, which itself expresses the past, has no need of *have*.

A redundant *have* also occurs sometimes with negated conditionals.

It would *have* not have happened in my time

Here the negative *would not have* has been confounded with the affirmative *would have*.

Redundant affixes

Sometimes a word is spoilt by the addition of an idle prefix or suffix. Thus the words *conjoin* and *self-confessed* do not need their first syllable; a thing is always joined with (*con-*) something else, and confession can never be vicarious. Other examples.

Prefixes: *co*-equal, *co*-partner, *inter*connect, *inter*mingle, *over*-exaggerate, *over*-idealize, *over*-simplistic, *pre*-book, *pre*-plan
Suffixes: much*ly*, over*ly*, thus*ly*

These three hyper-adverbs are products of the mania for spreading the suffix *-ly* to more and more adverbs. *Muchly* and *thusly* are harmless enough since they are used wittingly and facetiously. But *overly*, which is common American usage, has drawbacks when compared with the simple prefix *over-*, meaning 'excessively'. *Over-ripe* matches *under-ripe*, whereas *overly ripe* lacks a matching *underly ripe*. The matching usage is also consistent with that found in verbs, e.g. *overplay* and *underplay*.

Verbosity and circumlocution

Besides pleonasm and tautology there are two other kinds of redundancy: verbosity (long-winded phrasing) and circumlocution (roundabout phrasing). These two ills are cured by the surgery not of excision but replacement.

A liking for high-sounding phrases and convoluted sentences is typical of speakers and writers who suffer from logorrhoea. How much better than the pompous and ponderous 'We are not cognizant of his whereabouts at this particular point in time' is the simple 'We do not know where he is now'. The council official who said 'In the majority of instances the accommodation units are not marketable' could have put it more simply by saying 'Most of the flats cannot be sold'. The head of a civil service department who wrote 'I shall cause enquiries to be made with a view to ascertaining the facts' could have reduced this verbiage to a plain 'I shall find out what happened'. Official letters do not need to be padded out with such phrases as *it is appreciated that ...*, *it should be noted that ...* and *it may be recalled that*.

Circumlocution is a roundabout form of verbosity. In Dickens's *Little Dorrit* (1855–7) 'the Circumlocution Office' was a satirical name given to all government departments because of the devious formality with which they conducted their business, giving evasive replies, hiding behind heaps of paper and passing the buck. The finest specimen of circumlocution in Dickens, however, is to be found in a better-known novel. 'Under the impression,' said Mr Micawber, 'that your peregrinations in this metropolis have not yet been extensive, and that you might have some difficulty in penetrating the arcana of the Modern Babylon in the direction of the City Road – in short,' said Mr Micawber, in another burst of confidence, 'that you might lose yourself – I shall be happy to call this evening ...' (*David Copperfield*, 1849–50).

Circumlocution often appeals to those in office, or aspiring to it. An alderman once objected to the words 'He died poor', which Canning had used in his inscription beneath a statue to Pitt the Younger. In their place the worthy gentlemen proposed 'He expired in indigent circumstances', a sorry blend of circumlocution and euphemism. More recently an official wrote, after returning from a Third World country: 'Marked signs of malnutrition were exhibited by a considerable proportion of the non-adult population, who frequently utilized larvae for sustenance'. Stripped of its abstract Latinate vocabulary and translated into plain, direct English, this would read: 'Many of the children were starving and they often ate grubs'.

The intention is no doubt to amuse if one says 'He evinced a disinclination to depart' for 'He seemed unwilling to leave', or 'He requested vehicular assistance from the place of alcoholic refreshment' for 'He asked for a lift from the pub', but the humour, like the wording, is heavy. Except for some special effect, circumlocution, like other forms of redundancy, is to be shunned. The shorter, straightforward expression generally has greater force and is easier to understand. Your prose, like your rose, is better for a good pruning.

Further examples

She is not as bad as what he is.
They arrived here at 9 a.m. in the morning.
The main place of education is in the home.
The risks have been minimized to the utmost.
This is to the mutual benefit of both parties.
I do not like flying and nor does my husband.
The bill will be in the region of about £20 million.
The use of a title need not necessarily imply respect.
The council pay my rent, which I am grateful for that.
This reform is no panacea to cure all ills.
This was obviously a case of tit-for-tat retaliation.
What we are concerned with is what potentially could happen.
This strike activity led to many job losses.
He is more ready to blame others rather than himself.
These ingredients are combined together to make a thick dough.
She is on her fourth attempt at trying to give up heroin.
There was pressure from many quarters, including from the Treasury.
In terms of sheer numbers, far more women were killed than men.
Children are born with an innate ability to manipulate adults.
I'd have felt much more better if I'd have won.
In my own personal opinion, he is equally as blameworthy as his wife.
You can see the results of the crystallization process in these specimens.
Much beatnik poetry is improvised on the spur of the moment.
Out of 250 firms fifty of them are foreign.
He restricted his talk to only the most important features.

23. Grammatical Praxis

The sentences below illustrate various faults of grammar. Comments and suggested improvements are given at the end.

1. Quantitatively, America has the most historians of any other country in the world.
2. The number of errors are surprisingly few.
3. Your passport is required by the embassy secretary when applying for a visa.
4. Kay would have like to have played Lady Macbeth as a drama student.
5. When on his regular trips to New York, his love of jazz would emerge.
6. After receiving this notice, your refuse collection day will be on Friday.
7. When out of work, the state pays your unemployment benefit.
8. This would mean marriage, which I don't want to get into that situation.
9. What I am absolutely certain is that we must change the law.
10. Gorbachev cannot be attributed to the failure of perestroika.
11. He was reported to have asked for and was granted asylum in France.
12. If he were the oldest member of the club, he was also the fittest.
13. Temperance is one of those words that has changed its meaning.
14. This video film cannot be bought by children under 14, even if their parents wish them to.
15. The society having lost its subsidy, it now depends on donations.
16. Once safely back in the office, how satisfying to sip your coffee.
17. Though widely reported by the Irish media, the English press did not cover the President's visit to Gross Ile.
18. It didn't help the rich so much as harming the poor.
19. You could not pass his door without he heard you.
20. We worked out just how much food should the pandas have every day.
21. Like many former mining villages, work is scarce in Aberfan.
22. There seems to be as many scented blooms overhead as underfoot.
23. Can you afford not to miss another big-priced winner?

24. He said he'll be surprised if I came first.
25. He had no alternative but to resign.
26. Much as I dislike doing so, the blame must lie with the US Navy.
27. It is likely that the government may well alter this law.
28. Unmethodical and unpunctual, nobody could have been less suitable than Dennis for the job.
29. The European Union is far from perfect; no political institution is.
30. His hair was combed down over the forehead, as small boys do.
31. Looking at we journalists, our difficulties are considerable.
32. Not every school is doing as much as they could to stamp out bullying.
33. As a junior minister, there is no real power.
34. For most of us, we don't depend on hard drugs.
35. Few actors, except Gielgud, could have played the part successfully.
36. I'm going to show you something like you've never seen before.
37. He writes scrawl on purpose so you can't hardly read it.
38. We can now see what each of these items have in common.
39. It was sent to my old address, which I haven't been there for weeks.
40. No language is uniform, but exists in several varieties at all times.
41. He advised me to take a holiday, which I intend to do so.
42. They weren't doing anything other than to claim their rights.
43. They knew what each other was doing.
44. This was the snobbery so common among a certain type of middle-class woman.
45. Among the most important developments of recent years have been the discovery of pulsars.
46. This was the work of a group of friends, the most important of whom being Picasso.
47. We have long ago forgotten such dreams.
48. The more criminals arm themselves, so the public fear increases.
49. If the Danes fail to ratify the treaty, neither shall we.
50. No black soldier has yet to command a British regiment.

1a. 'The most historians of any other country' is an illogical crossed construction, which should be replaced by 'more historians than any other country' or 'the most historians of all countries'. In addition, the word *quantitatively* is redundant since *most* expresses quantity.
2a. False agreement. *The number of* takes a singular verb (*is*). And the co-occurrence of *number* and *few* is tautological. Say either 'The number of errors is surprisingly small' or 'The errors are surprisingly few'.
3a. False ellipsis. The words 'when applying for a visa' are attached to *the embassy secretary*, but it is clearly not the secretary, but an

23. Grammatical Praxis   179

applicant, who wishes to obtain a visa. The real subject should be inserted in the abbreviated clause to make it a full clause: 'when you are applying for a visa'.

4a. Crossed construction, arising from verb harmonization. The form 'would have liked to have played' is a double perfect. Moreover, the phrase *as a drama student* is misplaced, since it refers to the student Kay, not to Lady Macbeth. Amend to read: 'As a drama student Kay would have liked to play Lady Macbeth'.

5a. If only his love of jazz emerged on his trips to New York, what happened to the rest of him? To avoid the false attachment either delete *when* and the comma or begin with a full clause: 'When he was on his regular trips to New York'.

6a. The words 'After receiving this notice' are misrelated to *your refuse collection* and should be replaced by 'After you have received this notice'. And the day will be *Friday*, not *on Friday*.

7a. False ellipsis. The state, as we all know, is never out of work, but you might well be. Expand the first part to read: 'When you are out of work'.

8a. Crossed construction. The speaker produces a perfectly sound sub-clause 'which I don't want to get into', then spoils it by adding *that situation*, which turns the words after *which* into a main clause. Replace *which* by *and*, or delete *which* and say 'a situation I don't want to get into'.

9a. The word *of* or *about* is needed after *certain*. The omission no doubt comes from the speaker being unconsciously influenced by the synonymous statement: 'I am absolutely certain that we must change the law'.

10a. False attribution. Responsibility should be attached to the doer, not the action. Reverse to read: 'The failure of perestroika cannot be attributed to Gorbachev'.

11a. Broken construction. Like the request for asylum, the granting of it was part of what was reported, not an established fact. Thus the second verb form should parallel the first and read *to have been granted*.

12a. The pseudo-subjunctive *were* should be replaced by *was*, since the statement is one of fact, not supposition. And as the truth of the second part (*he was the fittest*) is not dependent on the truth of the first part (*he was the oldest*), the non-conditional *if* should be replaced by *although*.

13a. The verb form *has changed* mistakenly agrees with the singular subject *temperance* instead of the plural phrase *those words*. A second fault, consistent with the first, is the use of a following singular pronoun. The sentence should end 'that have changed their meaning'.

14a. The sentence should end with an active verb, i.e. *to buy it*, since the antecedent verb *be bought* is passive and therefore cannot be understood after *wish them to*. Alternatively, an active construction can be used in the first part, so that the sentence reads: 'Children under 14 cannot buy this video film, even if their parents wish them to'.

15a. An absolute construction has its own subject, which is different from that of the main clause. Its use is inappropriate when the subject is the same, as here. Delete *it* and place a second comma after *society*.

16a. It is acceptable to omit *it is* in the main clause after *satisfying*, but not to omit the subject and verb *you are* in the sub-clause, since the subject *you* is only referred to obliquely, by the pronoun *your*.

17a. False ellipsis, leading to false attachment. The English press was not widely reported by the Irish media. Either start with a full clause: 'Though it was widely reported by the Irish media', or convert the second clause into a passive: 'the President's visit to Gross Ile was not covered by the English press'.

18a. Non-matching verb forms. *Help* in the first part calls for *harm* in the second. Compare the sentence 'She wasn't singing so much as screaming', with matching *-ing* forms.

19a. The construction *without* plus a finite verb is good old English but bad modern English. Today an *-ing* form is used, giving here 'without him/his hearing you'.

20a. Broken construction. The word order of direct speech has been imposed on the reported version. Transpose *should* to stand after *the pandas*.

21a. False attachment, leading to false comparison. Work is likened to many former mining villages. The intended comparison is between Aberfan and many similar villages where work is scarce. Either replace *like* by *as in*, or recast the second clause to read: 'Aberfan has little work to offer'.

22a. False agreement. *There seems*, in the singular, is such a common initial phrase that the writer has been seduced from the *scented blooms*, which should *seem* to be overhead and underfoot.

23a. The writer has fallen into the hidden negative trap. As the verb *to miss* has the negative meaning 'not to get', the use of another *not* yields the sense 'not to not to get', which is the opposite of what is meant. Strike out *not*.

24a. False sequence of tenses, caused by confusing the forms of a real conditional and a hypothetical conditional. To express the first, use the future in the main clause and the simple present in the *if*-clause: 'He said he'll be very surprised if I come first'. To express the second, use the conditional in the main clause and the simple past in the *if*-clause: 'He said he'd (he would) be very surprised if I came first'.

25a. A common confusion of forms. Either 'He had no choice but to resign' or 'He had no alternative to resigning'.

26a. This broken construction, with its dangling *doing so*, requires repair to one or other of the two clauses. Either rebuild the first to read: 'Much as I dislike saying this' or the second to read: 'I must put the blame on the US Navy'.

27a. Double expression of probability, caused by crossing two different constructions. Either delete 'It is likely that' or substitute *will* for *may well*.

28a. It is not *nobody*, but *Dennis*, who is unmethodical and unpunctual. Amend to read: 'Nobody could have been less suitable for the job than Dennis, unmethodical and unpunctual as he was' or 'Unmethodical and unpunctual, Dennis was as unsuitable for the job as anyone could be'.

29a. False ellipsis. The second *is* should be followed by *perfect*, since the sentence as it stands states that no political institution is far from perfect.

30a. Broken construction. The active pro-verb *do* has no proper antecedent; what it refers to is the passive form *was combed down*. Either begin with 'He combed his hair down' or finish with 'like that of small boys'.

31a. Misrelated participle, nob's pronoun and logical gap. Whether one is looking at us (not *we*) journalists or not, our difficulties are considerable. The logical gap could be filled by saying 'Looking at us journalists, you can see that our difficulties are considerable'. But this still leaves an illogical link between the looking and the difficulties. The link can be severed by saying 'Look at us journalists; our difficulties are considerable'.

32a. The phrase *not every school* should be followed by a singular *it*. *They* requires a plural antecedent, i.e. *not all schools*, followed by *are*.

33a. False attachment. The *as*-phrase is hooked on to the dummy subject *there*, instead of a real subject. Replace *there is* by *one has* or *you have*.

34a. Confusion of forms. Amend the first part to read: 'As for most of us' or rephrase the second part to read: 'hard drugs are not a necessity'.

35a. False exclusion. The word *except* excludes Gielgud from the class *few actors*, producing the opposite sense to that intended. The fault arises from treating *few actors* in the same way as *no actor*. The word needed here is not *except*, but *besides*.

36a. The word *like* should be followed by a noun or a noun phrase, but is followed here by the clause 'you've never seen before'. Instead of *like* say *such as* or *the like of which*.

37a. *Hardly* goes with an affirmative verb, *can*, not the negative *can't*, and purpose is better expressed by *so that* than by *so* alone.

38a. False agreement. *Each* requires the singular verb *has*, and *in common*, which goes with a plural subject, should be extended to *in common with the others*. Alternatively, *each* may be replaced by *all*.

39a. *There* (= at that place) does not go with the relative pronoun

which. Say either 'which I hadn't been at for weeks' or 'where I hadn't been for weeks'.
40a. Overreaching negative. Insert *each* before *exists* or start 'A language is not uniform'.
41a. *Which* and *so* are both doing the same job, standing proxy for the phrase 'to take a holiday'. Say either 'which I intend to do' or 'and I intend to do so'.
42a. Non-parallel constructions. The participle form *doing* is matched by *claiming*, not *to claim*. The infinitive would be appropriate if there were also one in the first part, e.g. 'They weren't trying to do anything other than (to) claim their rights'.
43a. False distribution. The reciprocal pronoun *each other* serves as object, not subject. Here its parts should be distributed between the two clauses, making the sentence read: 'They each knew what the other was doing'.
44a. The word *among* takes a plural, but we cannot say *types*, because only one type of woman is mentioned. Instead we must change *woman* to *women* and make this, not *type*, the head word of the phrase. The sentence should thus end 'among middle-class women of a certain type'.
45a. The verb *to be* is not only in the wrong number (plural instead of singular), but also in the wrong tense (perfect instead of present). Replace *have been* by *is*.
46a. Crossed construction in the sub-clause. Say either 'the most important of them being Picasso' or 'the most important of whom was Picasso'.
47a. Clash of temporal viewpoint. *Ago* refers to a point of time in the past, whereas the present perfect tense indicates a period of time stretching from the past to the present. Say either 'We long ago forgot such dreams' or 'We have long forgotten such dreams'.
48a. Broken construction, caused by confusing two different pairs of correlatives. Say either 'The more criminals arm themselves, the more the public fear increases' or 'As more criminals arm themselves, so the public fear increases'.
49a. Neither shall we fail to ratify it? *Neither* needs to refer to something that is explicitly negative, not a word such as *fail*, which is negative in sense but not in form. Replace *fail to* by *do not* or *neither shall we* by *so shall we*.
50a. Confusion of synonymous expressions. Say either 'No black soldier has yet commanded a British regiment' or 'A black soldier has yet to command a British regiment'.

24. Stylistic Praxis

The sentences below illustrate various faults of style. Comments and suggested improvements are given at the end.

1. And why did they pay no notice?
2. The man who threw an egg at the mayor was forgiven by the civic chief after an apology to the town's first citizen.
3. The simplest solution in such a situation is simply to adopt the Latin word.
4. Both houses of the new Russian parliament met separately.
5. I once shot an elephant in my pyjamas.
6. We live in a nation that desperately needs reform.
7. Every single boy in the class with absolute unanimity voted her the best teacher.
8. She opened the envelope – it was not sealed – and found a love letter.
9. They recommended that the hospital closes and its work be transferred to clinics.
10. Men and women wear trousers and knickers and skirts respectively.
11. The end result of violence begets more violence.
12. We need to get more qualified people on the committee.
13. We believe that this is something we, unlike the Americans, do rather badly.
14. The minister did not recall being appraised about the trade deal.
15. It is very evident from many of the current essays being produced that standards have undoubtedly fallen.
16. The report shows that malignant melanoma has shown an overall increase over the period from 1979 to 1987.
17. We have to restore the standing of the BBC's reputation with the public.
18. These recent immigrants live in the oldest and most run-down housing.
19. However the reform may turn out in the end to have been a great mistake.
20. Russian women have a fascination for British men.
21. Usually there was some ulterior motive behind all his actions.

22. A man denied indecently exposing himself when he appeared before Leeds magistrates yesterday.
23. Should we teach the rules of spelling, and if so to what level of student?
24. Community problems have to be everyone pulling together.
25. Ask inside for further enquiries.
26. Jane is closer to her father than her mother.
27. That report from our Paris correspondent John Taylor.
28. Betts outwitted those who tried to stop him gaining power by various forms of bribery.
29. American tennis champion John McEnroe was involved in a heated dispute yesterday.
30. We saw the youth lying beside a girl with no clothes on.
31. Damage from the blast was kept to the lowest possible minimum.
32. His condition can only be improved by a liver transplant.
33. By definition, social workers come in for a lot of public criticism.
34. The sprightly humour of Andrew and the simple wisdom of Simon are among the characters who bring the tale to life.
35. These reforms were electorally very popular, including among trade unionists.
36. Each meal is microwaved, one at a time.
37. We sympathized with the President's decision to retire and expressed gratitude for his achievements.
38. The difficulty will be overcome by the commission sitting in Brussels.
39. The following categories will not have to pay, i.e. will be exempt.
40. There is no objection to the publication of exam results as such.
41. No sharp distinction between an artefact and a work of art can be made, however.
42. The blackmailer tried to extort Jackson for a large sum of money.
43. During this period the dictates of social Darwinism were embraced by the power structure.
44. Explain the reasons for your preference.
45. The importance of this law is because it protects children.
46. What the government should do is it should abolish the tax.
47. This sentence does not hang together.
48. If one wants to perfect one's French, you need to go to France.
49. This is a rare instance of where customers cannot choose.
50. You can expect congestion, heading in from South Wales.

1a. Mixed idioms. Either *take no notice* or *pay no attention*. It should be noted that there is no grammatical objection to beginning a sentence, as here, with the word *and*, but repeatedly doing so is bad style. The schoolteachers' ban is well motivated, but too extreme.
2a. *The civic chief* and *the town's first citizen* are examples of 'elegant variation', used here to avoid repeating the word *mayor*. Replace

24. Stylistic Praxis

the civic chief by *him*, and delete *to the town's first citizen* as unnecessary. Better still, rephrase in the active: 'After receiving an apology, the mayor forgave the man who threw an egg at him'.

3a. Clash of sounds and syllables. There are too many sibilants for euphony and the use of *simplest* and *simply* in the same sentence grates on the ear. These stylistic defects can be remedied by saying 'The easiest solution in such cases is to adopt the Latin word'.

4a. *Both* is used to denote two things or people which have something in common, e.g. 'Both rooms are full' and 'Both girls play hockey'. But here a difference is being expressed. The houses met at different times or in different places. Hence *Both houses* should be replaced by *The two houses*.

5a. In the film *Animal Crackers* Groucho Marx idiosyncratically follows this remark by saying 'How he got into my pyjamas I'll never know'. In the real world the pyjamas can be restored to their rightful owner by fronting the phrase *in my pyjamas*.

6a. Sloppy expression, confusing people (nation) with place (country). Say either 'We belong to a nation' or 'We live in a country'.

7a. Redundancy and number confusion. *Single* is not needed with *every boy*, and the phrase *with absolute unanimity* is not only redundant in the context of *every boy*, it is also inconsistent with a singular subject, since one person cannot be unanimous. Say 'Every boy (*or* All the boys) in the class voted her the best teacher'.

8a. Primitive syntax, of the kind used by semi-literate journalists, in which secondary matter is inserted without being integrated. The parenthetic main clause is better expressed as a dependent clause linked by a relative pronoun to the main clause: 'She opened the envelope, which was not sealed, and found a love letter'.

9a. Inconsistent verb forms. Use either subjunctives, *close* or *be closed* and *be transferred*, or non-subjunctives, *closes* and *is transferred*.

10a. A sartorial conundrum. As the three garments are distributed between the two sexes, the question arises 'Which has the knickers?' The word *respectively* is often misused, or used unnecessarily, as here. Write 'Men wear trousers; women wear knickers and skirts' (regardless of modern mores).

11a. A veritable dog's dinner. It is not the result of violence but violence itself that begets further violence. The word *beget* implies a result and the expression *end result* means no more than *result*, since a result necessarily comes at the end of any activity, so *end* can be dispensed with. Say either 'Violence begets violence' or 'The result of violence is more violence'.

12a. Ambiguity. In the phrase *more qualified people* the word *more* could refer to *qualified people* or to *qualified* alone. The ambiguity can be removed by saying either 'We need to get more people who are qualified (*or* with qualifications) on the committee' or 'We need to get better qualified people (or people who are more qualified) on the committee'.

13a. Confusingly, the word *we* is used in two different senses in the same sentence. The first *we* is the editorial *we*, while the second stands for the nation, i.e. *we British*. The latter could be replaced by *our people* or *the people of this country*.

14a. This sentence contains a malapropism and a misconstruction. *Appraised* (= evaluated) should be *apprised* (= notified). And *apprised* is constructed with *of*, not *about*, which has probably been taken from the synonymous *informed about*.

15a. This sentence carries excess baggage. If we throw out the words *very*, *undoubtedly* and either *current* or *being produced*, the sense remains the same.

16a. The word *overall* and the phrase *over the period*, contributing nothing to the sense, may be taken out. The perfect verb form *has shown* would be appropriate if the period stated were *from 1979 to the present* or *since 1979*, but as the period 1979 to 1987 does not relate to the present, the verb form should be *showed*. Since we already have one *show* in the sentence the second is best avoided by saying *increased* instead of *showed an increase*. The revised version now reads: 'This report shows that malignant melanoma increased by 50% from 1979 to 1987'.

17a. Tautology: either *the standing of the BBC* or *the BBC's reputation*, but not both.

18a. Bad diction: people live in houses, not in housing, just as they pay taxes, not taxation.

19a. A garden-path sentence. The reader is misled at first into thinking that the sense is 'Whatever the result of the reform may be'. The false scent is laid by using *however*, in the sense *nevertheless*, without a following comma. It could equally well be placed parenthetically ('The reform may, however, turn out in the end ...').

20a. This sentence could be misconstrued since the context in which it occurred did not make clear whether British men are fascinated by Russian women or vice versa. Until recently it could only have had the first meaning, but fascination is now often switched from the person or thing that fascinates to the one who is fascinated. The first, original sense can be expressed by saying 'hold (*not* have) a fascination for' and the second by saying 'have a fascination with (*not* for)'.

21a. Illogicality. If all the person's actions had an ulterior motive, than they always had such a motive, not just usually. Delete either *all* or *usually*, according to the sense intended.

22a. Misplacement. The two clauses should be reversed to make clear that the man did not expose himself indecently in the courtroom, but denied self-exposure somewhere else.

23a. False dependency. The question is whether spelling rules should be taught not to a level but to a student (i.e. students). Reverse the roles of head noun and dependent genitive, so as to say *to students of what level*.

24a. False equation. There is no existential connection between *community problems* and *everyone pulling together*. The logical gap in this badly worded sentence needs to be filled by inserting some such words as *dealt with by* between *have to be* and *everyone*.

25a. 'May I have further enquiries, please?' would be a stupid thing to say to a shopkeeper, but that is what the notice invites us to do. The co-occurrence of *ask* and *enquiries* is tautological. Substitute *information* for *enquiries*, or say 'Enquire further within'.

26a. Ambiguous comparison. Resolve the doubt by saying either 'Jane is closer to her father than to her mother' or 'Jane is closer to her father than her mother is'.

27a. Gimmicky mediaspeak. Similar *is*-less phrases are 'Today's newsreader – William Scott' and 'The number to ring – 01800-2121'. Complete the predicate by restoring the missing verb *to be*.

28a. Ambiguous placement. Make clear who did the bribing. If it was Betts move the phrase 'by various forms of bribery' to the head of the sentence. If it was his enemies rephrase the last part and say 'who used various forms of bribery in an attempt to stop him gaining power'.

29a. Timespeak. Cramming a descriptive noun phrase in front of a person's name is a device known as 'the false title'. Introduced by the magazine *Time*, it is now a common feature of journalese, though it runs counter to idiom, both in word order and in omission of the article. Instead of 'American tennis champion John McEnroe' say 'John McEnroe, the American tennis champion'.

30a. Ambiguous reference. Who had no clothes on, the youth or the girl? If the youth, put the phrase *with no clothes on* after the word *youth*; if the girl, say 'who had no clothes on'.

31a. Tautology. Delete the words *lowest possible*, since a minimum is by definition 'the lowest possible' or 'the least amount'.

32a. More precise wording is needed in order to avoid the ambiguity of the word *only*. Say either 'is bound to be improved by a liver transplant' or 'can be improved only by a liver transplant'.

33a. The phrase *by definition* is often misused, as here. Attracting public criticism is no part of the definition of a social worker, though it may be an occupational hazard. Instead of *by definition* say here *by the very nature of their work*.

34a. Loose style. The qualities of the characters are confused with the characters themselves. Recast the first part to read: 'Andrew, with his sprightly humour and Simon, with his simple wisdom'.

35a. An ill-constructed sentence. The phrase *electorally popular* is somewhat obscure and the word *including*, which here has no antecedent, never needs a following preposition. Reword to read:

'These reforms were very popular with the electors, including trade unionists'.

36a. The phrase *one at a time* refers to several things and therefore does not fit with the singular *each meal*. Say either 'The meals are microwaved one at a time' or 'Each meal is microwaved individually'.

37a. Misplaced sympathy and gratitude. It is people, not abstractions, that are the object of our sympathy and gratitude. Say 'We sympathized with the President in his decision to retire and expressed gratitude to him for his achievements'.

38a. Ambiguous *-ing* form. Is this a statement of expectation or a conditional statement? If *sitting* is a participle, this can be made clear by saying *which is sitting*. If *sitting* is a gerund, this can be shown by making it a possessive gerund, *the commission's sitting*.

39a. Cart-before-the-horse trouble. If the word *exempt* were used first it would be reasonable to explain its meaning, which is not familiar to everyone. But the phrase *will not have to pay* is transparent and needs no gloss. This explanation in reverse is like saying 'The king gave up the throne, i.e. abdicated'.

40a. As-suchery. The phrase *as such*, if taken with *exam results*, is redundant, since exam results can only be themselves. If *as such* is intended to refer to the publication of exam results, the idea could be better expressed as 'There is no objection in principle to the publication of exam results'.

41a. A top-heavy or, to be more accurate, front-heavy sentence. It flows much more easily if the long-delayed predicate and the adverb *however* are made to break up the lengthy subject, so as to read: 'No sharp distinction can be made, however, between an artefact and a work of art'.

42a. False construction. It is money that is extorted, not people. Rephrase to read: 'The blackmailers tried to extort a huge sum of money from Jackson'.

43a. Abstract jargon, typical of sociologese. Who ever saw a power structure embrace dictates? *The power structure* here presumably means not 'the hierarchy of power' but 'those in power', and *the dictates* appears to be used for *the doctrine*.

44a. We do not need both *explain* and *reasons*, since the giving of reasons is an explanation. Say either 'Explain your preference' or 'Give the reasons for your preference'.

45a. Misused conjunction. It is a fact, not a reason, that makes the law important, hence *that* should be used, not *because*. Alternatively one could say 'This law is important because it protects children'; here *because* is appropriate, since a reason is being given.

46a. Strike out the redundant *it should*, which merely echoes *the government should*.

47a. The criticism applies to the quoted sentence itself. *Together* goes with two or more things, but *sentence* is singular. To express the idea with precision change the subject and say 'The parts of this sentence do not hang together'.

48a. Change of standpoint. Be consistent and use either *one* or *you* in both instances, not a mixture of the two.

49a. The word *of* is introduced here needlessly, no doubt as a result of confusion with the synonymous statement: 'This is a rare instance of customers being unable to choose'.

50a. Back-to-frontery. This congestion, contrary to all experience, appears to be mobile. To restore it to its proper state of immobility put the phrase 'heading in from South Wales' at the beginning.

Punctuation

When speaking, we make use of rhythm, stress, intonation, pauses and gestures, in order to help make ourselves understood. But none of these are available to us when we write, so we must rely on punctuation to convey our meaning accurately. Thus punctuation marks are not optional frills, but an indispensable part of any writing. The different marks serve a variety of purposes, but their chief function is to make clear the relationships between the words and elements in a sentence, showing which are linked and which are separate. The golden rule is to use as few punctuation marks as the sense allows.

apostrophe: The raised sign (') is mainly used to combine with or replace the possessive ending *-s*. Singular nouns have *'s* (*the boy's room*, *Brown's room*, *an MP's pay*, *a month's time*); plural nouns have *-s'* (*the boys' room*, *the Browns' room*, *MPs' pay*, *three months' time*), but plurals not ending in *-s* add *'s* (*women's magazines*, *children's toys*). Nouns and names ending in *-s* in the singular usually add *'s* (*the boss's chair*, *Dickens's novels*, *Thomas's hat*, *Mavis's coat*, *Mr Jones's car*, *St James's Park*), but names ending in *-es*, pronounced *-iz* or *-eez*, may take an apostrophe with or without a second *-s* (*Bridges's/Bridges' poems*), and only without in the case of biblical and classical Greek names (*Moses' rod*, *Hercules' feats*, *Socrates' death*). The same rules apply to group genitives such as *the Duke of York's men* or *the man next door's dog*, and to possessives in which the name of a place has been dropped, such as *the doctor's [surgery]*, *the barber's [shop]* and *Emma's [house]*.

The apostrophe has two minor uses: (1) to express a plural form of letters (*dot your i's*) and cited words (*too many of 's*); (2) to indicate the omission of a letter or letters (*o'er* for *over*, *she'll* for *she will*, *isn't* for *is not*) or the figures denoting a century when a decade is referred to (*the '40s* for *the 1940s*): note that clipped words such as *flu* for *influenza*, and *phone* for *telephone*, no longer take an initial apostrophe.

Apostrophes are often misused. The possessive form *its* is frequently confused with the contraction *it's*, which is short for *it is* or *it has*, and the possessive *whose* ('belonging to whom') is confused with *who's*, which stands for *who is* or *who has*. But the commonest misuse is the so-called shopkeeper's (or greengrocer's) apostrophe, which is placed before nouns with a regular plural in -*s*, as in signs reading *Ripe Tomato's, Fresh Pie's, Propertie's Wanted, Video's for Hire*, and even – making a new singular – *Chee's*. The errant tadpole, as it has been called, has no place here. It is now commonly omitted in shop and other signs, partly perhaps through fear of misuse; nowadays many such signs read *Boys Shoes, Ladies Wear, Barclays Bank, Students Union*, etc. The best advice regarding the use of the apostrophe is: if in doubt, leave it out.

brackets: A pair of symmetrical signs, either round ( ), or square [ ]. The term brackets denotes the square type in American usage, but is normally used for the round type in British English. Round brackets (or parentheses) have four uses:

(1) to separate titles, dates, page numbers, and other references cited in a text, e.g. 'in a work by D. Crystal (*The English Language*, 1988, p. 62)', 'in the Bible (Job 5:18–24)', 'in the novels of Aphra Behn (1640–89)';

(2) to give or explain an abbreviation, as in 'the party's National Executive Committee (NEC)' and 'the role of the SAS (Special Air Service)';

(3) to enclose figures or letters used to distinguish items in a list, i.e. (1), (2), (3), etc. or (a), (b), (c), etc. (here a single bracket or full stop may also be used);

(4) to mark off parenthetic matter, e.g. an addition: 'He is (as he always was) a complete fool'; a definition: 'He drew an isosceles triangle (one with two sides of equal length)'; an example: 'The plural is formed by adding -*s* (dogs, eggs)'; or another name for a person: 'Cary Grant (real name Archibald Alexander Leach)' or place: 'in Ceylon (now Sri Lanka)'.

See also **square brackets**.

colon: The symbol (:) marks a break between two closely related statements that are not joined by a conjunction. Below are given its main uses, which are generally an alternative to some other form of punctuation and/or wording (here indicated in brackets after each example):

(1) to introduce a list or summary: 'You will need the following: a map, a compass, and a torch' (or a colon-dash, i.e. :–, but this is rarely used now);

(2) to introduce an explanation: 'I gave up: I was just too tired' (or a dash);

(3) to introduce quoted direct speech: 'I yelled: "Look out!" ' (or a comma);

(4) to introduce an example: 'It was a struggle: for one thing I had no help' (or a semicolon);

(5) to introduce a sequence of events: 'He shouted: he shouted again: we waited' (or full stops);

(6) to express a contrast: 'He is old: she is young' (or *but*);

(7) to point to a cause: 'He is yawning: he must be bored' (or *so*);

(8) to point to a consequence: 'They lost the match: they will go down' (or *and so*);

(9) to specify a reference: 'There's one thing I cannot stand: loud music' (or a comma and *that is* or *namely*).

Minor uses of the colon are to separate a main title and a subtitle, as in *Going Home: A Story of Joy*, and to express a ratio, as in *5:3*, meaning 'five parts to three'. In America a colon is used after the introductory salutation in business letters, e.g. *Dear Mr Hall:*, but a comma is used in personal letters, as it is in letters of both kinds in Britain.

comma: The sign (,) is used to separate words and groups of words within a sentence. Its various uses fall under three main heads:

(1) *Commas with single words.* Here they are used to separate items in a list or sequence. The items may be nouns (I keep rabbits, hamsters, and mice), adjectives (He is handsome, clever, and rich), verbs (She drinks, smokes, and takes drugs), or adverbs (They drive slowly, carefully, and nervously). In such sequences the 'serial' comma (the final one before *and*) is normally optional, but necessary when a final noun phrase itself contains *and* (The menu includes grilled dishes, toasties, and fish and chips). Commas are used if two or more adjectives qualify a noun in the same way, e.g. in describing someone's appearance (a tall, slim, elegant lady), but not if they qualify it in different ways (a poor old man), or if one adjective qualifies another, e.g. with colours (a bright red tie). Thus, if *and* can be inserted between the adjectives, commas are used, otherwise not.

Commas must be used with words addressing someone directly, as in 'You, John, can't play', but they are optional with comment adverbs, as in 'Unfortunately(,) the patient died' and 'He is (,) frankly(,) too old'.

(2) *Commas with phrases.* Parenthetic phrases are usually marked off by commas. Such phrases may be commenting (Generally speaking, the service is good), explanatory (He is an atheist, you see), illustrative (Some Indians, for example, have blue eyes), or appositive (Mr Smith, the chairman, spoke next). Most qualifying phrases also take commas (This is, in most cases, unnecessary), but common qualifiers of degree do not (This is more or less accepted now), unless they come at the end (This is accepted now, more or less). Commas are always used to separate the main clause and an absolute phrase (The party over, we all went home) or a participle phrase (Having read the note, she burnt it).

A comma is often used after an introductory phrase of place (In this zone, the climate is mild) or time (In 1994, he joined the army). This clause-splitting comma is normally unnecessary; it is needed only to keep the reader from going off on the wrong scent (In 1994, 1914 seemed very remote).

(3) *Commas with clauses.* When two clauses are joined by *and*, a

comma is used if there is a change of subject (He came later, and his wife came with him), but not normally if the subject remains the same (She is very old and she has a weak heart), unless an element of surprise or suspense is introduced. The neutral sentence 'I went to the shed and I found him there' acquires an element of the unexpected if a comma is inserted before *and*. *But* is treated in the same way: compare 'I am going, but she isn't'; 'He cut his leg but he did not cry' and 'He cut his leg, but he did not cry' (to my surprise). Other coordinating conjunctions are normally preceded by a comma, e.g. 'Don't keep laughing, or I won't tell you'; 'She doesn't like beer, nor do I'; 'We are late, so we must go'; 'He is well fed, yet he grumbles'.

With subordinating conjunctions the position is as follows. A comma separates a dependent clause from a following main clause, but not normally if the order is reversed; compare 'As we drew near, the dog growled' and 'The dog growled as we drew near'; 'When she came in, the boy blushed' and 'The boy blushed when she came in'; 'If you want, bring your wife' and 'Bring your wife if you want'. But clauses beginning with *(al)though* and *whatever* are always marked off by commas, e.g. 'Although he's poor, he is not unhappy' and 'He is not unhappy, although he's poor'; 'Whatever you say, I'm marrying her' and 'I'm marrying her, whatever you say'.

Commas should be used with commenting clauses, but not with defining clauses; compare 'The boys, who came late, were punished' and 'The boys who came late were punished'. A fault to avoid is the 'comma splice', i.e. the use of a comma to separate main clauses which are juxtaposed without a conjunction, e.g. 'I can't tell you her name, I promised not to'. In such a position the comma is not sufficient; a semicolon or full stop should be used instead.

Other uses of the comma are: to introduce direct speech (I said, 'Please explain'), including speech resumed after an interpolation ('Come in,' he said, 'and sit down'); to follow the salutation at the beginning of a letter (Dear John, ...) and the signing off at the end (Yours sincerely, ...), but commas are no longer needed in any part of the address.

The presence or absence of commas can crucially affect meaning. The sentences 'He didn't shout because he was scared', 'I left him convinced he was dying', and 'He has won three prizes more than anyone else' take on a different meaning if a comma is inserted before *because*, *convinced*, and *more* respectively. And the sentence 'After taking the panties, off she rushed to avoid the manager' paints a very different picture if the comma is put after *off*, not before it.

dash: This mark is a long horizontal stroke (—) or a shorter one flanked by spaces (–). Because of its versatility it is much overused, serving as a lazy writer's maid-of-all-work. Its indiscriminate use can lead to jerkiness or obscurity.

A single dash is used:
(1) to indicate a break in thought (He lost his ticket—the fool);

(2) to introduce an afterthought (He's quite clever—so is his brother);

(3) to introduce a quip or punch line (He only has one fault—he's impossible);

(4) to introduce an explanation (We can't give her that—she wouldn't like it);

(5) to specify something referred to (We want some grapes—black ones);

(6) to indicate a dramatic pause (He said he would win—and he did);

(7) to set off a final short appositive (He got what he deserved—nothing);

(8) to do the work of a colon (Ten were chosen—five boys and five girls);

(9) to mark a summing-up (Plenty of practice—that's the only way);

(10) to mark an omission (He doesn't give a d—).

Pairs of dashes are used to set off parenthetic words; in this use they are more informal and isolative than brackets or commas. They most often mark an aside or interpolation, e.g. 'He is—as he always was—a dreamer'; 'I know—don't interrupt—that isn't true'; 'He found—surprise, surprise—that mothers generally love their children'; 'There were troubles—conflict, anger, and infidelity—much of the time'.

In print a short dash, slightly longer than a hyphen, is used without spaces to join two names, e.g. *the Dow–Jones Index, the Iran–Iraq war, in May–October*, or letters, e.g. *The A–Z of Gardening*, or figures, e.g. *a score of 2–0, the 1914–18 war, pages 125–37*. Where short dashes are not available hyphens are used instead.

ellipsis (points): This is a series of three dots (...), used to signify an incomplete quotation or unfinished statement. Omission points may come at the beginning of a sentence (... even in wartime this was allowed), in the middle (There has been ... talk of peace), or at the end (He seems normal enough, but ...).

The same dots are used to represent a dramatic pause and then they are called 'suspension points', e.g. 'And the winner is ... Marlon Brando'. In this use they can be replaced by a dash.

exclamation mark: The symbol (!) is placed after forceful utterances and pointed remarks of various kinds. It is used in:

(1) interjections (Ah! Ouch! Wow!);

(2) emotional phrases (My God! Just great!);

(3) peremptory commands (Attention! Hands up! Fire!);

(4) warnings and distress calls (Look out! Help!);

(5) dramatic pronouncements (Hey presto! Lo and behold!);

(6) wishes and curses (If only I could! Rot in hell!);

(7) exclamatory questions (How dare you! Isn't he cute!);

(8) sentences with an exclamatory *how* or *what* (How sweet! What a lie!);

(9) expressions of surprise or disbelief (Well, I'll be damned! My husband a bigamist. Nonsense!);

(10) expressions of praise or disapproval (You clever girl! The stupid boy!);

(11) ironic remarks (Some lover! Such manners! The little dears!);

(12) contemptuous repetitions (You thought I 'wouldn't mind'!).

With imperatives such as *Come here* and *Give me that* an exclamation mark is used only if they are used emphatically, to express anger, impatience, and the like (Get out! Let's go!). An editorial exclamation mark, enclosed in brackets, is used to convey the writer's surprise or amusement, e.g. 'He called himself a leader of men(!)'.

The use of multiple exclamation marks, common in strip cartoons, is simply type-hype. Exclamation marks should be used sparingly, and above all singly, in serious writing.

full stop: The single point (.) is mainly used to indicate the end of a sentence, except where an exclamation mark or question mark occurs. Both full and minor sentences usually take a full stop (Some people think this is clever. Quite wrong.). No stops are normally used, however, in public notices (Keep off the grass), advertising slogans (Drink more milk), and newspaper headlines or sub-headings (Truman dies). Stops are also often omitted (as in this book) at the end of sentences being quoted for the purpose of grammatical analysis or commentary.

Points have traditionally been used with abbreviations (Dr.), initials (W.H. Smith), initialisms (U.S.A.), and acronyms (U.N.O.), but nowadays the unpointed style is used more and more frequently. Points are still generally used, however, as an alternative to brackets, with figures in numerical or alphabetical lists, i.e. 1. 2. 3., etc., or a. b. c., etc.

hyphen: The mark (-) is shorter than the dash and is a linking device, whereas the dash is generally a separator. The hyphen is used to join the parts of compound words, mainly as follows:

(1) *in noun compounds*. A block compound is often first written open (as separate words), then hyphenated, and finally solid (as one word), e.g. *key hole*, *key-hole* and *keyhole*. As a result, usage is often inconsistent (cf. *sea bird*, *sea-bed* and *seaboard*) and variable (e.g *gas light* and *gaslight*; *coal-face* and *coalface*). However, a hyphen is always used where the first element is not a qualifier, i.e. in appositional compounds such as *actor-manager* and *the space-time continuum*, and double-barrelled names such as *Jean-Paul* and *Douglas-Home*; when it is a single capital letter, as in *T-shirt* and *U-turn*; or where it is one of the prefixed elements *ex-* (*ex-wife*), *pro-* (*pro-life*), *quasi-* (*quasi-religious*), *self-* (*self-image*), *he-* or *she-* (*he-man*, *she-bear*), *yes-* or *no-* (*yes-man*, *no-ball*).

Compound nouns made up of more than two elements are always

hyphenated, e.g. *forget-me-not*, *mother-in-law* and *stick-in-the-mud*. So too are most compound nouns derived from phrasal verbs, i.e. where the second element is an adverbial particle, e.g. *stand-by*, *go-between*, *sit-in*, *take-off*, and *make-up*.

(2) *in adjectival compounds*. A hyphen is regularly used in compound adjectival modifiers of all types, e.g. *a left-handed child*, *an all-round athlete*, *an anti-roll bar*, *soft-boiled eggs*, *a bitter-sweet taste*, *profit-sharing schemes*. Likewise hyphenated are string compounds, i.e. extended adjectival modifiers, such as occur in *a hand-to-mouth existence*, *a happy-go-lucky person*, *a balance-of-payments crisis*, *a very spit-and-polish officer*, and *a take-it-or-leave-it attitude*. Hyphens also join a flat adverb to a participle, as in *hard-hitting* and *deep-rooted*, but adverbs ending in *-ly* are written separately, as in *rapidly moving* and *cleverly contrived*.

(3) *in numeral compounds*. Wherever numerals form part of a compound, hyphens are used, e.g. *a one-armed bandit*, *first-year students*, *two-thirds*, *fifty-one*, *a ten-hour delay*, *a 24-hour clock*, *a six-year-old boy*.

Adjectival and numeral compounds are still hyphenated when they follow the noun they qualify, if their original use was attributive; thus *a middle-aged man* is otherwise expressed as 'a man who is middle-aged'. But when the original form is postpositive (i.e. serving as a complement), then it stands on its own feet and needs no hyphens. Thus *a first-class ticket* needs a hyphen, but *to travel first class*, where *first class* is an adverbial complement, does not. Similarly, *an up-to-date guide* is 'a guide that is up to date', *a well-educated man* is 'a man who is well educated', and *a six-inch nail* is 'a nail that is six inches long'.

Less common uses of the hyphen are: to join a prefix and a date or a word beginning with a capital letter (pre-1980, anti-Darwinian), to avoid a clash of two identical vowels or three identical consonants (pre-emptive, shell-like), and to differentiate between otherwise identical forms (re-creation, recreation; co-op, coop; pro-verb, proverb). A clarifying hyphen avoids phrasal confusion, for example between *non-French speakers* (who are not of French nationality) and *non-French-speakers* (who do not speak French). A break hyphen marks the division of a word between two lines (litera-ture) and a suspended hyphen is used when the second element of two compounds is the same (full- and part-time teachers, gas- and water-cooled reactors).

Fewer hyphens are used in American English than in British English. The American preference for open or solid forms can be seen in *dining room*, *semiskilled*, and *nonnative*, compared with British English *dining-room*, *semi-skilled*, and *non-native*.

inverted commas: See **quotation marks**.
oblique: Another name for **slash**.

parentheses: The American English term for round brackets (one such bracket is a parenthesis). See **brackets**.

period: The American English term for **full stop**.

question mark: The symbol (?) is placed at the end of a direct question (Where have you been?), but not after an indirect one (I asked him where he had been). It is used when the form of words is declarative but the tone is interrogative (You're not going?), when the question is a disguised statement (Isn't she pretty?), and when it is rhetorical (Would you like a punch in the nose?). But there is no need of a question mark if the question constitutes a fairly lengthy request (Will you please supply us with details of this transaction, as we have no record of it). When a question is interpolated in the middle of a sentence, however, a question mark is required (We all know—don't we?—who is responsible).

If a question is exclamatory in tone an exclamation mark is used (Wasn't that marvellous!). And sometimes the two marks are used together to convey a mixture of doubt and surprise (Really?! Did you say he was humble?!)

A minor use of the exclamation mark is to indicate doubt (She is enjoying (?) all the publicity) or uncertainty of dating (William Tyndale (?1492–1536) was burnt at the stake).

quotation marks: Raised commas, either single ('...') or double ("...") are used in pairs to enclose a quoted word, phrase, or passage. They have four main uses:

(1) to quote the title of an article ('A reply to Dr Dawson'), a chapter ('The Second Front'), or a song ('Singing in the Rain'), but titles of books, magazines, films, TV programmes and the like are underlined in handwriting and italicized in print;

(2) to quote a single word or phrase, especially if it is slangy (He said he needed a 'fix') or new (He spoke of 'the feel-good factor') or inappropriate (I know what he means by 'corrective' measures) or objected to (He described my idea as 'crap');

(3) to quote a sentence or whole passage (Shakespeare said 'all the world's a stage' and described us mortals as actors on it);

(4) to quote direct speech (I asked him, 'Are you ready yet?').

In British English single marks are normally used for a main quotation and double marks for an interior quotation; in American English the reverse applies. Accordingly we write either: 'Me Tarzan. You Jane.' 'Correction: "I am Tarzan; You are Jane." ' or: "Me Tarzan. You Jane." "Correction: 'I am Tarzan; you are Jane.' " As this example shows, in both British and American English full stops (like commas) are placed inside the closing quotation marks for direct speech. In other circumstances, however, British English puts full stops and commas outside the quotation marks (She has been called 'the Queen of Hollywood'.). American English, by contrast, puts them inside the quotation marks (She has been called "the Queen of Hollywood.").

When a sentence ends with a question mark or exclamation mark, the closing quotation mark comes before or after, according to sense (I said to him, 'Why worry?', *but* Why did you say 'Don't worry'?).

semicolon: The sign (;) marks a break that is stronger than a comma and weaker than a full stop. It is most often used to join parallel or closely associated statements that are not linked by a conjunction or other connective, e.g. 'To err is human; to forgive—divine'. 'Some of us were disgusted; others were amused'. 'Such films are harmful; they ought to be banned'. 'Many people helped me; I could not have done it alone'. A semicolon may also be used in similar sentences where the parts are linked by a conjunctive adverb such as *however* or *moreover*, e.g. 'This is an expensive watch; however, it will last for years'. 'They respected each other; moreover, they were happy together'.

Semicolons are used instead of commas to separate phrases, some of which have their own commas, e.g. 'Our panellists are: Alan Jones, the chairman of the CBI; Mary Little, a headmistress; John Dixon, the MP for Macclesfield; and Joan Bright, the well-known political commentator'.

slash: The oblique stroke (/) has six main uses:

(1) to denote alternatives (either/or, his/her, Dear Sir/Madam, provided/providing);

(2) to divide the parts of an abbreviation (a/c 'account', c/o 'care of');

(3) to separate lines of poetry quoted continuously (I wandered lonely as a cloud/That floats on high o'er vales and hills);

(4) to indicate a financial or academic year (your tax return for 1994/95, in the session 1996/97);

(5) to express fractions and rates (23/24 'twenty-three twenty-fourths', 90 km/hr 'ninety kilometres an hour');

(6) to separate numerals in a date (6/2/90, 'June second 1990' in American English, but 'the sixth of February 1990' in British English).

square brackets: The matching signs [ ] are mainly used to enclose extra information, introduced for the sake of clarity. The interpolation may supply:

(1) an identification (The vicar [John's father] stood up);

(2) an explanation (The doctor said I had a thrombus [blood clot]);

(3) a clarification (These people [the protesters] would not move);

(4) an omission (The older type [of engine] was scrapped).

The interpolation [sic] is used to show that a mis-spelt or dubious form is given as it appears in the original source, e.g. 'Don't despare' [sic], I'll be there,' he wrote.

In dictionaries square brackets are often used to enclose etymological information, e.g. 'ampersand: noun. The character (&), signifying *and* [contraction of *and per se and*, i.e. the symbol & by itself (represents) *and*]'.

suspension points: See **ellipsis (points)**.

Basic Grammatical Terms

absolute: The term used to described a phrase, having its own subject, that is grammatically unrelated to the main clause (*Weather permitting*, we leave tomorrow. He approached, *dagger in hand*).

accusative: The traditional name for the object case when the object is direct (I love *her*).

active: The form of a verb used when its subject is in a state of being (He *sits*) or doing (He *works*). See **passive**.

adjective: A noun-describing word, i.e. a word that ascribes some quality, condition or relationship to anything denoted by a noun (*big* boys; *social* problems) or pronoun (He is *old*). Adjectives denoting qualities have three degrees: positive (*strong*), comparative (*stronger, more strong*) and superlative (*strongest, most strong*).

adverb: A word that modifies a verb (eat *quickly*), an adjective (*rather* good), another adverb (*very* soon), an adverbial phrase (*almost* at the top), a clause (I cry *only* when I am hurt) or a sentence (*Luckily*, he is safe). Adverbs formed with *-ly* from adjectives add *more* and *most* to express the comparative and superlative (*gladly: more gladly, most gladly*). Flat adverbs (those identical in form with adjectives) have both types of comparative and superlative (*slow: slower* and *more slowly; slowest* and *most slowly*).

adverbial: An adverb (*bravely*), an adverbial phrase (*in a brave way*) or an adverbial clause (*as he showed bravery*).

affix: An element attached to the beginning or end of a word or stem to make a derived form or an inflected form. See **prefix** and **suffix**.

agent: The doer, cause or instrument of an action expressed in the passive (I was bitten by *a dog*. He was killed by *lightning*. It was cut with *a saw*).

agreement: The inflection of a word to accord with the form of the word it refers to. The English verb agrees in number and person with its subject in the present tense, where the third person singular ends in *-s* (He/she *knows*) and the other persons have no ending (I/you/we/they *know*). Third-person pronouns agree in gender and number with their antecedents (The boy lost *his* way. The girl lost *her* way. The dog lost *its* way. The men lost *their* way). Demonstrative adjectives agree in number with the noun they modify (*this* book and *these* books).

antecedent: The word or words to which a following pronoun or adverb refers (It was *John* who phoned. *Father* said he would and he did. I like *driving fast*; it excites me. *He shouted at her*, which angered me. He lives *in Boston* and his parents live there too).

apposition: The placing of one noun or noun phrase after another in order to identify the person or thing more closely (Bill, *the drummer*, is our leader. I met the Minister of Health, *John Brown*).

article: A determiner used before a noun to give it a specific or general meaning. In English *the* is the definite article and *a(n)* is the indefinite article.

aspect: The grammatical expression of some feature of a verbal action or state, such as continuation (He *is reading*), habitual action (He *used to read*) or completion (He *has read*). See **perfect** and **progressive**.

attributive: The term used to describe an adjective that stands next to the noun it modifies, without a verb intervening (*her* ring, *numb* hands, hands *numb* with cold). See **predicative**.

auxiliary: A helping verb, i.e. one used with a main verb to form a tense or aspect. The chief auxiliary verbs in English are *be* (*is* helping, *will* help), *do* (*does* help, *did* help) and *have* (*has* helped, *had* helped, *will have* helped). See **modal**.

case: One of several noun or pronoun forms that are used to express different grammatical relationships. English nouns have a common case, used for both subject (The *boy* knows me) and object (I know the *boy*), and a possessive case (This is the *boy's* hat). The personal pronouns, apart from *it* and *you*, distinguish between the subject case (*I, he, she, we, they*) and the object case (*me, him, her, us, them*).

clause: A word group containing a subject and a predicate that forms part of a compound or complex sentence. In full clauses the subject and any auxiliary verb are expressed (*While he was swimming*, he drowned. I know the man *who is sitting in the car*), whereas in abbreviated clauses they are omitted (*While swimming*, he drowned. I know the man *sitting in the car*). Main clauses are capable of standing alone as simple sentences. Dependent (or subordinate) clauses are linked to a main clause or to another dependent clause by a subordinating conjunction or a relative pronoun (I'll tell you *if you like*. I was glad when I heard *that he was back*).

comparative: See **adjective** and **adverb**.

complement: Traditionally, a word or phrase that completes the sense of a subject-verb or subject-verb-direct object combination, where the verb is of the linking type. It may complete the subject (He is *mad*. He looks *a fool*) or the object (It made him *mad*. She called him *a fool*). Nowadays the term 'complement' is often used in a broader sense, to include objects (I like *tea*) and expressions of time or place (He is *at home*. The dance is *on Friday*).

complex: The term used to describe a sentence that contains one main clause and one or more subordinate clauses (*He is old, although he looks young*). See **simple** and **compound**.

compound: Consisting of more than one element, i.e. not simple. Compound nouns combine two or more words into a single entity or idea (*wallpaper, gas mask, cut-throat*). Compound tenses consist of an auxiliary and a main verb (*is seeing, has seen, will see*). Compound sentences are made up of two or more coordinate main clauses (*He is old and she is young*).

concord: Another word for **agreement**.

conditional: Expressing a condition, which is either (a) real or realizable (*If he comes*, I shall go) or (b) contrary to fact (*If he had come*, I would have gone). The conditional form of the verb, comprising the auxiliary *would/should (have)* and a main verb is used in the main clause of a conditional statement that is contrary to fact (I *would have gone*) or unrealized (I *would go*).

conjunction: A word or word combination that joins other words or groups of words. Coordinating conjunctions link equal grammatical elements (here *and* there, old *but* fit, hit *or* miss). Subordinating conjunctions link a dependent clause to a main one (I said *that* I was ill. I'll come *if* you ask me).

correlative: One of a pair of coordinating conjunctions that express a complementary or exclusive relationship (*both* tea *and* coffee, *either* whisky *or* brandy).

demonstrative: An adjective or pronoun that is used to indicate or single out some person(s) or thing(s) (*this* boy; I like *those*).

determiner: A word that modifies a noun and precedes any ordinary adjective modifiers. A determiner may be an article (*the* blue book), a demonstrative adjective (*this* new book), a possessive adjective (*my* son), a numeral (*six* eggs) or a quantifier (*some* eggs).

ending: See **suffix**.

finite: A verb form that is inflected i.e. marked for person, number or tense. *Does* is the third person singular present of *do*, and *did* is the past tense form of *do* for all persons. Non-finite verb forms (infinitives and participles) are not inflected.

gender: A set of two or three grammatical categories, masculine, feminine (and neuter), to which nouns are assigned in some languages. English has natural gender, based on sex and therefore restricted to names of males (*uncle, bull, William*), which are masculine, and those of females (*aunt, cow, Mary*), which are feminine. Some names of animate beings, such as *cousin, cook* and *kangaroo*, are of common gender, i.e. may be masculine or feminine.

genitive: The traditional name for the possessive case of a noun, pronoun or adjective. Many English nouns, mostly those denoting animate beings, have a so-called 'Anglo-Saxon genitive' in *-s* (*John's* book, *boys'* names).

gerund: A noun in *-ing* that is derived from a verb (*Cooking* is an art.

I like *skating*). Nowadays some grammarians prefer the term 'verbal noun'.

imperative: The form of a verb used to express a command (*Stop* that!), request (*Shut* the door, please), invitation (*Come* in), advice (*Borrow* the money) or warning (*Mind* your head). In English the imperative has the same form as the infinitive.

impersonal: A verb or adverb construction that has the dummy subject *it* or *there* (*It rains* often. *It is possible* he will win. *There is* no more. *There are* rats in there).

indirect speech: The reported form of an utterance. 'He said, *"You look cold"* ' is an example of direct speech; this becomes 'He said *(that) I looked cold*' in indirect speech.

infinitive: The base form of a verb that is unmarked for person, number or tense, i.e. the naming form given in dictionaries. English infinitives have a *to*-form (It is wrong *to kill*. I asked him *to come*) and a bare form without *to* (You must *come*. I saw him *fall*).

inflection: Variation in the form of a word to express different grammatical functions or relations. English inflectional endings include *-s* for the plural of nouns and the third person singular present tense of verbs, *-ing* for the present participle, *-ed* for the past tense and past participle, *-er* for the comparative and *-est* for the superlative of adjectives and adverbs.

interjection: A word used as an exclamation (*Ah! Help! Damn!*).

intransitive: See **transitive**.

inversion: Placement of the verb before its subject, as in direct questions (*Are you* ready? Where *is he*?).

linking verb: A verb used to identify or link the complement with the subject of a sentence (He *is* old. I *feel* sick. He *became* president).

modal: An auxiliary verb used to express ability (*can, could*), conditionality (*should, would*), intention (*shall, will*), necessity (*must*), obligation (*ought*) or possibility (*may, might*). Modal verbs have no infinitive and no inflected forms.

nominative: The traditional name for the subject case, distinguished in English from the object case only in pronouns (*I* and *me*; *he* and *him*).

non-finite: See **finite**.

noun: A word which denotes anything that can be perceived or conceived, i.e. a creature (*cat*), object (*box*), substance (*wood*), amount (*ton*), action (*riding*), event (*battle*), idea (*truth*), quality (*charm*), feeling (*love*) or state (*danger*). Proper nouns are individual names and start with a capital letter (*John, Paris, Sunday, Safeway*). Common nouns denote one of a class (*boy, city, day, store*).

number: The grammatical distinction between singular (one) and plural (more than one).

numeral: A word or symbol used to denote a number (*two, 2*). Cardinal numerals denote how many (*three, four*). Ordinal numerals denote position in a sequence (*third, fourth*).

object: A noun or noun phrase that is governed by an active verb or a preposition (I rear *pigs/them*; for *your son*). The direct object of a verb is the person or thing directly affected (I broke *the cup*). The indirect object is the recipient or beneficiary of a verb of giving or communicating (I wrote *Mary* a letter. I gave it *you*).

parenthesis: An explanatory or qualifying word, phrase, or clause inserted into a sentence with which it has not necessarily any grammatical connection. It is marked off by commas, dashes, or brackets (This is, *as far as I know*, the whole story. He is more intelligent – *and more sensitive* – than his father. The doctor suspected I had a thrombus (*blood clot*). The vicar [*John's uncle*] spoke next).

parse: Describe a word, clause or sentence in grammatical terms, specifying parts of speech, inflections and syntactical relations.

part of speech: One of the classes into which words are divided according to their grammatical functions. English has eight traditional parts of speech or word classes: adjective, adverb, conjunction, interjection, noun, preposition, pronoun and verb.

participle: A verb form used with the auxiliary *to be* or *to have*. The present participle, which ends in *-ing*, is used in the progressive aspect (He is/was *playing*). The past participle, which generally ends in *-ed* or *-en*, is used to form the present and past perfect (He has/had *played*) and to form the passive construction (It is/was *eaten*). Participles also serve as adjectives (*rolling* stones, *mixed* fruit).

passive: A verb form that combines the auxiliary *to be* and a past participle (*to be fed, is being fed, has been fed, will be fed*). The subject of a passive construction is the person or thing affected by the action (*He* was arrested. *They* were being beaten).

perfect: A verbal aspect, consisting of the auxiliary *to have* and a past participle, used to indicate completion of an action or state. The perfect aspect has three tenses: the present perfect (He *has gone*), the past perfect (He *had gone*) and the future perfect (He *will have gone*).

person: One of three categories to which personal pronouns and some verb forms are assigned, depending on whether they refer to the speaker (first person: *I, we*), the person(s) addressed (second person: *you*), or some other person(s) or thing(s) (third person: *he, she, it, they*). The present tense of the verb *to be* has the form *am* (first person singular), *is* (third person singular) and *are* (all persons plural).

phrase: In traditional grammar a group of words linked in meaning but lacking a finite verb (*Jack and Jill, little by little, in the bin, frankly speaking, covered in mud*). In linguistic structural analysis today a phrase may consist of a single word as well as a word group. Thus *people, these good people*, and *they*, being equivalent sentence elements, are all treated alike as noun phrases.

possessive: An adjective, a pronoun or an inflected form of a noun that expresses possession (*whose* book, *my* book, it is *mine*, *uncle's* shop, *Jane's* doll).

predicate: That which is stated about the subject of a sentence. The predicate may consist of a verb alone (He *lies*), a verb and complement (He *is a liar*) or a verb and object (He *tells lies*).

predicative: The term used to describe an adjective, pronoun or noun that serves as a complement, i.e. forms part of a predicate. Predicatives are separated from the subject by a linking verb (My hands are *numb*. The ring is *hers*. He feels *a fool*). See **attributive**.

prefix: An affix attached to the beginning of a word (*dis*respect, *pre*view, *over*load, *un*happy).

preposition: A word or phrase that indicates the relationship between a noun, pronoun or adverb and the word or words preceding it (*for* you, *to* mother, *in* here, *in spite of* that, *according to* reports). In English personal pronouns used with a preposition are put in the object case (of *them*, with *us*, between *you* and *me*).

progressive: A verbal aspect, consisting of the auxiliary *to be* and a present participle, used to indicate an action in progress or a continuing state. There are three progressive tenses: the present progressive (He *is going*), the past progressive (He *was going*) and the future progressive (He *will be going*).

pronoun: A noun-substitute, i.e. a word used to indicate, without naming it, anything that can be denoted by a noun or noun phrase, e.g. 'One cake was left and I ate *it*'. Besides the personal pronouns (*I, you, he, she, it, we, they*) there are demonstrative pronouns (*this, these, that, those*), indefinite pronouns (*all, any, anybody, both, each, either, everybody, neither, none, some, somebody*), interrogative pronouns (*who, which, what*), possessive pronouns (*mine, yours, his, hers, its, ours, theirs*), reciprocal pronouns (*each other, one another*), reflexive pronouns (*myself, yourself, himself, herself, itself, ourselves, yourselves, themselves*) and relative pronouns (*that, who, which, what*).

quantifier: An adjective or pronoun that denotes an indefinite quantity or number (*all* men, *few* boys, *many* times, *more* bread, *no* eggs. I have *none*. She has *some*).

sentence: A word or sequence of words that constitutes a complete utterance. Full sentences contain a subject and predicate (*Father is ill*). Minor sentences lack a subject (*Come here*) or a verb (*This way*) or both (*Just in time*).

simple: Consisting of only one grammatical element. Simple tenses consist of a single verb form (I *see*; simple present; I *saw*: simple past). Simple sentences consist of a single main clause (*He is old*). See **compound**.

stem: The base of an inflected word, to which various endings are added (*want* in *wanted* and *wants*).

subject: The word or words representing what is spoken about in a sentence. The subject, usually a noun or its equivalent, comes at the beginning of most English sentences (*John* is here. *He* has gone. *Seeing* is believing. *All children under 11* travel free).

subjunctive: A verb form used when speaking of hypothetical or contrary-to-fact situations, e.g. 'I wish she *were* here' and 'If I *were* you, I would go' (in such sentences the non-subjunctive *was* is just as acceptable as *were*). The commonest use of the subjunctive in present-day English is with expressions of necessity, desirability and the like, e.g. 'It is essential that he *attend*' and 'We insist that she *resign*', where the non-subjunctive forms in -*s* (*attends* and *resigns*) are equally acceptable.

suffix: An affix attached to the end of a word. Inflectional suffixes, or endings, mark some feature such as number (plural -*s* in *books*) or tense (past tense -*ed* in *wanted*). Derivational suffixes make a new word from an existing one (-*let* in *flatlet*, -*ly* and -*ness* in *sadly* and *sadness*).

superlative: See **adjective** and **adverb**.

syntax: The arrangement of words to form phrases, clauses and sentences.

tense: The grammatical indication of time expressed by a verb. There are three basic tenses: the present (He *works*), the past (He *worked*) and the future (He *will work*).

transitive: The term denoting verbs that are used with a direct object (I *like* coffee. He *raised* his hand). Intransitive verbs are not used with a direct object (You *snored*. She *laughed*).

verb: A word denoting an action or state that can be expressed in the past, present or future (*wrote, writes, will write*). Dynamic verbs denote actions (*do, go, take*). Stative verbs denote states (*be, live, sit*).

voice: The form of a verb that shows whether its subject is being or doing, or is acted upon. See **active** and **passive**.

Name Index

Addison, Joseph 7, 12, 51
Alford, Henry 9, 16, 37
Alfred the Great 21
Aristarchus 35
Aristotle 32-3, 35
Austen, Jane 50

Ballard, Philip Boswood 55-6
Behn, Aphra 191
Bevin, Ernest 142
Blair, Hugh 8, 152, 168
Blake, William 142
Bloomfield, Leonard 43
Boswell, James 16
Bradley, Henry 55
Brando, Marlon 194
Bridges, Robert 190
Brown, Goold 9
Bullokar, William 37
Burchfield, Robert 2, 17
Butler, Charles 37
Byron, Lord 11

Caesar, Augustus 7
Campbell, George 8, 29, 39-40, 53
Canning, George 175
Carlyle, Thomas 41
Carroll, Lewis 118
Caxton, William 17, 51
Chaucer, Geoffrey 26, 108, 140, 147
Chomsky, Noam 44
Churchill, Winston 13, 35
Clarke, John 27
Cobbett, William 37, 39, 152
Coleridge, Samuel Taylor 26, 33
Cooper, Christopher 37
Coverdale, Miles 13, 15
Crystal, David 191

Davies, Hugh Sykes 56

Defoe, Daniel 7
Dickens, Charles 11, 138, 175, 190
Dionysius Thrax 35
Donatus, Aelius 36-7
Donne, John 11
Dryden, John 7, 12-13, 21-2

Einstein, Albert 42
Elizabeth II 19
Erasmus, Desiderius 35

Fielding, Henry 134
Fowler, Francis George 54-7, 59
Fowler, Henry Watson 2, 13, 16-17,
  23, 37, 51, 54-7, 59, 74, 84, 171

Gibbon, Edward 29
Gill, Alexander 37
Goldwyn, Samuel 107, 142
Gowers, Ernest Arthur 17, 19, 57-9
Grant, Cary 191
Greaves, Paul 37
Greenbaum, Sidney 3, 44
Greenough, James Bradstreet 54, 59
Greenwood, James 27

Hall, Fitzedward 48
Hall, Robert Anderson 31
Hardy, Thomas 50
Herbert, Alan Patrick 140
Hercules 190
Homer 41
Horace 39, 58
Hurd, Richard 12

Jespersen, Otto 16, 35, 41-3
Johnson, Samuel 8, 21-2, 38
Jones, Hugh 27
Jonson, Ben 28, 37, 39
Joyce, James 41

Kames, Lord 152
Keats, John 118
Kenyon, John Samuel 19
Kingsley, Charles 72
Kittredge, George Lyman 54, 59

Lamb, Charles 26
Latham, Robert Gordon 31, 41
Leech, Geoffrey 3
Lily, William 37
Locke, John 51
Louis XIV 88
Lounsbury, Thomas Raynesford 47
Lowth, Robert 8, 12, 23-4, 27, 29, 37

Maittaire, Michael 13
Malory, Thomas 108
Mason, George 13
Meres, Francis 7
Mill, John Stuart 33-4
Milton, John 27, 40, 50, 108
Moon, George Washington 9
Moses 190
Murray, Lindley 8-9, 12, 21

Nash, Walter 44
Nesfield, John Collinson 37

O'Neill, Eugene 135
Orwell, George 34, 57-9, 146

Phillips, Edward 7
Pitt, William 175
Plato 32
Pope, Alexander 13
Poutsma, Hendrik 84
Priestley, Joseph 37, 39
Priscian 36-7

Quiller-Couch, Arthur 56-9, 171
Quintilian 39
Quirk, Randolph 3, 44

Ramus, Petrus 37
Reagan, Ronald 57, 126
Richards, Ivor Armstrong 42-3, 46
Roche, Boyle 141

Sapir, Edward 71-2
Saussure, Ferdinand de 43
Schopenhauer, Arthur 62
Shakespeare, William 7, 13, 15, 21, 23, 26, 28-9, 38, 40, 50-1, 71, 83, 108, 134, 140, 197
Sheridan, Richard Brinsley 134
Sidney, Philip 27, 51
Smollett, Tobias 134
Socrates 35, 190
Spencer, Herbert 55
Stubbs, Michael 44
Svartvik, Jan 3
Sweet, Henry 39, 53, 84
Swift, Jonathan 7, 29

Taylor, Richard 11
Tegnér, Esaias 41
Tennyson, Alfred 28
Thackeray, William 118
Trench, Richard Chenevix 33
Tyndale, William 71, 197

Voltaire 148

Wallis, John 13, 37
Webster, Noah 9
White, James 13
White, Richard Grant 41, 43
Wordsworth, William 33, 50

Subject and Word Index

-*a* plurals 78-9
abbreviated clauses 94, 100-1
abbreviations 61, 195, 198
absent agents 87, 92, 94, 100
absent antecedents 83
absent connectives 101-2
absolute constructions 92-3, 95
absolutes 146
abstract appendages 170-1
abstract nouns 54-6, 59, 62, 159, 170
accusative 17
acronyms 195
adjective phrases 87, 132
adjectives 38, 58, 70-1, 135-6, 144-9, 170-1
adverb phrases 92, 163
adverbials 70
adverbs 30, 58, 69-71, 136, 144-8, 153-4, 172-4
advertese 103, 132
affixes 174
agentless passive 56-7
aggravate 47
ago/since 123
agreement 2, 21-2, 38, 76-86
ain't 29-30, 64
all manner of 85
ambiguity 50, 53, 60-1, 106, 153-5, 158-67
American usage 13-14, 19, 46, 67-9, 76, 78, 84, 121, 127, 174, 191-2, 196-8
among 22
ampersand 198
anacoluthia 125
analogy 8, 35-7, 71, 74, 102, 173
and 77, 101, 184, 192-3
antecedents 24, 50, 61, 72, 82-3, 126-7, 155, 160-1
any 107
any other 122

apposition 87-8
appositional compounds 195
articles 38, 80, 97, 160
as ... as 16, 23, 97-8, 122
as if 73
as/like 72-3
as such 89, 188
as well as 89, 166
as with 73, 106
as-phrases 73, 88, 164-5
attachment 61, 87-96, 100, 155
attenuators 145, 147
attraction 21, 79-81, 84
attribution 121-2
attributive nouns 160
attributive queues 160
auxiliary verbs 38, 99-100, 127, 162, 174

back-formations 49
back-shifting 130
back-to-frontery 154-5
bare infinitives 11
barely 116, 122
because 51, 123, 126, 164
besides 89
between 22, 123, 173
blended genitives 107-8
blends 118-19, 173
block compounds 160, 195
boosters 145
both 185
both ... and 123
British usage 46, 76, 127, 191-2, 196-8
broken constructions 125-33
by -ing 94, 155

can/could not help 118
cardinal numbers 30
case 26, 38

case confusion 15
categorial confusion 159-60
change of standpoint 83-4
circumlocution 55, 58, 60-1, 175
cleft constructions 102, 119
clichés 57-8
clipped words 190
collective nouns 76-7, 79
comma splices 193
commas 164-5
comment adverbs 47
commenting clauses 24
commenting phrases 92
comparatives 28-9, 107-8, 163, 173
comparison 14-16, 73, 97-8, 105-10, 125, 128, 144-6
complement 17, 70, 80
compound subjects 77, 79
compounds 48, 69, 95
concrete nouns 54, 56-7, 59, 159
conditional sentences 74, 128-9
confusables 135-8
conjunctions 72, 89, 92, 95, 101, 107, 123, 131
conjunctive adverbs 198
connectives 101-2
contact clauses 101
conversion 48-9, 95, 159-60
coordinates 26, 101
correlative comparisons 128
correlatives 81, 113, 122-3, 128, 153
countable nouns 21, 23, 81
covert subjects 94
cross-association 15
crossed constructions 61, 112, 118-24

dangling participles 49-50, 90, 132
dangling subjects 125
defining clauses 24
dependent genitives 17, 21, 79-81, 84
descriptive grammar 3, 43-5
detached relative clauses 155-6
determiners 85
dialect forms 28-9, 40
different from/to/than 36, 52
direct speech 126, 130
disinterested 47
disjuncts 47
displaced adverbs 153
displaced negatives 112-13
divided usage 36, 42-3, 45-53, 62-4, 76, 93

doctrine of norm 41-3
doctrine of usage 39-42
doesn't/don't 29-30
double comparatives 28-9
double conditionals 120
double marking 28
double negation 34, 64, 111-13
double perfect 120
double plurals 78-9
double superlatives 28
doubt if/that/whether 36-7
downgrading 147
downtoners 145
due to/owing to 19-20
dummy subjects 88, 92, 156, 161

each 80
each other 23
either 46, 80-1
either ... or 81, 113
elatives 145-6
elegant variation 184-5
ellipsis 2, 72, 93, 97-106, 112
endings 38, 76-7, 84
epicene pronouns 82-3
etymological fallacy 21-2, 47
euphemism 55, 175
exiled phrases 156

false titles 187
far from 92
fewer/less 23
fillers 62, 168
final prepositions 12-13, 71
first/firstly 70-1
first two/two first 30
flat adverbs 30, 69-70
fore-and-aft prepositions 173
foreign phrases 57-9
foreign plurals 78-9
French language 14-15, 48, 116
function words 38, 173-4
fused participles 16-18, 163

garden-path sentences 101
gender 38, 82-4
genitive 84, 165
German language 28
gerunds 16-18, 163
gobbledygook 55
gradability 144-5
grammar teaching 8-9, 38, 63-4

Indexes

grammatical terms 38, 63, 199-205
Greek language 7, 28, 33, 35-6, 43, 48, 78, 108, 111, 125, 134
group genitive 190

hardly 116, 122
headlinese 97, 160
hidden negatives 115-16
hopefully 47
however 9
hybrids 48
hyper-adverbs 174
hyperbole 148
hypercorrection 67-75, 78
hyphens 78, 164

I/me 14-16, 67-8, 71
-ics nouns 78
idiom 17, 30, 34, 68, 70, 101, 112-13, 118-19, 127, 153, 169
if-clauses 74, 101, 128-9, 131
if not 166
illogical forms 34-5, 107-8, 113, 153
imperative 94
impersonal expressions 15, 88, 93-4
inclusive exclusion 107-8
indefinite pronouns 82-4, 94
indirect comparisons 73, 106
indirect speech 74, 129-30
infinitive phrases 89, 93
infinitives 11-12, 17, 37, 99, 102, 126
inflection 29, 38, 71, 152
-ing forms 37, 131-2, 163
initialisms 195
instead of 89, 92
instructionese 102-3
intensifiers 20, 28, 145, 147-9
interjections 194
interrogatives 72, 126
intransitive verbs 56
inversion 113, 115, 130-1
irony 145, 195
-ize verbs 49

jargon 57-9
journalese 91, 132
just 153

Latin fallacy 9
Latin language 7-9, 11, 27, 29, 33, 36-40, 43, 45, 48, 63, 74, 78, 108-9, 111, 134-5

levelling 29
like-phrases 34, 73, 106-7, 164-5
linking verbs 105
loan-words 7, 78-9, 135
logic 8, 27, 30, 32-5, 42, 112, 114-15, 123, 146, 153
logical gaps 131
lubricators 168
-ly 30, 69-71, 174

malapropisms 61, 134-6
many a one 81
matching forms 71, 105, 120, 126
may/might 129-30
merely 153
metaphor 57, 141
miscoupling 144-51
misplacement 106, 152-7
misrelated participles 49-50, 61, 89-90
mixed agreement 77
mixed comparisons 97-8
mixed idioms 142
mixed metaphors 61, 141-2
mixed subjects 81
mixed voices 127
modal verbs 76, 162, 174
more than one 81
multiple negation 26-7, 111-12
myself 68

near-negative words 116, 122
negation 26-8, 111-17, 164-5
negative transference 112
neither 21-2, 80-1
neither ... nor 22, 81, 113
neologisms 48
no other 122
no sooner 122
nob's adverbs 69-70
nob's pronouns 67-9
non-conditional *if* 129
non-matching forms 89
non-restrictive clauses 24
non-standard forms 28-9, 32, 36, 40, 63-4, 67, 69-70, 72, 78, 80, 101, 111, 116, 118, 127, 130, 140, 173
none 21, 61, 81, 115
nor 113-14, 170
norms 31-2, 40-1, 42-4
not 26, 113-16, 164
not as/so ... as 23-4

not so much 122
not only ... but also 113
not un- 34-5, 111
not without 34-5, 111
noun phrases 87-8, 123, 131-2
nouns 68, 123, 137-8, 150, 159-60
numerals 30, 78

object case 67-9
object pronouns 14-16
object swapping 120-2
one (pronoun) 81-4
one another 23
one of ... who/which 50-1, 82
one-legged constructions 128-9
only 34, 153
ordinal numbers 30
other 107-8, 122
ought to 127
overly 174
oxymoron 148

parallel constructions 153
parsing 10, 38
participle phrases 50, 89-94, 131, 155
participles 16-18, 20, 29, 49, 56, 89, 95, 99, 131, 150, 156
parts of speech 38, 199-205
passive voice 20, 38, 56-7, 99-100, 126-7, 160
perfect aspect 120
phrasal verbs 172
phrase transference 17, 19, 67-8
pleonasm 61, 168-9
plural anomalies 78-9
plural endings 36, 77-8
portmanteau words 118
possessive 24, 36, 38, 106, 165
predicate 118, 125
prefer 108-9
prefixes 174
premodifiers 160-1
prepositions 12-13, 68-9, 72, 89, 95, 98-9, 123, 163, 173
prescriptive grammar 1-2, 9-10, 31, 43-6
progressive aspect 35
progressive passive 35
pronoun anomalies 84-5
pronoun confusion 15
pronouns 14-16, 22-5, 68, 81-5, 98, 115, 150, 160-1

pronunciation 40, 46, 67
pro-verb *do* 127-8
proximity rule 152
pseudo-absolute phrases 93
pseudo-subjunctive *were* 74
pseudo-synonyms 139-40
punctuation 163, 190-8

quantifiers 163
question tags 127

rather than 92, 172
reason ... because/that 51, 119
reciprocal pronouns 23
redundancy, 27, 61, 115-16, 168-76
reflexive pronouns 36, 68
relative clauses 24-5, 91, 155-6
relative pronouns 24-5, 52, 71-2, 101-2, 126
reliable 48
repetition 60, 62, 168
restrictive clauses 24
rhetoric 1, 8
rhetorical questions 168
rules of diction 56, 61
rules of grammar 8, 10-25, 31, 35, 43, 61, 91
rules of style 53-9, 61

scarcely 116, 122
second/secondly 70-1
secondary grading 144-5
semantic reversal 140-1
sentence fragments 132
sequence of tenses 129-30
sesquipedalian substitutes 138-9
shadow pronouns 126, 173
shall/will 13-14
should/would 13, 120
so (that) 102, 166
spelling 32, 38, 163
split infinitives 11-12
squinting modifiers 154
standard English 32, 40, 46
string compounds 196
strong verbs 29, 36
subject case 67-9
subject pronouns 14-16
subjunctive 38, 74
such as 89
suffixes 49, 69, 174
superlatives 28, 107-8, 122

synonyms 47, 111, 138, 169
syntax 40-1, 61, 103

tautology 51, 61, 109, 119, 145, 168-70
technical terms 58-9
than 16, 97-8, 108-9, 114, 122
that-clauses 24
the ... -er 173
the ... -er, the ... -er 128
thee/thou 15, 83
these kind/sort of 84-5
they/their 82-3
transitive verbs 56

unchanged plurals 78, 85
uncountable nouns 21, 23, 81
understatement 145, 148
unlike-phrases 34, 106-7
upgrading 147-8
usage manuals 2, 46

vagueness 62
verb derivation 48-9

verb harmonization 120
verbosity 61, 175-6
verbs 29, 36, 48-9, 71, 76, 99-100, 105, 136-7, 159-60, 162
very 20, 144, 148-9
voice 56-7

was/were 29-30
weak verbs 29, 36
weakening intensifiers 149
wh-questions 12
what-clauses 80
when-clauses 131
when -ing 94
where-clauses 131
which-clauses 24, 156, 161, 173
who-clauses 24
who/whom 71-2
whose 24
who(so)ever 72
word confusion 134-43
word order 38, 130, 152

ye/you 15, 83